KV-637-805

Applying Conversation Analysis

Applying Conversation Analysis

Edited by

Keith Richards
University of Warwick

Paul Seedhouse
University of Newcastle upon Tyne

First published 2005 by
PALGRAVE MACMILLAN
Houndmills, Basingstoke, Hampshire RG21 6XS and
175 Fifth Avenue, New York, N.Y. 10010
Companies and representatives throughout the world

PALGRAVE MACMILLAN is the global academic imprint of the Palgrave
Macmillan division of St. Martin's Press, LLC and of Palgrave Macmillan Ltd.
Macmillan® is a registered trademark in the United States, United Kingdom
and other countries. Palgrave is a registered trademark in the European
Union and other countries.

ISBN 1–4039–4233–1 hardback

This book is printed on paper suitable for recycling and made from fully
managed and sustained forest sources.

A catalogue record for this book is available from the British Library.

Library of Congress Cataloging-in-Publication Data
Applying conversation analysis / edited by Keith Richards, Paul Seedhouse.
        p. cm.
    ISBN 1–4039–4233–1 (cloth)
    1. Conversation analysis. I. Richards, Keith, 1952–
    II. Seedhouse, Paul.

    P95.45.A66 2005
    302.3′46—dc22

                                                        2004048939

10   9   8   7   6   5   4   3   2   1
14   13 12 11 10 09 08 07 06 05

Printed and bound in Great Britain by
Antony Rowe Ltd, Chippenham and Eastbourne

Contents

Notes on Editors and Contributors

Editors

Keith Richards is a Senior Lecturer in the Centre for English Language Teacher Education, University of Warwick, UK. His research interests lie in the area of professional interaction and development, particularly in the field of education. He is the author of *Qualitative Inquiry in TESOL* (Palgrave Macmillan, 2003).

Paul Seedhouse is Postgraduate Research Director in the School of Education, Communication and Language Sciences, University of Newcastle, UK. His area of research interest is in applying CA methodology to institutional interaction. His monograph *The Interactional Architecture of the Language Classroom: A CA Perspective* was published by Blackwell in 2004.

Contributors

Paul Drew is Professor of Sociology at the University of York, UK, where he has taught since 1973, though with periods teaching and researching in the US and Europe. His research in conversation analysis focuses on communicative practices that underlie social interaction, and on interactions in workplace and institutional settings such as courtrooms and medical consultations (e.g. he is the co-author, with Max Atkinson, of *Order in Court* 1979; and co-editor, with John Heritage, of *Talk at Work* 1992). He is currently working on a project in collaboration with colleagues in the linguistics department, on affiliation and disaffiliation in talk-in-interaction.

Paul Dickerson is Senior Lecturer in Psychology, **John Rae** is also Senior Lecturer in Psychology, and **Penny Stribling** is a doctoral student in the School of Psychology and Therapeutics Studies at the University of Surrey Roehampton, UK. **Kerstin Dautenhahn** is Professor of Artificial Intelligence and **Iain Werry** is Lecturer in Computer Science in the Adaptive Systems research group, School of Computer Science at the University of Hertfordshire, UK.

Steven Bloch is a Lecturer and clinical tutor at the Department of Human Communication Disorders, University College London, UK. He has previously worked as a speech and language therapist for 12 years specialising in long-term community management of adults with progressive neurological conditions. His research interests include the effects of motor speech disorders and augmentative and alternative communication systems on conversation between adults.

Hilary Gardner is a Lecturer in Human Communication Sciences at Sheffield University, UK. She has been a Speech and Language Therapist practitioner for over 20 years. Ongoing research interests include i) the application of CA to educational interactions, especially those where non-professionals are supporting Speech Therapy work; ii) what CA can tell us about the nature of Specific Language Impairment in children; and iii) the production of CA-based assessment of clinical outcomes.

Nicky Britten is Professor of Applied Health Care Research at the Peninsula Medical School at the Universities of Exeter and Plymouth, UK. She is a sociologist with a long-standing interest in patient–doctor communication about prescribed medicines. She is a co-editor of the *Oxford Textbook of Primary Medical Care.*

Joseph Gafaranga is a Lecturer in Theoretical and Applied Linguistics at the University of Edinburgh, UK. In addition to teaching and research, he is Programme Director for the MSc in Applied Linguistics. A sociolinguist with interest in Conversation Analysis, he has published in the area of bilingual conversation as well as in the area of doctor–patient interaction.

Erik Vinkhuyzen is a member of the research staff at the Palo Alto Research Center (PARC), USA, where he is a workplace ethnographer. His research has focused on technology in the workplace, especially the impact of so-called intelligent systems on the work practices of employees. His current research concerns the work practices of employees in local copy centers as well as those of dimensional engineers in a large truck manufacturing plant.

Margaret H. Szymanski is a member of the research staff in the Systems and Practices Laboratory at the Palo Alto Research Center. She earned her PhD from the University of California, Santa Barbara, specializing in the study of language, interaction and social organization. Her research interests include collaborative learning activity, copresent and remote states of incipient talk, and interaction around technology.

Maria-Carme Torras is Senior Academic Librarian/information specialist at the Arts and Humanities Library at the University of Bergen, Norway.

She has previously taught English and Linguistics at the Universitat Autonoma de Barcelona. She has published on bilingual talk-in-interaction, especially in institutional settings.

Bethan Benwell is a Lecturer in English Language and Linguistics at the University of Stirling, UK. Her research interests include the study of popular discourses of masculinity and the analysis of constructions of student identity in tutorial talk. She is the editor of *Masculinity and Men's Lifestyle Magazines* (Blackwell, 2003) and is currently co-writing a book, *Discourse and Identity* (EUP) with Elizabeth Stokoe.

Elizabeth H. Stokoe is a Lecturer in Social Sciences at Loughborough University, UK. Her current research interests include the analysis of talk in educational and neighbour mediation settings, and the links between gender and discourse.

Salla Kurhila is Assistant at the Department of Finnish, University of Helsinki, Finland. Her publications include an article in *Journal of Pragmatics* (2001) and a chapter in an edited volume (*Second Language Conversations*) by R. Gardner and J. Wagner (2004). She is currently working on native–non-native interaction, kindergarten interaction, and correction in conversation.

Jean Wong is Associate Professor of Special Education, Language and Literacy at the College of New Jersey (Ewing, NJ, USA). Her articles have appeared in *Research on Language and Social Interaction, Applied Linguistics, International Review of Applied Linguistics*, and *Issues in Applied Linguistics*. Her main research interest lies in bridging connections between in conversation analysis and applied linguistics.

Maria Egbert is 'Privatdozentin' (Associate Professor) at the University of Oldenburg, Germany. She is a specialist in conversation analysis, intercultural communication and German as a Foreign Language. Her publications focus on multiperson practices, repair and membership categorization.

Numa Markee's primary research interests are in the emerging field of CA-for-SLA, the Management of Curricular Innovation, and Language-in-Development. He teaches Applied Linguistics at the University of Illinois at Urbana-Champaign, USA.

Donald Carroll is a full Professor at Shikoku Gakuin University, Japan, where he teaches courses in the areas of applied linguistics, intercultural communication, conversation analysis and EFL. He has also taught EFL/

ESP/EAP at universities in Mexico, Oman and Kuwait. He is currently completing a PhD in Communication Studies at the University of York, UK.

Andrew Packett teaches English to students of journalism at the University of Coimbra, Portugal. His research interests are in applications of CA in the field of teaching English for Specific Purposes.

List of Illustrations and Tables

Illustrations

Tables

Transcription Conventions

A full discussion of CA transcription notation is available in Atkinson and Heritage (1984). Punctuation marks are used to capture characteristics of speech delivery, *not* to mark grammatical units.

[	indicates the point of overlap onset
]	indicates the point of overlap termination
=	a) turn continues below, at the next identical symbol
	b) if inserted at the end of one speaker's turn and at the beginning of the next speaker's adjacent turn, it indicates that there is no gap at all between the two turns
(3.2)	an interval between utterances (3 seconds and 2 tenths in this case)
(.)	a very short untimed pause
<u>word</u>	underlining indicates speaker emphasis
e:r the:::	indicates lengthening of the preceding sound
-	a single dash indicates an abrupt cut-off
?	rising intonation, not necessarily a question
!	an animated or emphatic tone
,	a comma indicates low-rising intonation, suggesting continuation
.	a full stop (period) indicates falling (final) intonation
CAPITALS	especially loud sounds relative to surrounding talk
° °	utterances between degree signs are noticeably quieter than surrounding talk
°° °°	considerably quieter than surrounding talk
↑ ↓	indicate marked shifts into higher or lower pitch in the utterance following the arrow

> <	indicate that the talk they surround is produced more quickly than neighbouring talk
( )	a stretch of unclear or unintelligible speech
(guess)	indicates transcriber doubt about a word
.hh	speaker in-breath
hh	speaker out-breath
→	arrows in the left margin pick out features of especial interest

Additional symbols

((T shows picture))	non-verbal actions or editor's comments
ja *yes*	translations into English are italicized and located on the line below the original utterance
[gibee]	in the case of inaccurate pronunciation of an English word, an approximation of the sound is given in square brackets
[æ]	phonetic transcriptions of sounds are given in square brackets
< >	indicate that the talk they surround is produced slowly and deliberately (typical of teachers' modelling forms)
☺	smiley voice
☹	serious tone (contrasts with smiley voice)
#	creaky voice
X_____	the gaze of the speaker is marked above an utterance and that of the addressee below it. An unbroken line (_____) indicates that the party marked is gazing towards the other; absence indicates lack of gaze. Dots (. . .) mark the transition from nongaze to gaze and the point where the gaze reaches the other is marked by X. Commas (,,,) indicate the moment when gaze is shifted.

Foreword: Applied Linguistics and Conversation Analysis

The scope of applied linguistics (hereafter AL) has in the recent past begun to expand beyond its origins in language learning and second language acquisition. It is, for instance, beginning to encompass fields of 'application' such as the study of language deficits and severe speech disorders, social and interactional deficits such as autism, and classroom or pedagogic interactions, whether or not they involve language learning. It is fairly easy to trace the connections between these fields and AL's origins; moreover, the objective of informing professional practice and training, for example in (speech) therapy and counselling, remains at the heart of AL's research in these emerging areas. But as Keith Richards points out in his Introduction, that focus on professional practice has reached out into areas which are less closely connected with AL's origins in language learning/SLA. These include business and commercial language, for instance in meetings and negotiations; service encounters; language in the media; medical interactions; scientific inquiry; legal language and so on. In some respects AL has begun to encompass such fields of study in so far as they represent different genres of spoken language; since these genres are forms of everyday talk in which we engage, then they have a part to play in teaching (spoken) language (as I think McCarthy (1998) has argued so cogently).

The recent expansion of the boundaries of AL is due in part also to the influence of conversation analysis (hereafter CA), and of both its analytic perspective, and of its investigations of forms of talk-in-interaction which are not 'ordinary' conversations, but perhaps more 'institutional' in character (there is some controversy about whether a distinction can be made between ordinary conversation and institutional forms of talk-in-interaction, but I shall side-step this for the present). 'Conversation analysis' was always something of a misnomer, since it emerged from Harvey Sacks's investigations, joined by those of Emanuel Schegloff and Gail Jefferson, and later by others, into such 'institutional' interactions as calls to a suicide prevention centre and group therapy, as well as ordinary or mundane conversation during telephone calls between family and friends. While the basic concepts and findings of CA have emerged from its studies of mundane conversation, it is equally applicable to examining second language acquisition in the classroom (e.g. Seedhouse 1996, 2004) and in daily life (such as checking into or out of a hotel abroad; see Kurhila 2003), speech disorders and speech therapy (Goodwin 2003), emergency services' telephone call handling, TV and radio news interviews (e.g. Clayman and Heritage 2002), forms of counselling (for instance on AIDS counselling, see Peräkylä 1995) and interactions in medical settings (e.g. Heritage and Maynard, in press); which is why we generally refer to our field as *talk-in-interaction*. CA studies in such 'institutional' areas as these (Drew and Heritage 1992b) have contributed significantly to AL's expanding programme and scope. This has in part been a direct consequence of the ways in which the application of CA's methods in such fields reveals aspects of 'professional practice' which seem to have implications for practice and for training (see e.g. the account by Heritage and Stivers (1999) of the way doctors' use of 'on-line' commentary when making a physical examination of the patient works to overcome patient resistance when, contrary to patients' expectations, doctors are not going to prescribe antibiotics).

So put very simply, there is a congruence, even a convergence, between certain aspects of the programmes of AL and CA; and this is very clearly represented in the chapters in this volume, which cover much of the expanded scope of AL, from (second) language teaching, to speech disorders and therapy, educational settings that do not involve language teaching, service encounters, and medical interactions. These studies are either CA investigations, or have adopted CA's perspective and concepts in their analyses. At the core of CA's perspective is, of course, *sequential analysis* – that is, that in their turns at talk speakers conduct social actions of various kinds; and that all aspects of linguistic production, including lexical, syntactic, phonetic and prosodic, are organized in terms of, and fitted to, a turn's position in a sequence of turns/actions (for overviews, see e.g. Drew 2004; Heritage 1984b; ten Have 1999). I think it is fairly clear that studies in AL, and certainly those represented in this collection, have adopted a sequential approach to linguistic production; so that language is being examined in its *interactional* environment, rather than in the form of single 'utterances' abstracted from the surrounding talk (in the manner of the exploration of 'well-formedness' in generative grammar). However, there are certain aspects or features of CA's programme and approach, even perhaps its 'theory', around which there have been and may remain some tensions between AL and CA. Some consideration of these is necessary in assessing how far AL and CA can converge; or rather, since AL is a discipline, and CA an analytic perspective, and only one of the perspectives adopted within AL, I might be better advised not to regard them converging, but instead to frame these issues in terms of how far CA can be applied to and exploited in AL's project to intervene in (professional) practice, either in the form of design or training. Plainly CA *is* being applied to AL; and so the question is really, how successful is the adoption by AL of the methods of CA likely to be, in view of the distinctive programme and 'analytic attitude' of each? Here is a very brief summary of some themes in CA's perspective, which in some respects may be the sources of some tension with AL's programme and studies – and which in a variety of ways are addressed in chapters in this volume.

- *The normative character of conversational patterns*: CA research aims to identify the patterns, practices and devices through which talk-in-interaction is orderly and coherent; these have a normative character. They are therefore not (or more than) statistical patterns, and represent the outcomes of speakers orienting to what they should properly or appropriately do in certain (sequential) circumstances. A simplest example is the expectation associated with *adjacency pairs* (that a second pair part should follow a turn hearable as a first pair part). But other examples include the *preference organization* associated with some actions, and practices for designing questions in media (news) interviews so as to preserve their neutralism (see Clayman and Heritage 2002). The normative character of (verbal as well as non-verbal) conduct points to social rather than purely linguistic factors in interaction. And it is not clear whether, or how far, this normative character of talk-in-interaction is accepted or represented in AL research.

- *Participants' orientations to conversational patterns*: In some respects as a corollary of the normative character of interactional patterns, research in CA shows not just that some sequential or other patterns are to be found in talk, but that participants *orient to such patterns* in their conduct. Again, a simple example: the (normative) expectation that a turn at talk will be connected to its prior turn, topically, and in terms of the action sequence etc. (connections that are displayed linguistically though repetition, ellipsis and deixis, which thereby lie at the heart of discourse cohesion) is oriented to by speakers about to take turns that are *not* so connected, which are for instance going to be about a quite new and different topic. They do so through using markers of topical disjunction, instructing the recipient not to look for a topical connection between the turn they are about to take, and what came before. The use of such markers is then a systematic conversational *practice*, a device or technique understood to be employed to handle certain interactional contingencies. The importance of showing that participants orient to some pattern(s) is beginning to be accepted in AL, explicitly so in the work of McCarthy (1998) and others.

• *Procedural relevance of identities in talk*: Any participant in interaction possesses an indefinite range of identities, or ways they might be categorized or described. But the sheer possession of an identity does not guarantee the relevance of that identity in accounting for some conduct. That is, the simple matter that someone *is* a male, a patient, middle aged, a father or whatever does not warrant, without further explication, that one of those identities is the basis for some particular (verbal) conduct, or explain why someone said something, or said it in a particular way. For instance, the fact that someone is a learner of a second language, which they are attempting to use in a certain situation (such as registering for a university course, or checking into an hotel), does not automatically mean that (all) their conduct in a given interaction is governed by that identity. Kurhila (this volume) shows that certain systematic aspects of the interaction between a foreign student and a university secretary (the former speaking the language of the latter only very uncertainly) are related to their identities as client–service provider respectively, and *not* to their identities as NNS–NS. The challenge for analysis is to show which of a speaker's identities is salient to a particular moment in interaction, or to a particular interactional 'move', and to show precisely how it is thus procedurally relevant (on which see Schegloff (1992b), and also Benwell and Stokoe, this volume).

• *The practices for interacting and reasoning are not setting-specific*: There is a potential tension between CA and AL in terms of the setting-specific nature of AL research. AL investigations tend to focus on a given type of setting, such as language learning in the classroom, particular kinds of service encounters etc., whereas CA investigations stress the setting-independence of its findings concerning the interactional practices that are identified. An example is the pattern to be found when one speaker makes an assessment, to which the recipient does not immediately respond; a gap or silence ensues, in response to which the speaker may back down from their assessment (or its strength), thereby securing the agreement of their recipient. This pattern/practice is to be found in ordinary conversation, news interviews, medical interactions, indeed in any form or genre of interaction. However, the complex interplay between speech setting and activity (such as cross-examination) offers the prospect of a more fruitful connection between CA and AL. There is scope for comparative analysis of speech settings. Consider, for example, the 'choral' response of children answering a teacher's question in classroom lessons, and the teacher's third turn assessment of that response (often a repeat), and how that pattern is almost uniquely associated with classroom instruction.

- *Talk as action*: A starting point of CA enquiries is the actions or activities that participants conduct in their turns at talk. When we analyse talk, we look first of all at what speakers are doing in the talk, whether these are the kinds of activities that are common in mundane talk, such as complaints, invitations, assessments, criticisms, requests and the like; or whether they are activities more closely associated with or bound to certain settings, such as (medical) examination and diagnosis, (cross-) examination in court hearings, service requests ('I need to make some copies...'), or lecturing (see also Schegloff 1996b, on actions for which there are no easy vernacular names). By contrast, the starting point for enquiry in AL is commonly a linguistic feature, such as the patterns of co-occurrence of a specific verb form, or a vocabulary item (see e.g. McCarthy 1998). It is fair to say, I think, that this is a source of tension not only between AL and CA, but within CA itself, since although we may begin with the social actions being managed through talk, the practices that we identify tend not to be related to a specific social action. Furthermore, analysis may indeed focus entirely on a lexical item, and the work that item does, an exemplary case being Clift's (2001) account of the different interactional work that 'actually' does when placed in turn-initial position, and in turn-ending position.

- *Intervention and designed output*: As I have mentioned above, and as Keith Richards stresses in his Introduction, one of the aims of AL is to design intervention which in some way will inform and improve (professional) practice in a given field of speech, e.g. improving language teaching strategies, doctor–patient communication, therapeutic interventions with people with speech and other disorders etc. Basic research in CA has focused only on investigating and identifying the practices that underlie our competence as users of a language; to document these practices, and not to evaluate them. Thus, as Peräkylä and Vehvilainen (2003) point out, CA has generally not addressed itself to such matters as degrees of professional competence and 'best practice'. Peräkylä and Vehvilainen explore some of the ways

in which CA studies (relating to AIDS counselling, primary care medical consultations and educational/employment counselling) might
be relevant for practitioners in these fields. Indeed, some moves in
this direction have already been made; these include my own work
for the Metropolitan Police, Silverman's (1997) summary of the
lessons to be drawn from his analyses of AIDS counselling; and in
particular Atkinson's (1984) findings about the construction of
political speaking. These had an immediate and palpable impact on
practitioners; it was widely believed that (British) MPs all bought
a copy of Atkinson's book, and certainly the speaking style of Paddy
Ashdown (then leader of the Liberal Democrats) owed much to
Atkinson's work. Much recent CA research on medical interaction
has the explicit aim of informing medical practice and training. And
I think that the implications for practice of Maynard and Marlaire's
(1992) study of the interactionally contingent nature of the outcomes
of certain educational tests are particularly clear. CA will, I think,
remain focused on unsponsored 'basic' research; but the signs are
(judging from by Peräkylä and Vehvilainen 2003, and these others
more practically-oriented studies) that CA is becoming more 'applied'
(though for a more fully considered view on this, see Schegloff *et al.*
2002). However, the principal analytic challenge will be whether
studies of practitioners' behaviour in natural settings can yield results
pertaining to the evaluation of performance (i.e. to assessments about
degrees of competence), and hence to design recommendations that
are based solidly on systematic research evidence.

- *Large corpora and quantification*: CA research is characterized by close,
  detailed and intensive analysis (often too detailed for some people's
  taste) of relatively small data sets. There is generally nothing particularly 'representative' about CA data corpora; most commonly they
  have been assembled as and when opportunities arose, although
  more recent studies, especially of medical interactions in the USA,
  Finland and to a small extent in the UK, have been more systematic
  in their approach to data collection. Of course the qualitative and
  inductive analytic stance of CA has been associated with a rejection
  of a statistical approach towards documenting phenomena (see e.g.
  Schegloff 1993 and Heritage 1995). But the collection of larger and
  more systematically representative data corpora in CA studies has led
  to a certain re-evaluation of the role of coding in research, and
  whether and how findings might be subject to statistical evidence
  (and even testing). So some research in CA is beginning, to a certain

extent, to converge with the tendency in AL to work with large data corpora. In some respects this arises from the issues outlined in the previous section, concerning the practical applications of CA research: for instance, medical practitioners are likely, quite reasonably, only to accept recommendations for changing practice, or for training, if these recommendations are based on statistically significant findings. They want to know that such-and-such a communicative practice will have a given result, in a statistically demonstrable number of cases. Generally speaking, of course, it is difficult to demonstrate that certain outcomes are directly related to particular communicative practices, in the kind of determinate fashion that could be depicted statistically. However, this can sometimes be achieved, as Mangione-Smith *et al.* (2003) have shown in their statistical exploration of 'on line commentary', initially identified through detailed qualitative analysis of primary care consultations.

A few years ago, I would have said that AL and CA were wide apart; but now I think differently. I think that this brief review of some of the distinctive features of CA's approach shows that there is an increasing convergence between the two. The possible complementarity between AL and CA is multi-faceted, and so I will resist trying to come to an unambiguous conclusion. However, two points stand out for me: it is fairly clear that applying CA to AL will involve investigating what is distinctive about talk-in-interaction in different settings, or speech activities in different settings, which in some respects is an extension or specification of a sociolinguistic programme. Second, whether CA can be applied to or exploited in pursuing the intervention and design objectives with respect to professional practice (e.g. in training recommendations etc.) that are part of AL's programme, cannot easily be resolved; it is a matter on which those in CA differ, and rests in part on the kinds of relevancies which studies of practice and competence can be shown to have for (professional) practitioners. The chapters in this volume reflect the broadening scope of AL, and the profound contribution that the methods and perspective of CA are making to AL's developing programme.

PAUL DREW

1
Introduction

Keith Richards

> To every human problem there is a neat and easy solution –
> and it's wrong.
>
> H. L. Mencken

One of the strengths of Conversation Analysis (CA) as a research discipline is its capacity to direct researchers' attention to apparently tiny features of interaction and explode their dimensions beyond all expectations, revealing delicacies of design and management that resist the assaults of clumsier instruments. The unwillingness of CA researchers to settle for easy solutions and their concern to elaborate the complexities of human action as revealed through talk have led to an impression in some quarters that the products of their investigations are too delicately wrought to bear the strains of application in the rough and tumble of practice. However, professionals in a range of disciplines from medicine to broadcasting have come to recognize the value of research that respects their peculiar achievements, and the field of Applied Linguistics (AL) has begun to acknowledge the contribution that CA can make to its programme. This book celebrates this important connection and anticipates some of its potential outcomes.

A recognition of the possibilities inherent in exploring the applied dimension of CA gave rise to the seminar that was the genesis of many of the chapters in this book. It brought together conversation analysts from a range of academic and professional contexts and invited them to present examples of CA which arose from or pointed towards the possibility of professional intervention. However, no restrictions were placed on the form that this relationship might take, since the aim was to explore dimensions of application rather than to establish procedures for this. The resulting collection ranges from chapters that begin with practical problems or conundrums and use CA as a means of understanding and responding to these, to chapters where CA has revealed hitherto unrecognized aspects of interaction that suggest possibilities for productive intervention. So far, issues of application in CA have remained largely unexplored, but developments over the last decade mean that the time is ripe for a consideration of the different forms that this might take. This volume is a first step towards representing the many perspectives – some recognizably mainstream, others more contentious – that will need to be considered if CA is to develop coherently as an applied discipline.

Dimensions of application

In his review of CA at 'Century's End', John Heritage argued that 'part of the claim of any framework worth its salt is that it can sustain "applied" research of various kinds' (1999: 73), and he indicated that this aspect might feature prominently in developments within the discipline.[1] Although CA has always been interested in talk in institutional settings (Sacks 1972a), this observation is to some extent a reflection of the rapid growth of CA studies in such settings following Drew and Heritage's important collection on the subject of talk at work (1992a), embracing not only traditional professions such as medicine or law (e.g. Heritage and Maynard in press, Travers and Manzo 1997), but fields such as business (e.g. Boden 1994), broadcasting (e.g. Clayman and Heritage 2002) and counselling (Peräkylä 1995). It is only natural that professional interest should extend beyond description and towards the potential of such research in terms of training and development interventions, encouraging the emergence of 'applied CA' almost by default. However, the concept of 'application' is by no means straightforward and in this section I briefly consider the claims of three different models with a view to developing a perspective that is consistent with the nature of CA and within which the wide range of issues raised by the chapters in this volume can be accommodated.

Theory → practice

The traditional view of applied research, associated particularly with work within (post-) positivist paradigms, is that it derives from, and is in some way subordinate to, 'pure' research. Crudely put, the aim of pure research is to develop theories that can then be applied in practical situations, an understanding of the process of application being the business of applied research. In the context of AL, discourse framed in these terms has been described as dysfunctional (Clarke 1994), but debates about the relationship between theories of second language acquisition and language teaching, or the part that interaction has to play in our understanding of these, have over the years generated considerable heat (e.g. Beretta 1993; van Lier 1994; Firth and Wagner 1997, 1998; Gass 1998; Wagner 1996; Seedhouse 1998).

In terms of CA, which is interested in the normative characteristics of interaction and eschews theory-building, this model has no currency, but there is still scope for misunderstanding. In a recent discussion of applied CA, ten Have drew a distinction which, while never designed to promote or even suggest such an orientation, is nevertheless cast in terms associated with it:

> In 'pure CA', the focus is on the local practices of turn-taking, sequential organization, etc., in and for themselves, while in 'applied CA' attention shifts to the tensions between those local practices and any 'larger structures' in which these are embedded, such as institutional rules, instructions, accounting, obligations, etc.
>
> (ten Have 1999: 189)

In so far as ten Have uses the term 'pure CA' to draw attention to the important issues of speech setting and activity, discussed by Drew's 'Foreword', its inclusion seems harmless enough, but abstracted from this particular context its use is more problematic because of a hierarchy implicit in theory-practice models in which 'applied' research is inferior to 'pure' research. It is therefore important to insist that such a distinction has no validity in CA, which refers '– perhaps pre-eminently – to a method of inquiry' (Schegloff *et al.* 2002: 4): however we may choose to characterize applied CA, it must above all meet the analytically rigorous demands of all CA practice worthy of that name.

As far as applied CA is concerned, then, the fact that the data are collected in institutional settings and the findings have relevance to practice in these settings does not imply that the approach to analysis should be fundamentally different from that of the broader discipline. If a distinction is to be drawn between CA and applied CA, it is not to be found in methodological difference but rather in terms of the phenomena to which attention is directed and the relevance of the research to training or professional development.

Discovery → prescription

A model that reflects the importance of directing attention is one in which the researcher discovers some feature(s) of social and/or professional behaviour and on the basis of this prescribes – or proscribes – certain courses of action. To take a well-known example, if there is a 'procedural rule...that a person who speaks first in a telephone conversation can choose their form of address, and in choosing their form of address they can thereby choose the form of address the other uses' (Sacks 1992: 4), this information can be incorporated in relevant professional training and perhaps established as 'standard operating procedure'. There are good reasons for believing that a model of this kind is suited to CA-based research, three of which seem particularly persuasive:

- CA is empirically grounded and therefore well placed to generate the sort of discoveries that can inform practice;
- its focus on practical accomplishment through interaction establishes a natural link with professional practice;
- because its raw materials are publicly observable phenomena, these are available as resources in any subsequent training interventions.

Despite the immediate appeal of this model, it suggests an approach not entirely consistent with CA's methodological principles. One of the dangers – inherent in any research undertaken with application in mind – is that when a researcher sets out to discover something with a particular end in view, this inevitably serves to direct attention to those aspects of the data that are most likely to serve that end, an approach that is antithetical to CA's insistence on open-mindedness. At worst, this could lead to a narrowing of vision, influencing treatment of the data and violating a primary consideration in CA that 'nothing that occurs in interaction can be ruled out, *a priori*, as random, insignificant, or irrelevant' (Atkinson and Heritage 1984: 4). But even if the analyst avoids this pitfall, as Sacks noted, such an approach precludes the possibility of unexpected discovery inherent in 'unmotivated examination' (1984: 27).

Even if analytical dangers are avoided, the notion of prescription brings its own dangers, not least the underlying assumption that it is possible to specify exactly what actors should do in particular circumstances. One of the significant contributions that CA can make to our understanding of social and professional life is its ability to identify regularities in talk and action and this can serve as an invaluable guide to action, but this is not the same thing as laying down laws of behaviour. Unfortunately, it is the latter which has the most allure to materials designers and trainers, with inevitable consequences:

There seems to be a tendency in such situations to summarize the conclusions of a consideration of practical problems and general interests in terms of relatively simple recipes or 'rules of thumb'.

(ten Have 1999: 199)

Problems such as this could be dismissed as peripheral to the main concerns of CA or as matters of the relationship between researcher and client, but if we are to take seriously the issue of applying CA and if it matters to us how our work is understood, we cannot afford to sweep them under the table. One way of addressing the issues they raise is to direct our attention to the way we represent our work, and this is where the choice of model is so important. A representation in terms of discovery and prescription would serve only to reinforce the impression that the application of CA findings is essentially unproblematic, a mere matter of finding the best way of parcelling up and delivering the goods. Something more in tune with the conceptual realities of the discipline is required.

Description → informed action

The model that best represents the range of application possibilities covered by the chapters in this book is one that relates the nature of the primary research to possible modes of intervention, recognizing its potential for enriching professional practice rather than reframing it in prescriptive terms. Such a model would represent the primary research as oriented predominantly to description rather than discovery, allowing for the possibility of unexpected insights arising from the sort of unmotivated investigation recommended by Sacks. In emphasizing description it would reflect CA's methodological orientation, implying no fundamental distinction between primary research and research undertaken with a view to possible applications, allowing that both might generate insights with the potential to transform practice. All three of the advantages summarized under the previous model would apply here, and description would, of course, embrace discovery.

In terms of application, the emphasis on informed practice would have two important implications. The first of these would be the establishment of a relationship in which CA would be seen as performing an enabling rather than an enacting role in professional development. Instead of thinking in terms of narrow prescription, clients would be encouraged to consider more broadly the ways in which CA might impact on their practice. Taking the findings in the chapter by Dickerson *et al.* (Chapter 2) as an example of this, professional therapists could be sensitized to interactional possibilities that they had not hitherto considered, not in terms of procedures that they might follow (how far and in what ways these might be specifiable is a professional issue) but in terms of responding to competencies that CA has been able to expose. By thinking in terms of raising awareness, directing attention, developing sensitivity, challenging assumptions, etc., CA can contribute to informed professional action, helping professionals to deepen their understanding and develop new competencies. The aim of this book is to suggest the wide range of possibilities available through CA, extending from what might be described as core professional concerns to work that does no more than suggest where its influence might be felt.

The second important concomitant of a focus on informed professional practice is that it allows for the possibility that CA will become involved in describing not only aspects of professional practice but also the processes of training or development that might be associated with these. The chapters in the final section of the book illustrate what form this might take. Markee's chapter (Chapter 12), for example, shows how CA can be used to reveal aspects of classroom behaviour that may have implications for an approach to teaching using tasks, while Packett's contribution (Chapter 14) demonstrates how CA can be used as part of the teaching process in order to sensitize trainees to aspects of their practice. It is conceivable that over time this aspect of applied CA, which takes it closest to the concerns of AL, is one that will grow significantly.

Dimensions of competence

Instead of working from the assumption that competence is something that one either has or does not have, CA provides a means of exploring the ways in which such competence is constructed in particular circumstances by the participants involved. In adopting this perspective, CA sets aside participant roles such as teacher and student or expert and novice as *a priori* analytical resources and relies instead on a careful analysis of the ways in which the talk is designed – and the purposes and orientations revealed *through* this. What matters in CA is the extent to which identity is procedurally relevant for the participants themselves, and it may well be that the identities oriented to are not those normally associated with the activity taking place. Examined from this perspective, competence cannot be treated as a taken-for-granted quality to be merely assigned or withheld (as a whole or in part), but must be regarded as a subject for scrutiny across different dimensions.

The implications of this for AL, as the chapters here reveal, are profound, and the issues raised in terms of understanding, awareness and sensitivity have ramifications far beyond the confines of the classroom. The book begins with three chapters that explore the nature of competence in the context of therapy, where it is a focus of professional concern. All of them expose aspects of competence that for one reason or another had previously remained unexamined but which point to the possibility of therapeutic advances.

The work of Paul Dickerson, John Rae, Penny Stribling, Kerstin Dautenhahn and Iain Werry (Chapter 2) in examining interaction with an autistic child exposes the limitations of assumptions about the 'asocial' characteristics of such children. Drawing on a careful analysis of visual and verbal coordination, they are able to show that subtle and previously unnoticed orientations to speakers reveal interactional competence of a higher order than had previously been acknowledged. Their subtle and insightful examination of the strategic use of gaze direction as an interactional resource is important not only in terms of the light it sheds on the nature of interaction with autistic children but, perhaps more importantly, in the extent to which it exposes the shortcomings of approaches derived from assumptions of linguistic deficit and highlights the need for a re-assessment of our view of such children based rather on the recognition of competencies.

Steven Bloch's chapter (Chapter 3) also reveals previously unrecognized competence, but this time the spotlight falls on the ways in which this is revealed in talk between an individual with a severe speech disorder (dysarthria) and a lay person, in this case his mother. As the author points out, although previous studies of dysarthria have included theoretical discussion of message co-construction, they have not extended to detailed analysis of everyday talk. Once attention is shifted away from the mechanics of speech production, and from dysarthria as a medical condition, towards the social dimension in which two participants achieve together what in normal circumstances might be the product of a single individual, this exposes hitherto unrecognized interactional resources. What is perhaps most interesting, and certainly most moving, about Bloch's sensitive and insightful analysis, is the way that the participants 'make ordinary' talk which is to an outsider so clearly different from the exchanges with which we are familiar in our everyday encounters.

Interaction between parent and child is also the focus of Hilary Gardner's chapter (4), but where Bloch's study revealed what specialists can learn from lay persons doing 'ordinary' talk, here attention is directed to the non-specialist acting as therapist. The outcomes are strikingly different. The chapter concentrates on a mother's attempt to help her child overcome phonetic problems, showing how, despite her extended efforts, this does not lead to improvement and in some cases actually serves to introduce new errors. When these efforts are compared with those of a professional therapist, interesting differences emerge, the most obvious of which is the length of the *bouts* (or number of turns used for dealing with a target word) involved. In showing how the professional therapist achieves success in much shorter bouts than those of the mother, Gardner highlights significant differences in the turn types that feature in their talk. By exposing underlying assumptions through the careful analysis of particular stretches of talk, Gardner is able to establish a basis for helping the lay therapist develop awareness and skills that will improve the quality of therapeutic engagement with the child and so extend the latter's exposure to remedial intervention.

The three chapters concerned with therapy all offer a widening of traditionally conceived views of what constitutes interactional compe-tence, elaborating aspects of its social construction. Although none of them offers prescriptions for intervention, all three indicate clearly the dimensions along which such intervention would operate and the considerations that would inform its shape and character. They are all characterized by a respect for existing professional practice and are essentially augmentative in orientation. The outcomes of applied research, however, need not necessarily be augmentative; its programme can also embrace work that revisits sites of professional talk and reveals aspects that challenge everyday assumptions about, or interpretations of, its construction. This is where the contribution of the next three chapters is to be found.

Challenging assumptions

The four treatments of professional interaction in this volume range much wider than those in any other section, in terms of both professional and interpretive focus. In different ways, however, all of them challenge natural or commonly held assumptions about interaction in the institutional settings with which they are concerned.

Joseph Gafaranga and Nicky Britten's study (5) provides a valuable example of how CA's interest in local orderliness can deepen our understanding of small but significant aspects of professional practice. Their research, which builds on earlier work, examines the apparently innocuous topic initial elicitors such as 'How are you?' or 'What can

I do for you?' that occur at the start of General Practice consultations, showing how these are significant in terms of the professional encounter taking place. The chapter serves as a powerful challenge to comfortable assumptions about 'professional language', demonstrating conclusively that what might easily be dismissed as a necessary social preliminary in such consultations, a mere prelude to the business in hand, is in fact fundamental to them, a constituent activity with procedural implications.

Although Erik Vinkhuyzen and Peggy Szymanski (6) also focus on a very specific interactional sequence, the motivation for their study in professional – or more specifically organizational – terms is specifiable at the outset: where provider and customer goals conflict, how can a company maximize customer satisfaction while minimizing costs (via inconvenience, extra work, etc.) to itself? Their interactional interest lies in the ways that customer requests are formulated and how employees manage the non-granting of these. By examining a range of examples involving new and experienced customers with different service expectations and studying the sequential development of the talk and the service provider's management of this, the authors are able to identify strategies used by employees to maximize benefits to the company. Their work challenges the assumption that meeting service requests is a matter of orienting to customers' needs in terms of services available, showing that such exchanges are embedded within wider organizational concerns to which employees orient in the design of their talk. This connection between particular linguistic or interactional constructions and wider social or organizational goals lies at the heart of AL, and this chapter serves as a useful reminder that an orientation to client interests does not commit the researcher to constraints associated with a purely instrumental approach to applied research.

Maria-Carme Torras (7) also takes service encounters as the source of her data, but her interest lies in how linguistic identity bears on the ways in which talk is constructed. She demonstrates that the institutional character of service encounters lies not only in the participants' ascription of the membership categorization device 'service parties', but also in their display of other identity sets in the talk. The chapter examines the ways in which 'acquaintanceship' and 'language preference' are managed and in the case of the latter shows how participants resort to renegotiation of identities in order to deal with actual or potential unsuccessful compliance. With increasing globalization, where intercultural communication is likely to become the norm in some service encounters, this work has important implications for staff training and development. Its discussion of one-in-a-series encounters also connects with Gafaranga and Britten's research, and its interest in the way that compliance is achieved links it to Vinkhuyzen and Szymanski's work. Taken together, these chapters show how AL might widen its interactional horizons away from the 'standard' encounter that currently appears in most coursebooks featuring interaction and towards a broader view of the multiple dimensions brought into play in such encounters.

The work of Bethan Benwell and Elizabeth Stokoe (8) shifts attention away from service encounters but remains firmly in the sphere of awareness raising. Their contribution represents a case for broadening the scope of university teacher preparation beyond teaching methodology to include sensitivity to the way in which students orient themselves to the teaching and learning process. In an interesting extension of the considerable body of research providing strong evidence of male resistance to academic identity in compulsory education in the UK, the authors direct their attention to post-compulsory education, where much less research has been done and where the same assumption persists. By adopting a CA approach and thereby rejecting 'male' and 'female' as *a priori* categories within which their investigation is framed (a feature of earlier research), they are able to explore how students construct aspects of their institutional identity through engagement with tutorial tasks. Their analysis suggests that, at least as far as university settings are concerned, resisting academic identity and appearing not to work hard is a prevalent interactional characteristic and not gender-specific. By challenging the extension of traditional conceptions of gendered performance in education to post-compulsory contexts, this research therefore opens up new avenues of investigation that should eventually be used to inform the design of materials for the induction of students and the preparation of university teachers.

Orienting to grammar

The third part of this book sees a move from the professional contexts in which AL is typically involved and towards two topics that have always lain at its intellectual core: the relationship between native speakers (NS) and non-native speakers (NNS) of a language, and orientation to grammatical issues, the latter a subject in which CA also has a keen interest (e.g. Ochs *et al.* 1996). Once again, our aim has been to encourage a rethinking of traditional assumptions and approaches in the light of the distinctive contribution that CA can make. Although there is a considerable body of work in AL on NS–NNS interaction, most of it has relied heavily on approaches that concentrate largely on linguistic form, taking social identity for granted, though there is evidence that a more balanced picture is emerging, and the chapters in this section suggest directions this might take.

The chapters demonstrate clearly that CA does not take linguistic competence for granted, but rather offers a way of examining how it is constructed through talk. The participants are not all monolingual speakers and each chapter features a different language, a balance that is in fact atypical of AL, where the traditional concentration on English suggests a narrower research base than is actually available.

The language on which Salla Kurhila (9) draws is Finnish. Although her focus is on grammatical self-repair, the author's interest lies in the ways in which speakers orient to grammatical correctness and specifically how the linguistic competence of NNSs, far from being a point of orientation within the talk, is actually constructed through it. An important difference between this work and most of the work on this topic in AL literature is that, while CA recognizes NS and NNS as descriptive terms, they are not used as analytic categories. Kurhila shows how they may or may not be relevant at different points in the talk and how the NS can decline to adopt the role of linguistically knowledgeable participant, exploring what kind of interactional consequences or problems may emerge as a result of this. The importance of such work is that it underlines the importance of looking beyond matters of grammatical accuracy as such and exploring the ways in which participants orient to this.

Jean Wong's chapter (10) also adopts this perspective, but where Kurhila's interest lies in how participants orient to grammar, her attention is directed specifically to non-attendance to grammatical error. Using examples from NS–NNS conversation, she presents evidence of native speakers side-stepping or disattending to NNS error in pursuance of social goals. The author shows how other repair of the talk, as opposed to other correction of the grammar, is an interactional achievement of the participants involved, reflecting aspects of their social and linguistic identities. By focusing on 'what is displayed (in the data) *for the participants* as *acceptable talk*' she throws refreshing light on old debates about the place of 'accuracy' in NNS talk and the nature of communicative competence. Her work has important implications for the teaching of 'conversational' English in a classroom context, where 'disattending' to grammar may have other implications, and for our notions of competence in terms of the relationship between grammar and social interaction.

The three previous chapters all have direct relevance to the immediate concerns of AL; the relationship of Maria Egbert's work (11) is more oblique, but no less important for that. Her analysis is situated in the uncertain and contentious waters of discriminatory practice and her conclusions must at best be tentative. Concentrating on a single telephone exchange that was described as discriminatory by native speakers who listened to it, she tries to account for how such an impression might have arisen, something that none of these was able to do. The call, in German, is between a lessor and a caller in search of an apartment, and Egbert is able to show how responsibility for an early lexical error made by the lessor is represented as a mistake on the part of the non-native speaker caller. Her analysis of the subsequent talk and the ways in which the caller is discouraged from pursuing her enquiry raise awkward questions about identity and power, particularly salient in the context of debates on the relationship between critical discourse analysis and both CA (Billig 1999; Schegloff 1999) and AL (Widdowson 2000). More broadly, research of this type raises very important questions about the way data should be presented in sensitizing those who are likely to have to deal with discriminatory situations as part of their professional lives.

Language learning

The final part focuses explicitly on language learning from a classroom perspective. Interest in interaction in the language classroom has a respectable pedigree in AL dating back at least 30 years, and its importance has long been explicitly recognized (e.g. Allwright 1984). Although specific features of talk associated with the work of conversation analysts, such as repair (e.g. van Lier 1988), have received attention, evidence of a genuine CA approach is more recent, though the situation is now changing (e.g. Egbert 1998; Hosada 2000; Iles 1996; Jung 1999; Lazaraton 1997; Markee 1995, 2000; Seedhouse 2004; Wong 2000b) and it is interesting to note that CA featured as one of the three traditions chosen to feature in a recent special edition of *Applied Linguistics* on microanalyses of classroom talk (Zuengler and Mori 2002). The three chapters featured here approach language learning and teaching from very different perspectives, each of them important.

Behind Numa Markee's interest in a topic of current concern in AL (12), task-based learning, lies a radical shift in perspective on the concerns of classroom researchers. His notes on video recording and transcription provide more than a mere appendix to an interesting chapter; they address methodological issues classroom researchers in AL cannot afford to ignore. By carefully examining the choreography of on-task and off-task behaviour in a language class, he is able to show how students orient to two different interactional agendas, managing each within acceptable institutional parameters. His discussion explores an interesting tension between the benefits in terms of second language acquisition of off-task talk and the potential importance of on-task learning. The commonplace claim that interesting and motivating materials and tasks matter is here given interactional substance, albeit in terms of the potential these students reveal through their off-task behaviour. Using CA to expose 'what really happened', Markee is able to suggest subtle shifts in our ways of seeing and understanding that have the potential to change how professionals go about their business in both teaching and research.

Don Carroll's data (13) are not collected from the classroom, but his research is concerned with language learners and provides a powerful demonstration of what can be achieved when CA is used to explore prominent but previously unexamined aspects of learner talk. Investigating the interaction of novice Japanese speakers of English and directing his attention to the common practice of adding vowels to word-final consonants, he challenges an assumption that language teachers (in common with others) have taken for granted: that this is a pronunciation problem arising from negative transfer and that it should be corrected accordingly. He is able to demonstrate conclusively the inadequacy of this explanation and reveal instead that such *vowel-marking* is far from random, serving as an important interactional resource. In terms of practice, the implications of Carroll's research are clear and important, and of particular relevance to ESL teachers world-wide working with Japanese learners, highlighting the potential value of raising awareness of 'interactionally equivalent micropractices' as an alternative means of addressing certain so-called pronunciation errors. However, it has even more profound implications in at least two respects, both touched on by Carroll in his conclusion. The first raises issues of the NS–NNS relationship from the perspective of the analyst and the methodological demands associated with the treatment of non-native discourse. The second, in common with the chapters in the first section, lies in its shift of attention away from a linguistic deficit model based on grossly apparent features of talk and towards a recognition of the subtle ways in which interactional competencies may be revealed through the careful analysis of interaction.

The following chapter (14) serves as an example of the direct relevance of CA to the pedagogic context and as a refutation to those who challenge its potential for application. Andrew Packett teaches English to Portuguese students of journalism and uses CA in his work at the

University of Coimbra. In this example he illustrates how the effective deployment of insertion sequences in broadcast interviews can be taught using CA data as classroom materials. The analytical base of the chapter, highlighting an interactional feature of broadcast interviews not previously noted in the literature, is impressive in itself, but what makes it particularly valuable is the way the author develops a coherent 'CA-informed pedagogy' that enables him to pin down the sources of learners' difficulties and help them to develop vital professional skills through the comparison of their own efforts with those of accomplished performers. Packett provides helpful outlines of the pedagogic context and relevant procedures together with an analysis sensitive and detailed enough to enable the reader to see how a minimal exchange can produce a 'key pedagogic insight'. The success of this project as an example of CA and of classroom practice serves as a final resounding endorsement of the contribution CA is already making to AL.

Conclusion: openings and closings

How far and in what ways applications of CA will develop over the coming years will be determined in part by the extent to which its contributions are understood and valued by those who are asked to learn from them and make use of them: therapists, doctors, teachers, salespeople and interviewers, to name just some who might be influenced by this book. That CA has much to offer, in a field hitherto dominated by psychologists and communication specialists relying on secondary data sources such as reports and interviews, is perhaps an argument that no longer needs to be made, but the dimensions of its contribution in terms of both mode and content have yet to be explored. This book represents a first step towards mapping the contours of this new territory and showing in what respects it might relate to a field where matters of application have long been of prime concern. Its emphasis lies in exploring possibilities rather than laying down parameters, secure in the knowledge that the rigours of CA offer adequate protection against the seductive appeal of the neat and easy solutions.

Notes

1 This section should be read in the light of a categorization of potential markets for applied CA proposed by Heritage at the 2004 annual conference of the American Association of Applied Linguistics (Portland, 1–4 May). He identified three potential markets:

Disorganized markets, with a 'tell us what to do' orientation, where the aim is to solve problems, a small evidential base provides an adequate resource, and participants are interested in sharing common experiences and understandings.

Organized markets, where a different order of persuasion is needed to convince policy-makers, who require evidence that an intervention is worthwhile before they introduce it. Here, the outcomes of CA will need to be supported by quantified evidence of their impact.

Resistant markets, where there is no interest in acting on the findings of CA, which may expose uncomfortable evidence of, for example, racist or sexist behaviour. These require very different strategies of persuasion.

Part I
Speech and Language Therapy

2
Autistic Children's Co-ordination of Gaze and Talk: Re-examining the 'Asocial' Autist

Paul Dickerson, John Rae, Penny Stribling, Kerstin Dautenhahn and Iain Werry

Introduction

Autism is generally conceptualized as a childhood neurodevelopmental disorder resulting in life-long disability and high care requirements for the majority of individuals concerned. In the UK there are around 500 000 persons so diagnosed (NAS 1999), attracting much research interest. Contemporary accounts of Autism emerging from both research and practitioner perspectives draw upon 'Wing's triad of impairments' (e.g. Wing 1993): 'core' categories referring to impairments in language, social interaction and, more variably, imagination/flexible thinking. Their presence, which may be accompanied by a host of other 'secondary' symptoms, are central to the diagnosis of the syndrome; they underpin and validate most taxonomic and psychiatric classificatory systems of Autism e.g. DSM IV (APA 1995) and ICD-10 (WHO 1993).

Despite this apparent clarity around the behavioural markers of Autism, the lack of a clear aetiology, prognosis or definitive account of the pathological processes involved mean that Autism has been the target of many scientific and other approaches to modelling its characteristics. Some early models emerging from practitioner and clinical perspectives did not always prove useful (e.g. Bettelheim 1967), so in an effort to improve validity there has been a shift towards empirical research.

Previous empirical research into Autism has largely derived from experimental or sometimes clinical/observational data, such that research criteria and hypotheses are often based on previously published 'findings'. Much research is comparative, framed around notions of identifiable 'deficit' in Autism and juxtaposed against assumed 'normal' capabilities in 'neurotypical' development or other types of developmental disorder e.g. Downs' Syndrome. Moreover, they tend to use a methodology that removes the participant with Autism from naturalistic and familiar interactional contexts and substitutes a research environment based on prior assumptions or the current research hypothesis. Even observations of 'free play' with an associate adult tend to be at least semi-structured with the aim of eliciting particular types of activity e.g. generating questions.

Despite considerable research, a central conceptual challenge for those researching Autism is that it remains easier for even experienced clinicians to recognize than adequately describe, hence a plurality of paradigms has emerged that compete to account for such 'deficits'. In relation to the 'core impairment' in social-interactional skills, three contemporary theories of domain-specific 'deficit' are worthy of note:

a) *The Asociability Hypothesis*. This postulates that the autistic child lacks social interest in others (Jordan 1999; Powell 1999) and is therefore unmotivated to avail him/herself of the basic 'tools' of social interaction. One problem here is that non-production of linguistic skills in Autism is potentially conflated with lack of social intent, and the empirical support for such an assumption is weak.

b) *'Theory of Mind' Deficit*. In this experimentally-derived model it is claimed that children with Autism lack the 'metarepresentational' capacity to see things from other people's exclusive perspective, which has considerable implications for the management of joint interaction (Yirmiya *et al.* 1999). Acquisition is developmental, attributed to 'neurotypical' children at age 3–4 (see Baron-Cohen *et al.* 1985; Leslie 1987). However, in embedding validation in verbal responses to Piagetian tasks it becomes difficult to isolate task failure attributed to 'abnormal' social development from spoken language disability (see DeGelder 1987).

c) *Joint-Attention Deficit*. This empirically-derived model rests on Autistics' apparent failure to initiate or respond to joint attention bids, most strikingly non-verbal *referential* attention to some object or third person (see Curcio 1978; Leekam *et al.* 1998; Mundy and Crowson 1997; Mundy and Sigman 1989). 'Joint attention deficits' have come to be treated as one of the most developmentally significant features of the syndrome. For example, it has been proposed that in Autism 'nonverbal communication is characterized by a lack of *joint attention*, defined as behaviours used to follow or direct the attention of another person to an event or object to share an interest in that event or object' (Siller and Sigman 2002: 77).

These theories' focus on non-verbal activity reminds us that a whole range of interactive resources can be deployed to undertake referencing work in interaction, some specifically highlighted in diagnostic criteria as prone to 'deficiency'; e.g. DSM IV refers to 'marked impairment in the use of multiple non-verbal behaviours such as eye-to-eye gaze, facial expression, body postures and gestures to regulate social interaction' (APA 1995). Such resources can be used flexibly and pragmatically to accomplish a whole range of interactional tasks, either singly or concurrently, to meet local interactional requirements.

The study of the deployment of gaze is especially relevant since 'gaze abnormalities' (notably gaze aversion) have long featured in iconic representations of the child with Autism (Kanner 1943, 1946; O'Connor and Hermelin 1967; Wolff and Chess 1964) and continued to be a focus of interest (e.g. Mirenda *et al.* 1983; Volkmar and Mayes 1990). Although initial interest in gaze focused on it as a potentially syndrome-demarcating behaviour, it later emerged as an emblem of social communicative impairment. Frith (1989) for example, asserted that autistic children possess a deficit of understanding of the significance of the eyes in communicative activity. Such a claim would benefit from further inquiry before being treated as axiomatic.

There are methodological issues that constrain the validity of experimental work in this domain. Gaze activity can, as the joint-attention paradigm highlights, be used to undertake object referencing work, but can also be harnessed in activities such as recipient-selection, or even averted to decline another's nomination for a subsequent turn. If one functional use is absent, can we safely assume others are similarly impaired? Setting up an experimental trial or observational context that assumes eye-to-eye gaze (or perhaps more accurately eye-to-face gaze) performs only referencing work may miss the diversity of possible activity in progress. The method of eliciting gaze in many studies may invite erroneous generalization, for example Van der Geest *et al.* (2002) assume that gazing at photographs experientially matches face processing in everyday life. The practice of reporting gaze fixation or eye contact as a percentage of interaction time (e.g. Arnold *et al.* 2000) does not tell us anything about the local events that occasion its use.

Theories b) and c) above can be located in the domain of pragmatics, an inability to use practical resources to achieve particular kinds of interactional work (Baltaxe 1977). One problem with the experimental work undertaken is its exclusive focus on the activities of one party (i.e. the child with Autism) on the tacit assumption that some measure of experimental 'control' can make the activities of interlocutors (e.g. researchers, accompanying carers etc.) functionally irrelevant. However, real life interactions involve the activities of at least two persons, and often other environmental resources such as objects. Thus interaction is always co-authored, and the contributions of each party will all be relevant to managing ongoing proceedings.

Since the study of pragmatic skills is more ecologically valid when undertaken in the naturalistic, co-constructed environments in which their deployment becomes appropriate to maintaining social interaction, utilizing a research method able to orient to those conditions becomes imperative. Conversation Analysis (CA), with its unique sensitivity to the local sequential organization of multi-authored activity, seems to add dimensions apparently lacking in other approaches considered above. In implying a concern with spoken language, the name Conversation Analysis can detract attention from its capacity to explore the sequential placement of a whole gamut of spoken and non-spoken interactive resources including gaze (e.g. Goodwin 1981; Heath 1986; Lerner 1996).

There is a further rationale for using Conversation Analysis. Much previous work has focused on what children with Autism *cannot* do, CA allows us to refocus on *competence*, what communicative skills children deploy in interaction and how/when they use them. In this we concur with the principle advocated by eminent researcher Beatte Hermelin, i.e. the need to concern ourselves less with what these '. . . children can or cannot do but rather how they do it'. (1972: 289). In according equal recognition to the actions of all parties to an interaction, CA transcends unhelpful pathologization to demonstrate how conversational partners can actively design their contributions to facilitate communication. Furthermore, its flexibility facilitates research across the whole Autistic Spectrum, including non-verbal children.

Moreover, CA's considerable data bank offers the researcher much comparative material without engaging in the vexed politics of matching control participants. Although CA developed through the analysis of non-impaired interaction, its detailed empirical approach has recently made an immense contribution to our understanding of other areas of 'impaired communication', most notably aphasia. For example Goodwin (1995, 2003a and b), Schegloff (2003), Wilkinson *et al.* (2003) provide analyses of interactions involving aphasic participants in a range of settings including home environments and clinical assessment contexts. Furthermore, its appropriateness as an applied research tool for studying social interaction in Autism has already attracted CA researchers, specifically in the area of echolalia (e.g. Dobbinson *et al.* 1998; Local and Wootton 1995; Tarplee and Barrow 1999; Wootton 1999).

Given CA's primary focus on data, we would like to devote the largest part of the chapter to our discussion of some interaction involving children with Autism and their co-participants. But first, a brief introduction to the data source is necessary. The interaction we shall explore involves videotaped activity of pupils at a residential primary school for children with Autism in England. They have been recruited as participants in an experimental trial as part of the 'Aurora Project' (for discussion see Dautenhahn and Werry 2000; Werry *et al.* 2001; further details may be found at http://www.aurora-project.com/). This therapeutic project is centred upon developing mobile robot technology to assist this client group (who are assumed to find human-to-human interaction stressful) in developing interaction skills. In using these minimally-intrusive data collection methods and data sharing we aim to counter ethical concerns around research with this sensitive group of participants. Other participants involved in these activities include two researchers from the project, and school staff responsible for safeguarding the welfare of these vulnerable pupils.

Analysis

Our analysis will focus on some gaze-related practices we have observed children with autism employing. We begin with the co-ordination of gaze with talk. In extract 1 (lines 01–03) Lenny is gazing at a robot which has just ceased moving; several other participants are present. In line 04, still gazing at the robot, he produces a turn that is grammatically a question 'Why'z it stopped' and interactionally a sequence-initiating action, specifically a first pair part of an adjacency pair constructed as a single TCU. As this unit comes to an end he starts to move his gaze to one of the adults, a staff member (Tina), who is present but seated just off camera. Lenny's gaze reaches Tina during line 05 and remains on her for about one second until Lenny looks down at the robot as it make a sudden, and audible, movement (line 06). Our focus will be on Lenny's gaze in lines 04 and 05.

Extract 1[1]

[Aurora Pairs: Lenny & Colin 14:59] JR 13/06/02
Lenny, Colin, Robot and sometimes a Teacher and Researcher are visible
View is through camera1.
Nonvocal conduct: Irrespective of speaker-
<u>above line</u>: Lenny, <u>below line</u>: as indicated
The robot has just stopped moving.

```
                         ((starts to sit back))
                      R→
01    Lenny:         Can I go 'ome


                         ((sits back))

02                       (---------1---------2---------3)


                                 ((small head rotation))

03                       (---------4---------5------)


             →    R→
04    Lenny:  →   Why'z it stopped


             →       ..(Tina)
05                   (---------1---)


             →       . R→
06    R:      →      xxXXXXXXXXXxx


                  ((R moves to left of Lenny))
                  ((moves over))

07                   (---------1----)
```

The gaze redirection Lenny engages in (in lines 04 and 05) constitutes
a recurrently used format for the organization of gaze: bringing gaze to
the recipient of an utterance near the completion of that utterance.
This practice may be used by a speaker to show *who* they are addressing
and also to show that they are available to receive subsequent talk. For
example, in his analysis of talk and body movement in medical settings
Heath (1984) reports the following extract.

Extract 2 (Heath, 1984)

D= doctor, P=patient

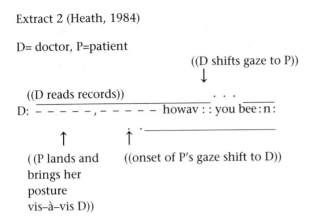

In his analysis of this extract Heath is concerned with the availability of the patient for interaction with the doctor and how the doctor orients to this. (The patient's availability is accomplished through such things as their postural alignment with the doctor and their bringing their gaze to the doctor.) Heath locates how the doctor moves from scrutiny of patient records to gaze at the patient and how this is co-ordinated with the production of the utterance 'How have you been'. As he starts to produce this utterance the doctor is gazing at the patient records, but during the production of the utterance his gaze moves to the patient so that the doctor is gazing at the patient as the unit comes to a possible completion.

A similar organization is shown in Lenny's shift of gaze in lines 04 and 05. Lenny moves from gazing at the robot to gazing at Tina as he completes the question 'why'z it stopped'. The shift of Lenny's gaze from the robot to Tina commences at the transition relevance place as the word 'stopped' is completed. Furthermore it can be noted that Lenny's gaze is directed not just anywhere but towards Tina who, as a member of staff, can be viewed as an appropriately selected recipient and next speaker. That is, both the timing and the direction of Lenny's gaze shift orientate to the possibility of Tina being able to provide an answer to Lenny's question regarding the robot's lack of movement.

In Heath's data there are apparently only two participants present (the doctor and the patient). So, an utterance addressed to another party is uniquely addressed to the other party present. Consequently, using resources such as gaze to accomplish the selection of a recipient would not seem to be relevant. Nevertheless, displaying that the doctor is no longer engaged in reading records and is available for talk is interactionally relevant. (See Rae 2001, for further consideration of gaze and the management of participation in different activities.) However, in multi-party settings, such as the one in which Lenny finds himself, the selection of a specific recipient for some talk may involve the use of body movement practices. As part of his analysis of the second person pronoun 'you', Lerner (1996) has examined how 'The use of you can, on occasion, demonstrate to co-participants that someone has been selected, but where recipients only subsequently determine just who has been addressed by locating, e.g., the recipient of the speaker's gaze.'

Extract 3 [Chicken Dinner] Lerner (1996, p. 291)

```
01      Nancy:      let's watch Rocky three.
02                  (0.7)
                    ((8 lines omitted))
11                  (1.6)
12   →  Vivian:     have you been watching it a lot?
13                  (1.2)
14      Shane:      ner–nahwuh–(.)well
```

In Extract 3, Lerner notes that Vivian's turn in line 12 could be addressed to any of the co-present parties (Nancy, Michael or Shane). However as she begins line 12, Vivian turns to look at Shane, a position she sustains until the end of line 14. Nancy and Michael each look up at Vivian, their gazes reaching her during 'it'. Shane (who has been engaged in eating a forkful of food) turns towards Vivian during the silence in line 13. And it is Shane who subsequently replies to Vivian's question. It appears then that Shane is able to see that Vivian's question has been addressed to him. Thus Lerner demonstrates that 'you' can be used to show that *a* party has been selected and that *gaze* can be used to show *which* party has been selected.

As with Lerner's data, Lenny is not merely displaying his state of recipiency for a response to the sequence initiated by 'Why'z it stopped', he is also selecting a particular party as the recipient of his talk. That is, he is using gaze to accomplish addressing. It may be noted, though, that comparing Lenny's gaze practices (Extract 1 lines 04–05) with those of Vivian (Extract 3 line 12) reveals that his gaze reaches his addressee much later than Vivian's gaze reaches hers. Lerner reports that Vivian's gaze reaches Shane, her addressee, as she *starts* her turn whereas Lenny's gaze reaches Tina just after he *finishes* his turn. These different gaze practices may be produced by reference to the design of the turn with which they each occur. As Lerner notes, Vivian's turn involves the term 'you', a pro-term that is disambiguated by her gaze. This term occurs very early in her turn and it is plausible that there is a push to show just who the 'you' is addressing/referring to close to its production, so the early placement of 'you' in the turn may create a push for early gaze at the recipient in the case of Vivian's turn. By contrast, Lenny is not using the pronoun 'you' and is therefore free of the constraint that may occur through the use of this term. On the other hand, he is using another pronoun 'it' which refers not to a *recipient* but rather to the *referent* of his turn – the robot. For Lenny's turn then, displaying what 'it' refers to might be being accomplished through bringing his gaze to the robot rather than to a recipient.

Lenny continues to direct his gaze at Tina during the 1.3 sec silence in line 05, but when the robot moves he returns his gaze to it, demonstrating that he is responsive to the changing situation which the movement of the robot brings about. The direction of gaze at a recipient which Lenny displays is not a unique occurrence in our data. In another session the robot's cessation of movement leads another boy, Tim, to produce the same question as Lenny: 'Why'z it stopped?'

Extract 4

[Aurora Pairs: Chris & Tim 14:41:14.5] JR 06/06/02
Chris, Tim and sometimes Robot are visible. Researchers
E1 and E2 are present, but off-camera; probably behind cameras, C1
and C2 respectively. View is through C1.
Nonvocal conduct: Irrespective of speaker-
above line: Tim; below line: Chris.

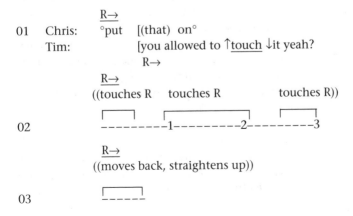

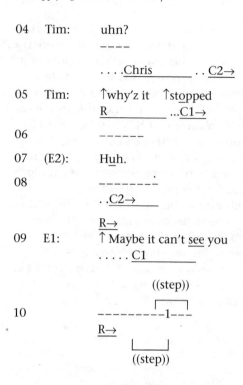

As Extract 4 shows, as he says 'Why'z it ↑ stopped', Tim brings his gaze to one co-present party, Chris (another boy) then relocates his gaze towards one of the researchers (presumably behind C2, camera 2). However, before examining this, some earlier actions need to be described. First, from the start of the extract Chris and Tim display joint attention to the robot. Previously in this session Chris has presented himself as having prior knowledge of the robot; he was already present in the room when Tim arrived and has also previously drawn Tim's attention to some of the things the robot does. Thus in inquiring about whether they can touch it (in line 01) Tim orients to Chris as being knowledgeable about the robot. Following three careful touches to the robot it stops moving and Tim moves back and monitors the stationary robot.

In line 06 he seeks to initiate a sequence through producing a first-pair part, the question 'Why'z it stopped', and as he does so brings his gaze to Chris. Here, Tim produces the same format as Vivian in Lerner's data (Extract 3): bringing gaze to the recipient of an utterance near the start of that utterance. Chris however continues to gaze at the robot and then brings his gaze to C1. As Chris's gaze reaches C1, Tim moves his gaze from Chris to C2. By bringing his gaze to Chris as he starts his turn it is apparent that Tim's question is (at least initially) being addressed to Chris. However, Chris displays a different proposal about what is underway. By moving his gaze from the robot to C1, Chris's conduct suggests that that although he understands that an inquiry is underway, he does not treat himself (or does not wish to be treated) as its addressee. Rather, by looking at one of the researchers it appears that he is monitoring that researcher, thereby treating them as the addressee of Tim's question. Tim, who is monitoring Chris throughout this, is thus faced with the prospect of a proposed recipient not merely failing to display recipiency but displaying a counter proposal about who the relevant addressee is. Following this, Tim looks away from Chris and brings his gaze to another researcher C2 who, from his line of sight, is just to the right of Chris.

Apparently then, Tim has undertaken an analysis of the state of recipiency of an intended addressee and has found an alternative addressee for his inquiry. It should be further noted that this is all accomplished while his turn is in progress. Goodwin (1981) has carried out extensive research on speakers' resources for securing gaze from non-attending co-participants, or, as happens with Tim in this extract, finding alternative recipients. An example of this is shown in Extract 5.

Extract 5: Adapted from Goodwin (1981: 150–3)

Pat, Jere and Chil are teaching Ann how to play bridge

```
01    Pat:     now Ann you gotta count points.
02             (1.0)
03    Ann:     oh okay.
04             (15.8)
                                                    ...Ann
05  → Pat:     now if you have thirteen points: , (---------1)
    → Ann:     └_____
                        ((gazing towards cards))

               _____ , . . . . . Chil          . . . . . . . . Jere   , ,
06    Pat:     counting: voi:ds? s:ingletons and doubletons. = right?
```

Goodwin identifies how Pat's talk in line 05 is designed for Ann, the novice bridge player, not for the others present who already know how to play bridge. (Note, however, that unlike the other utterances examined in the earlier extracts Pat's talk does not constitute the first pair part of an adjacency pair.) During the production of the turn-so-far in line 05, the speaker (Pat) does not use gaze to show who is being addressed. However, during the pause that follows her talk, Pat looks at Ann and sees that Ann is gazing at her cards. Rather than attempting to secure Ann's co-participation, Pat embarks, in line 06, on *another* action which Goodwin examines in detail: namely she modifies her talk in order to make it relevant for *other* parties who are present. She does this by transforming what has thus far been a statement into something else, namely a form of request for verification. This is in part accomplished by the elongated, questioning intonation on 'voids' and the appending of 'right'.

In Extract 4 Tim does not undertake any addition to his turn-so-far when faced with non-recipiency from Chris. There is nothing comparable in his action to the talk Pat produces in Extract 5, line 06. However there is no reason why there should be. In Extract 5, Pat only looks up to monitor what her intended recipient is doing *after* some talk has been produced. By monitoring his intended recipient *during* the course of his turn, Tim is able to redirect his turn prior to its completion and thus circumvents the kind of remedial talk which Pat produces.

Extracts 1 and 4 thus show that two children who have been diagnosed as autistic can, at least on these occasions, show competent and sophisticated eye gaze practice. They are able to produce a recurrently used format for the organization of gaze: co-ordinating the bringing of gaze to a recipient with the production of a sequence-initiating turn. Furthermore, they show competence in modifying gaze when transformations occur to the situation that affect the relevance of where their gaze is currently located. Thus in Extract 1, line 06, when the robot starts moving, Lenny abandons gaze at his addressee and looks down at the robot. In Extract 4, line 05, Tim abandons gaze at his addressee when that proposed addressee gazes at another co-present party.

Although both Pat in Extract 5, and Tim in Extract 4, use gaze direction to identify new recipients, it can be further noted that as Pat's gaze reaches her new recipient she utters words that refer to matters she is now presenting i.e. as she says 'voids' her gaze reaches Chil. Although Tim's redirection of gaze prior to turn completion meant that he didn't produce subsequent talk, precisely this kind of management of address through the timing of gaze and talk is demonstrated in Extract 6.

Extract 6

[Aurora Single: Chris]
Chris, Robot and sometimes Researcher (E) are visible, other adults (A)
are present but not on camera throughout
Nonvocal conduct: Irrespective of speaker-
<u>above line</u>: Chris; <u>below line</u>: Robot.

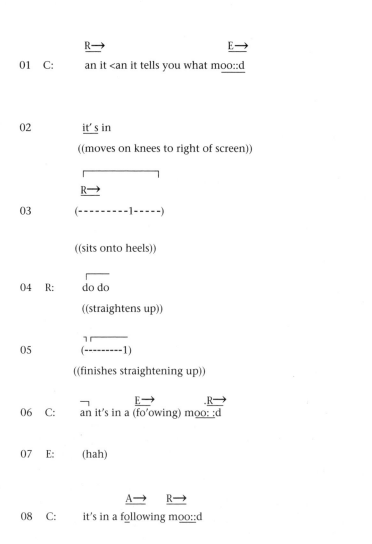

		R→ E→
01	C:	an it <an it tells you what m<u>oo::</u>d
02		<u>it' s</u> in
		((moves on knees to right of screen))
		R→
03		(---------1-----)
		((sits onto heels))
04	R:	do do
		((straightens up))
05		(---------1)
		((finishes straightening up))
		¬ E→ .R→
06	C:	an it's in a (fo'owing) m<u>oo: :</u>d
07	E:	(hah)
		A→ R→
08	C:	it's in a f<u>o</u>llowing m<u>oo::</u>d

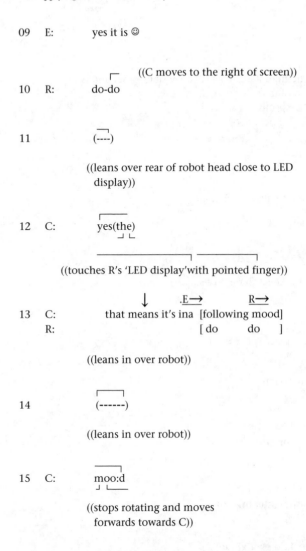

09   E: yes it is ☺

                        ┌   ((C moves to the right of screen))
10   R: do-do

11   (----)

        ((leans over rear of robot head close to LED
          display))

12   C: yes(the)

        ((touches R's 'LED display'with pointed finger))

13   C: that means it's ina [following mood]
        R: [do   do   ]

        ((leans in over robot))

14   (------)

        ((leans in over robot))

15   C: moo:d

        ((stops rotating and moves
          forwards towards C))

In Extract 6, Chris is playing with the robot in the company of two adults (A & E), but no other children. Across the extract Chris produces four turns each consisting of one turn constructional unit (TCU) (lines 01 & 02, 06, 08 and 12 & 13). In producing each of these turns Chris shifts his gaze between referent (robot, or some part of it) and recipient (adult). For example, in line 01, Chris's utterance 'an it <an it tells you what <u>moo::d</u> it's in' involves a shift from gaze at robot for the first part of the utterance to gaze at E as the turn completes.

Furthermore through his use of gaze, pointing and body orientation Chris orientates to the different levels of specificity required across the sequence of interaction.

The gaze shifts manage two key interactional aspects of each utterance (noted with Extracts 1 and 4): *who* is being addressed and *what* is being referred to. Thus as the utterances are produced Chris co-ordinates his gaze between the object being referred to (the robot) and the potential recipient (E or A). Second, Extract 6 shows a recurrent progression in Chris's gaze shifts from referent (robot) to recipient (adult) as the turn progresses (sometimes returning to the robot at turn completion).

In Extract 6 each iteration of 'it' and 'that' *co-occurs* with a gaze to the robot – thus the lexical term is disambiguated by the accompanying gaze to the referent, providing the necessary specificity for his interlocutors without having repeatedly to articulate 'the robot' or to find and produce the potentially complex term 'the LED display'. It can be noted that Extract 4 presents a deviant case in comparison to Extracts 1 and 6 in that the autistic child (Tim) gazes at the potential recipient (rather than referent) as he utters the indexical term 'it'. However, this discrepancy can be accounted for by noting that in Extract 4 joint attention was clearly established: Tim's interlocutor (Chris) was already gazing at the referent (the robot) prior to and concurrently with Tim's articulation of 'it' and this gaze activity was visible to Tim. In Extracts 1 and 6 by contrast the adults are positioned much further from the referent (and indeed might not be, from the autistic child's perspective, seeably gazing at it) and hence the issue of confirming the indexical term by gaze at referent is of heightened relevance.

Chris's gazes at (and pointing and body orientation to) the robot also show sensitivity to the particular level of specificity which the interaction at hand makes relevant. In shifting between talking about the robot as a whole and talking about a relatively small indicator that forms part of the robot, Chris adapts his gaze, pointing and body orientation behaviour to manage the different levels of specificity required at specific places in the interactional sequence. In Chris's talk in lines 01 & 02 'an it <an it tells you what m<u>oo</u>::d <u>it's</u> in' he is referring to a highly specific part of the robot (the LED display). In this case the necessary specificity of reference has been established by the sequence immediately prior to lines 01 & 02 of Extract 6 in which Chris *points* to the LED display in the brief pause between uttering 'that' and 'that': 'that (.) that thing tells you what's its mood is'. Indeed, this turn was followed by E's 'that tells you yeah (.) what's its programme is', a response in which E also uses 'that' without problematizing it as an ambiguous indexical item. This exchange suggests there are grounds for supposing that the referent 'it' in line 01 is at this stage not problematic, following as it does from a disambiguating pointing which itself received a response that did not indicate uncertainty regarding the indexical term used.

Chris's turns in lines 06 and 08 comprise a side sequence in which he has moved from talk about a specific part of the robot to talk about the robot as a whole. The surrounding talk of Chris which refers to the robot's mood indicator is therefore interposed with (related) talk in lines 06 and 08 which refers to the robot globally. The shift in focus from the robot's LED display to the robot as a whole is accompanied by a shift in Chris's specificity of referring. Thus rather than using gaze or gesture to indicate a precise part of the robot, in lines 06 and 08 he gazes more generally at the robot such that the indexical item 'it's' can be disambiguated as now referring to the robot as a whole rather than to a particular part of it.

In line 13, however, Chris is no longer referring to the robot in general but (once again) to the small LED display that forms part of the robot. Here, as in his talk immediately prior to line 01, his interlocutors may need an increased level of specificity regarding what the 'that' refers to in line 13. Chris attends to this issue by not only briefly touching the LED but also by moving his head close to and directly over the LED – his gaze and head position are configured to conspicuously display a highly specific referent and thereby attend to the increased level of specificity that is now relevant in the interaction. Furthermore, this very pronounced movement of head and gaze not only indicates that the 'that' (uttered after the movement has commenced) refers to the LED display, it also further underscores the shift from side sequence (in which the robot was referred to globally) to the prior concern with a specific part of the robot: the 'mood' display device or LED. Therefore Chris's use of an extremely close head position and gaze at the LED (made conspicuous for his interlocutors) both accomplishes clarification of indexical terms and by its very enactment denotes a shift from the side sequence to the prior topic of the interaction.

Conclusion

This study has investigated and described competencies in the use of gaze and pointing which previous research has claimed to be an area of particular deficiency for autistic children. The pragmatic practices we have described include:

- using gaze in accomplishing addressing
- using gaze in accomplishing referring
- using pointing in accomplishing referring
- coordinating gaze and pointing with talk.

Given such evidence of some complex pragmatic competences, how does our analysis relate to the theories of social impairment that we outlined previously? First, in our participants with Autism, it is difficult to establish a 'joint attention deficit' in the terms used by researchers reviewed above. We have presented multiple examples of 'triadic joint attention' initiated by children with Autism, designed to draw adult attention to the activities of the robot platform via the interactional placement of gaze for indexing and recipient selection. Often this gaze is co-ordinated with talk and sometimes gesture, and it may be used to mark changing situations. Here these children with Autism manage skilfully to initiate and maintain both bi-partite and tri-partite joint attention effectively. We are therefore not able to furnish support for Siller and Sigman's (2002) centrality of a joint attention deficit.

Another potentially surprising finding, given the labelling of Autism as a severe communication disorder, was the organizational congruency of autistic speakers' practices with the activities of non-impaired speakers reported in other CA literature as displayed in the contrasted data fragments above. Our data extracts featured concurrent and/or sequential placement of multiple communication resources frequently designed to allow eliciting information from or informing other participants. This tends to indicate at the very least some social orientation on the part of participants with Autism. Such evidence is difficult to relate to both the 'Asociability Hypothesis' and in the case of Extract 6 the TOM hypothesis. It is plausible to suggest in the latter that participant 'Chris' was somewhat aware that his participants had different knowledge from himself in relation to the robot's functional capacity, hence the persistence of the 'informings' highlighting aspects of the robot's 'mood'.

However, it is not our intention to dismiss the psychiatric taxonomies or the 'theories' of social impairment in Autism; other considerations must be taken into account. First, it should be remembered that 'gaze impairment' – however iconic it is treated by those who work with children with Autism – may not be *critical* to diagnosis in a menu-based approach. This said, diagnostic criteria may benefit from being sharpened by taking into account CA-based details. For example, the use of gaze, as a resource at specific interactional junctures, may be an advance on notions of 'regulation' in social interaction. Secondly, there may be an age-related issue here, since 'poor eye contact' is construed as most markedly apparent in pre-school children, although persisting as a feature for many. If this claimed 'eye contact deficit' is, however clumsily articulated, intended to describe (social) interactional use of gaze, then a rigorous approach should also use CA to examine gaze activities in this age group. Third, there may be issues of context. We have seen that in conditions in which the child is granted a fair amount of agency to shape his/her own activities this small sample is not deficient in the capacity to spontaneously accomplish a remarkably flexible range of socially-oriented gaze activities. We need to explore how this operates in other contexts because, together with the efficacy of CA as a research method, this may account for why other experimental research has previously failed to identify these skills.

It is also clear that this work reported here can only make at most a very modest contribution to a necessarily greater CA project in describing pragmatic skills in Autism. There is a whole range of interactional resources we have not attended to here, for example prosody. We also urgently need to examine transcripts from differently-able participants with Autism, such as those with preferences for designing interaction with other resources (e.g. foot gestures) to develop an account of how they manage interaction, however idiosyncratic and 'non-communicative' their practices may appear on first inspection. Such work could provide insights for a range of remedial approaches, and it is to the practice or applied implications of our analysis that we turn next.

There are tremendous challenges involved in teaching many children with Autism, and direct, complex interventions will place their own challenges, including delivery stress on teachers, parents and practitioners. However, we cautiously suggest that CA work could potentially inform pedagogic and other therapeutic interventions in a variety of ways.

First, developing practitioners' use of CA-oriented observation and assessment skills can potentially extend the ways in which children's displayed skills and capacities can be acknowledged, both pre- and post-intervention. This would require an extensive training programme for Speech & Language Therapists and other interested parties. If research priorities are re-ordered then the identification of competencies rather than deficits may emerge. Identifying the specific interactional prac-tices used by a child may assist familiar interlocutors such as parents and teachers to design their communicative activity such that the child can participate in them. Second, in terms of popular intervention models like Applied Behaviour Analysis, CA's attention to the precise placement of interactive practices such as gaze activity could sharpen therapeutic strategies, e.g. developing those that apply behaviourist-type programmes to reinforce 'looking' during interaction. Sequential placement could form an initial training priority or an advanced programme for developing communication skills. This may need to take the form of directly teaching autistic children precisely where context-sensitive resources (such as gaze) may be placed in a way that is accessible to them. The development of a specialist data bank to support programmes of this kind requires concerted CA research into interaction involving autistic persons.

Note

1   Transcription of talk follows the Jefferson orthography usually used in CA work. Transcription of nonvocal actions and events largely follows Goodwin's system of annotations to the Jefferson orthography. That is, descriptors of movements, and labels showing gaze direction, are shown in parallel with ongoing talk, or sound, or silence. Silences are shown graphically as dashed lines, each dash corresponding to one-tenth of a second and with each whole second numbered. However, rather than showing speakers' details above their line of talk, which details correspond to which participant is indicated in the notes for each transcript. Also, although gaze is shown by labelled lines, in order to simplify the amount of detail on the page, where gaze continues for a prolonged period at a certain place, e.g. at the robot, R, this is shown as R→, this should be read as gaze directed at R until indicated otherwise.

3

Co-constructing Meaning in Acquired Speech Disorders: Word and Letter Repetition in the Construction of Turns

Steven Bloch

Introduction

For an individual with a severe speech disorder (*dysarthria*) relating to an acquired neurological condition such as Parkinson's disease, motor neurone disease or multiple sclerosis the ability to produce intelligible speech can become increasingly difficult as the underlying pathology progresses (Duffy 1995; Yorkston *et al.* 2002). This unintelligibility may then lead to troubles in interaction. Robillard (1994, 1999) for example reports specific problems relating to the timing of turns and the context of prior talk as well as difficulties in initiating repair. Additional work highlighting socially consensual 'real time' in talk, states that problems in temporal co-ordination may be seen as contributing to the perception of communicative (in)competence among people with speech disorders (Higginbotham and Wilkins 1999).

   While there is a traditional focus upon the *individual* in communication impairment research and clinical application, the accomplishment of co-constructed talk within an environment of speech and language difficulty has received increasing attention over the past decade, specifically in the field of aphasiology (the study of acquired language impairment). Goodwin (1995, 2003) describes the strategies employed by a man with aphasia, describing ways in which someone with severely reduced language resources (restricted to: 'yes' , 'no' and 'and') is able to collaboratively establish meaning through specific sequential activities – including the use of gesture. Further work has examined how joint productions are utilized as a conversational strategy in aphasia (Oelschlaeger and

Damico 1998) and also how traditionally labelled symptoms of aphasia (e.g. telegrammatic speech) may be understood from a collaborative perspective (Heeschen and Schegloff 1999). However, despite a growing interest in understanding the social action of disordered communication, acquired *speech* (as opposed to language) difficulties have received little attention.

Through the use of Conversation Analysis (CA) this chapter describes a pattern of turn design displayed by participants in the co-construction of meaning within an environment of dysarthric speech. Where one would expect to find an utterance produced by one person alone (e.g. a single word) the examples given below show the work of two participants engaged in both single and multi-word turn construction. It shows that the participants (an intelligible speaker and a severely dysarthric speaker) have developed specific routines and patterns of action through talk that form a joint action strategy. Examples of utterance completion are also presented – demonstrating further joint action. These are seen as distinct from component completion practices previously described in the literature (Lerner 1996). The chapter concludes with a consideration of the potential applications of CA to work with people with dysarthric speech.

Dealing with problematic talk

It has previously been reported that problems in speech, hearing and understanding may be addressed through an 'organization of repair' (Schegloff *et al.* 1977). The ways in which participants deal with problematic talk and the sources of problematic understandings have been described with reference to a number of features including: sequential environments (Drew 1997) and prosodic contextualization (Couper-Kuhlen 1992). One of the most striking features to emerge concerning repair is that it appears to be the only action that can supersede others. At next turn position there is always the opportunity for other initiated repair if a problem has been encountered. Given its purpose perhaps this is not surprising, repair is a practice that concerns a problem, and for other-initiated repair this will relate to a problematic understanding of prior action (prior turn or sequential context). In this way the continuation of prior social action is restricted until any problem has been addressed. However, given the strength of repair and its ability to alter the sequentiality of ongoing talk 'any action type with this immensely powerful privilege of displacing any other item must surely be restricted in its privilege of occurrence' (Schegloff 2000a).

For dysarthric speakers and their co-participants repair has the potential to become a central feature of any interaction. Not all action proves to be problematic, but data collected for the study from which the following examples are extracted show that speech (un)intelligibility is regularly located as a trouble source through other initiated-repair. This is shown in Extract 1 where Stan initiates repair (line 3) upon Mary's prior turn, which is moderately dysarthric. Stan not only signals a problematic understanding but also locates the specific part causing difficulty. Mary takes the third turn (line 5) to complete the repair by re-doing the trouble source. Stan then shows his understanding in line 7 and the action proceeds.

Extract 1

```
001      M    and my getting in (0.6) the ⌈(↓car.)                        ⌉
                                           ⌊((drops hand & looks to S)) ⌋
002           (0.9)
003   →  S    getting in what?
004           (0.5)
005      M    the ⌈↓ car:                    ⌉
                  ⌊((drops hand & looks to S)) ⌋
006           (0.8)
007      S    the car (.) oh yeah.
008           (1.0)
009      M    was ⌈very good          ⌉
010      S        ⌊that's a that's a ⌋(.) that's a huge improvement (.) ⌈isn't it⌉
011      M                                                              ⌊mm    ⌋
```

Given that participants use repair sequences to deal with problematic talk in this way, it may be that no further strategies are required. As speech becomes increasingly unintelligible there is the option of using communication aids or augmentative and alternative communication (AAC) systems,[1] but there is clearly a period in the progression of dysarthria where so called 'natural' speech is used in increasingly problematic circumstances. Thus, what is of interest here are the ways in which a speaker using *natural* speech (albeit severely dysarthric) achieves understanding through collaborative action.

Analysis

The following examples are presented from a video recorded conversation between two adult family members: John and Sheila. John has a severe dysarthria and severely restricted trunk, limb and facial movements due to motor neurone disease (MND). His cognitive and language abilities are intact. Sheila (John's mother) is the non-dysarthric speaking conversation participant. The action takes place in John's room within a nursing home. John's speech is characterized by weak lip, tongue, jaw and soft palate movements. He also has reduced respiratory support.

Two processes are described in this analysis: joint turn adaptation to co-construct utterances for meaning, and completion of utterances by the non-dysarthric participant.

a) Repetition as a resource for the co-construction of meaning

From an initial observation of the following examples it is clear that a non-typical talk activity is occurring between the participants. A common sense expectation may be that meaningful utterances consisting of strings of words are generally created by one participant at a time. However, this analysis shows that the participants may orientate to units smaller than individual words while those words are being created. This operates through single word or grapheme units being built up jointly over a number of successive turns to complete a multi or single word utterance.

Two types of *repetition sequence* can be observed: those involving whole word units and those utilizing single grapheme or phoneme units. Both types of sequence operate in paired turns: John's production of a unit and Sheila's repeat of that unit. The repeats continue until an agreed end point is reached. The end point is displayed through Sheila's action consisting of a complete production of John's full multi-turn utterance or an action that demonstrates her understanding of the previous sequence of turns. The following examples are presented to demonstrate these features of talk, with the final example showing an alternative end point to the routine in which the meaning of the prior sequence of repeated turns is embedded within the ongoing talk rather than through an explicit utterance.

In Extract 2 Sheila asks John if he knows when he will be moving into a new room within his nursing home. His response is established over two separate turns (lines 3 and 7).

Extract 2

```
001      S    so when (0.5) do you know when you're going to be moving?
002           (0.6)
003  →   J    ((1 syllable)) (in a)
004           (0.3)
```

```
005      S    in a,
006           (0.4)
007   →  J    (few days.)
008           (0.5)
009      S    in a few days.
```

In response to Sheila's utterance in line 1 John takes next turn (line 3) to respond. John's turn in this case produces the first part of a complete intended utterance. The words 'in a' are followed by a short pause. At this point it would be possible for John to continue his turn construction and complete a meaningful TCU. John has no knowledge at this point whether Sheila has understood his prior talk. It is Sheila's next turn (line 5) that demonstrates the joint strategy for working with this construction. Sheila repeats back what she has heard 'in a'. This repeat is not produced in a way that would indicate an other-initiated repair strategy – it is produced promptly with a level intonation, and contrasts with other occasions where a trouble source has been located. This is critical in that it displays Sheila's awareness to John what she has understood. Also, that through *only* repeating what she has heard she may be projecting the next turn action as a continuation of John's utterance. John then adds further information at line 7 – 'few days' confirming this interpretation – i.e. by completing the noun phrase production. This is shown to be highly efficient in that John does not attempt to produce the whole unit 'in a few days' but simply the necessary elements ('few days') to complete the unit. Sheila then repeats back John's two preceding turns – again displaying her understanding to John. This serves the function of bringing their joint understanding together – it provides a check for both participants that they agree where they are in the talk. This summary may be of importance in such a setting where extra work is being conducted in maintaining meaning.

The status of Sheila's repeat turns may be worth highlighting at this point. A number of options are available to Sheila on receipt of a partial utterance – she may not chose to say anything – thus allowing John the chance to continue, or she may acknowledge John's turn and affirm that she has heard the sounds produced. However, these alternative routes do not achieve the same action that is being achieved by Sheila's actual turn design. Through repeating she is explicitly demonstrating her understanding to John. This is an unequivocal understanding check – it is doing an action of 'this is what I understand from the prior turn'. In addition and more fundamentally, this construction is also doing an acceptance of the prior turn as a unit that has some sort of meaning in the local context. The production of a single word (or grapheme as discussed below) could have the ability to raise questions of competence in 'normal' talk, but here we have evidence of an agreed system legitimizing the action of single word/letter production.

A third outcome from this process is one of efficiency in talk. The displays of understanding by Sheila are acknowledged through John's next turn actions but (unless there is a problematic understanding) John does not make an explicit confirmation of each of Sheila's understanding displays – rather his next turn action holds an embedded assumption of adequate understanding of his prior turn. This process enables the construction of larger utterances by the speech impaired speaker without adding additional accountable actions – i.e. the speech impaired speaker does not have to respond to the repeat turn with explicit affirmation but does have the option of initiating repair if the repeat does not match the first turn.

Multi-turn utterance creation and associated word repetition is shown above to be one strategy for dealing with reduced speech signal intelligibility, but it is notable in this data that grapheme repetition is also used as an ongoing resource. The following two examples demonstrate co-constructed spelling for meaning.

In Extract 3 John tells Sheila that a phone will be needed for his new room. Again, the production of the key word 'phone' is a joint achievement produced on a turn-by-turn basis. Here the word 'phone' is constructed through a number of turns in which each grapheme or letter name is spelt out aloud by John. Sheila is then seen to produce the same letter name in each next turn position.

Extract 3

```
001      S    someone's got to come and do ⌈it have ⌉ they.
002      J                                  ⌊ mm   ⌋
003           (0.6)
004      S    right
005           (0.9)
006  →   J    a:-a-a: an a=
007      S    =an a
008           (0.5)
009  →   J    ef
010           (0.3)
011      S    ef
012           (0.3)
```

```
013  →  J    o:
014           (0.2)
015     S    o:
016           (0.2)
017  →  J    en
018           (0.2)
019     S    en
020           (0.8)
021  →  J    ee((slight downward movement of lower lip))
022           (0.2)
023     S    ee
024           (0.7)
025     S    and phone.=
026     J    =((blinks & moves lower lip down))
```

In line 6, John produces a turn that signals a link to the previous talk as well as a projection that more is to follow. Sheila then takes next turn to repeat or, more accurately, re-do what she has just heard. At line 9 John produces the grapheme name 'ef' which Sheila then repeats at next turn position. It is at this point that both participants display an orientation to the spelling sequence. After John's first spelling turn, Sheila has the opportunity to initiate repair but she does not do this and in repeating the previous turn with a level intonation (line 11) and nothing more she is displaying to John a) her understanding that they have moved into 'spelling rules' and b) that she has no more to add at this point, thus enabling John to continue. John in next turn (line 13) implicitly acknowledges Sheila's acceptance of the sequencing rules and produces the next grapheme name 'o:'. The speed with which this spelling exchange occurs is also significant – there is the minimal amount of time required between each turn – again providing supportive evidence that this is a normative sequencing strategy for the participants. The spelling continues with 'en' and 'ee'. After his production of 'ee' (line 21) John moves his lower lip down slightly – a possible indicator of end of word. However, rather than taking this as a completed word Sheila repeats the last unit with the preceding intonation 'ee' (line 23) – indicating that further letters might be added. A short silence is followed by Sheila offering the full unit of 'and phone' to which John immediately confirms with an eye blink and lower lip movement.

   A second example of this resource combines the word repetition with the grapheme repetition units. John is telling Sheila that aside from a new phone, the maintenance men have two more power points and a Possum[2] to install into his new room.

Extract 4

001	J	(they have)
002		(0.6)
003	S	they have,
004		(0.4)
005	J	(two more)
006		(0.5)
007	S	two:
008		(0.4)
009	J	more
010		(0.4)
011	S	more,
012		(0.5)
013	J	(power)
014		(1.3)
015	S	((very slight lean forward))
016	J	(power)
017		(0.6)
018	S	power (0.4) ⌈points. ⌉
019	J	⌊((1 syllable))⌋ and a
020		(0.3)
021	S	and a,
022		(0.6)
023	J	pee o:
024		(0.7)
025	S	pee o:
026		(0.4)
027	J	es ⌈es ⌉
028	S	⌊°es°⌋
029		(0.5)
030	S	the Possum to sort out.

In line 1 John begins this example with 'they have'. This is repeated by Sheila in next turn with a level intonation (line 3). John then adds two more words (line 5). In line 7 Sheila initiates a repair on John's prior turn by locating the trouble source specifically at the second unit of the two produced. This is displayed primarily by Sheila's elongation of 'two' (line 7) – a different production to that found in the other examples. John then repeats the word that Sheila signified as causing difficulty, which Sheila then goes on to repeat. Despite this being a repair sequence inserted within an ongoing message construction routine, Sheila's intonation on 'more' brings both participants back to the main process. John's next turn (line 13) shows his own awareness of this return to the routine by adding additional information. Sheila responds to this initiation by repeating his prior turn. At line 18 Sheila repeats the word 'power'. This is followed by a short gap before Sheila produces 'points' and John overlaps with one syllable and then 'and a' which Sheila repeats. At this point there is the introduction of the spelling routine. Having established that more is to come, John takes next turn (line 23) to produce two sounds 'p' and 'o'. There is no explicit context given for these sounds, but Sheila does not take significantly longer to respond than in previous turns. She repeats back what she has heard with a level intonation. John then continues with two more sounds 'es es'. At this point Sheila produces a full interpretation – 'the Possum to sort out' – and it is established from the data that both John and Sheila are using pairs of graphemes in successive turns to build up a key word for meaning.

John and Sheila are capable of jointly managing talk through an explicit turn-by-turn display of understanding. Sheila (as the non-dysarthric speaker) uses repetition to display her understanding on a turn by turn basis while John builds up both full messages and/or full words over a number of successive turns. This is only seen to work because both participants display a shared understanding of the routine rules.

b) Word completion as a conclusion to repetition

A further feature that draws attention to the shared activity between John and Sheila is that of word completion. This describes the way in which Sheila completes a word unit prior to a full joint construction. The completion of words during spelling work reduces the amount of work and time required by the impaired speaker to produce each turn.

Prior to the sequence in Extract 5 John and Sheila have been talking about John's lunch. John mentions one of the catering staff at the nursing home (Sarah) and goes on to tell Sheila that Sarah is a 'd-i-e-t'. Sheila is shown to offer a completion to this construction at line 33 where she expands 'diet' to 'dietician'.

Extract 5

```
001   J    (she is)
002        (1.2)
003   J    (she is)
004        (0.3)
005   S    she is
006        (0.7)
```

007	J	a
008		(0.2)
009	S	a
010		(0.5)
011	J	dee eye
012		(0.6)
013	S	dee eye
014		(0.5)
015	J	ee
016		(0.6)
017	S	ee
018		(0.3)
019	J	(tee)
020		(1.2)
021	S	dee eye ee:
022		(0.3)
023	J	(tee)
024		(0.4)
025	S	see?
026		(0.6)
027	J	t
028		(0.2)
029	S	tee=
030	J	=((blinks & moves lower left lip down))=
031	S	=a diet=
032	J	=((moves lower left lip down & lips forward))=
033 →	S	=dietician?=
034	J	=((blinks & moves lower left lip down))
035	S	what Sarah is?

Between lines 1 and 9 John and Sheila use word repetition to establish 'she is a'. John follows with two letter sounds 'dee eye' (line 11), followed by an 'ee' (line 15). The following letter sound causes some difficulty. John's attempt to produce a voiceless alveolar plosive [t] is compromised by his dysarthria – resulting in unwanted nasalization and friction to the sound. The result is the production of a sound similar to [s]. At line 21 Sheila does not offer her understanding, but repeats back what she has already understood – i.e. 'd - i - e'. At this point she has initiated repair on John's previous turn. John then repeats his turn (line 23) – again with similar intelligibility problems. This time, Sheila displays her understanding and locates both the trouble source and, crucially, its form. John now has knowledge of Sheila's difficulty and modifies his production by producing not the letter sound 'tee' but rather the speech sound [t]. Sheila now repeats back John's target sound which he immediately confirms as correct via facial movements. At this point (line 31), Sheila now brings together her understanding of the built-up utterance and says 'a diet'. John confirms this and also moves his lips forward slightly. Sheila then produces a candidate for the whole word 'dietician', which John immediately confirms. Given that the topic of 'Sarah' has already been established prior to this sequence it is unlikely that Sheila's final turn is a problematic understanding, but rather one relating to the truth of John's utterance (they have also discussed Sarah as having trained as a nurse prior to her catering role). Sheila's talk after this sequence indicates her doubts as to Sarah being a nurse, caterer and dietician.

The word completion work does not always work smoothly. The need to contextualize a word to the prior talk is important, and if extended time is used in constructing a word via spelling there is a risk that this relationship may be lost thus requiring further repair work.

In Extract 6, John and Sheila continue to discuss the room adaptations and the need for assistance from the environmental control company 'Possum'.

Extract 6

```
001  J    ((4 syllables))
002       (0.7)
003  J    ((2 syllables))
004       (0.9)
005  S    they will?
006       (0.6)
007  J    ((4 syllables))
008       (0.3)
009  S    em
010       (0.7)
011  J    (ay en)
012       (0.3)
013  S    ay
014       (0.5)
015  J    (en)
016       (0.2)
017  S    en
018       (1.1)
```

```
019  S   man-maintenance man?=
020  J   =no=
021  S   =no.
022      (0.2)
023  S   man
024      (0.8)
025  J   from
026      (0.4)
027  S   from
028      (0.7)
029  J   Possum
030  S   =Possum!
031      (0.7)
032  S   someone's got to come and do ⌈it have⌉ they.
033  J                                 ⌊mm    ⌋
034      (0.6)
035  S   right.
```

The extract begins with John's turn in line 1 which is particularly difficult to understand. He then takes a second turn, again with only the syllabic pattern identifiable. Sheila's first turn is a candidate interpretation indicated by rising/questioning intonation (line 5). John again produces a turn that is unintelligible. This time Sheila signifies a trouble in understanding by picking up on one letter sound for spelling (line 9). John provides two more letter sounds spelling the word 'man'. In line 19, Sheila produces the full word that displays her understanding of what they have already spelled – 'man'. She then adds additional information relating to her understanding of the reference and relevance of 'man' – that is, Sheila is offering a candidate understanding by expanding what John has said and furnishing the agreed unit 'man' with the role of 'maintenance'. John initiates repair at this point very promptly (line 20) and Sheila also immediately shows recognition that what she has offered is not what John had intended to produce. In line 23 Sheila returns to the previous understanding by repeating her last 'successful' turn. This serves the purpose of returning the participants to the last position they were at when things were 'working'. This also allows John to take next turn to provide further information required. It is then established that John is referring to the man from Possum and not a 'maintenance man'.

The above examples demonstrate actions characterized by repetition and word completion units. The repeats are shown to work as individual paired units, but with the realization that these units form part of a larger meaningful entity – i.e. either a full utterance as in 'in a few days' or a full word as in 'phone'. The significant feature here is that such units are created through the joint-actions of both participants. Both John and Sheila have adapted their talk to create a specific turn pattern that would normally appear incomplete on an individual turn basis. The co-construction routines are extraordinary phenomena: they are not characteristic of everyday conversation. However, the participants do manage to integrate these methods into their everyday talk – thus making these routines ordinary in practice.

A final feature of this 'creation of ordinary' is shown in Extract 7. When the spelling for meaning works it can be so successful that it becomes implicit within the ongoing talk and meaning is shown to be extracted and understood without recourse to explicit meta-routine talk.

Prior to the conversation in this sequence , John has asked Sheila if she has bought him some CDs for his computer. He now goes on to ask Sheila if she has bought a shelf for his new room. The word 'shelf' is constructed through letter repeat turns but it is never stated as a full word. Its understanding is established through Sheila's action in line 35.

Extract 7

```
001   J    ((widens eyes & moves jaw forward)) (0.2) (( 3 syllables))
002        (0.5)
003   S    ((moves lips silently)) ⌈mm?                    ⌉
                                   ⌊((slight lean forward)) ⌋
004        (0.8)
005   J    ((1 syllable)) ⌈    ((2 syllables))       ⌉
006   S                   ⌊((moves lips in sync)) ⌋
007        (0.6)
008   S    ((leans forward)) ara⌈mat?               ⌉
                                ⌊((lowers brow))⌋
009        (0.5)
010   J    ⌈    ((3 syllables))          ⌉
011   S    ⌊((moves lips in sync)) ⌋
012        (0.6)
013   S    how about
014        (0.5)
015   J    the
016        (0.4)
```

017		S	the
018			(0.5)
019		J	es
020			(0.5)
021		S	es
022			(0.4)
023		J	h:
024			(0.4)
025		S	aitch
026			(0.5)
027		J	ee (.) el
028			(0.7)
029		S	ee (.) el
030			(0.5)
031		J	ef
032			(0.5)
033		S	ef,
034			(0.6)
035	→	S	I've been into B&Q:=
036		J	=((lowers eyelids & slight nod))=
037		S	=and they're dearer.

Following an initial repair sequence between lines 1 to 10, Sheila displays her understanding of John's prior talk 'how about' at line 13. This is followed by production of 'the' (lines 15–17). John then switches to letter/sound level in line 19. The notable action is found at the end of the joint production of the word 'shelf'. At line 31, John produces 'ef' and Sheila repeats at next turn (line 33). Sheila's production of 'ef' is not accompanied by a fall in intonation (all the sounds in this sequence have a level intonation) or by any facial/body movements, which might indicate end of word. The repeat of the 'f' is important here in that it shows Sheila is not acting upon a possible prediction of the word prior to its full completion. Her understanding of this sequence as a full turn is displayed in her next turn selection which demonstrates: a) that she has been able to piece together the individual sound units to produce the word 'shelf', and b) that she can relate the action of this turn to the topic of conversation prior to this sequence – namely that John is asking Sheila if she has done anything about the shelf despite not having taken action regarding the CDs.

Having finished the spelling work together, Sheila's next turn (line 35) is not used to clarify her understanding by saying the word in total, but

by dealing with the action as she understands it by providing a response to John's utterance 'how about the shelf'. Her action displays her understanding of John's utterances as a comment about the expected purchase of a shelf for his room. John participates in this 'realignment of topic' (line 36) by acknowledging Sheila's understanding of his spelling and allowing Sheila to continue her turn.

Discussion

The analysis in this chapter has described two resources used by participants within an environment of dysarthric speech. These resources are characterized by the use of short turn units followed by next turn repeats, and also the practice of turn completion. In an examination of repetition in conversation Tannen (1989) considers a number of possible functions of repetition including 'interaction' and 'interpersonal involvement'. However, CA analysis goes further in revealing that next turn repetitions by other may be used to perform number of different social actions (Schegloff 1996b; Tarplee 1996). The argument here is that the repetition of dysarthric turns does not function in a reparative way, but is instead part of an established routine of sequencing that enables the understanding of talk through a successive build-up of turns. Further prosodic analysis is required to examine the ways in which the routines are seen to work, but at this stage it can be stated that the dysarthric speech has a much reduced prosodic range. The non-dysarthric participant's prosody indicates a differentiation between the feature associated with repeated words and letters and intonation more commonly associated with other-initiated repair (e.g. rising intonation).

Of particular note is the way in which the dysarthric speaker produces only part of what may be considered a full utterance at each turn position. In showing how an utterance may be started by one person and finished by another, Sacks (1992) suggests that the idea that a sentence is 'somebody's property' is 'considerably weakened'.[3] In the current work the majority of dysarthric speech turns are responded to with a repeat, culminating in an action that summarizes or contextualizes the incremental turns. In this way the non-dysarthric participant's action achieves both a 'TCU building' and turn contextualising function. It can also be noted that the data presented shows two participants achieving what would normally be done by one alone – i.e. the production of single word units and multi-word utterances. This is an unusual pattern of talk and yet the participants display a close alignment in its operation – suggesting that this has become a regular mode of interaction.

The turn constructions described in this chapter rely upon joint action between the participants. Throughout the repetition sequences each turn is used by the participants to monitor and feed back the progression of an intended utterance. The maintenance of intersubjectivity between John and Sheila would not be possible without this form of action.

It has previously been suggested that spontaneous *language* in dysarthric speakers may change in response to increasingly effortful speech (Wilkinson *et al*. 1995). In addition, it has been reported that dysarthric speakers present as 'less participative' in conversation (Comrie *et al*. 2001). The current study supports the view of conversation change but would contend that it is not necessarily language content or amount that needs to be considered but rather the ways in which co-constructed talk is adapted to achieve different activities. Recent work on aphasia turn taking (Wilkinson *et al*. 2003) identifies adaptive language within turn taking environments, and it would appear that such activity may also be present in dysarthric talk.

Implications

Traditionally the investigation and subsequent management of dysarthria have been based upon a speech signal intelligibility model – with the degree of severity being based upon a perceptual or instrumental analysis (Chenery 1998). In this way dysarthria has been understood largely in terms of the deviation of speech from culturally acceptable norms. The focus of investigation and clinical assessment has been upon the mechanics of speech production in relation to the dysarthric speaker. In this respect dysarthria is a medical label that describes a form of speech production but does not indicate the consequences of that production upon conversation or social action. Any links between the severity of speech function and the effects upon interaction are assumed.

The work presented in this chapter does not negate or attempt to challenge the value of speech impairment investigation and therapy. However, for individuals with severe dysarthria who can make no physical improvements there may be a role in applying the principles of conversation analysis to dysarthric talk in order to examine how such talk-in-action is achieved. There are two potential implications of such an application:

1. *Understanding how participants manage dysarthric speech: complementary information for the assessment process*: Current dysarthria assessment tools used clinically in the UK fall into two categories: speech

subsystem assessments (e.g. 'The Robertson Dysarthria Profile' (1982)) and speech intelligibility assessments (e.g. Yorkston and Beukelman's 'Assessment of Intelligibility of Dysarthric Speech' (1981)). Both approaches focus upon the perceptual analysis of a dysarthric's speech. They do not address interactive communication. The application of CA principles and methods to the analysis of dysarthric conversation may provide additional information regarding the individual strategies and resources used by participants. The addition of such work would not only complement traditional speech assessment but could also contribute to treatment outcome measurements. Thus, understanding *how* talk is working could be used as a potential baseline for intervention measurement.

2. *Offering an additional resource for the management of progressive speech disorders*: For people with acquired progressive dysarthria (moderate to severe) there is a general consensus that therapeutic intervention should aim to reduce disability through the development of functional strategies for the maintenance of communication (Royal College of Speech and Language Therapists 1998). The aim at this level is not to improve the speech mechanism physiology but rather assist in optimising communicative abilities in whatever way possible. A range of strategies are typically proposed – e.g. slowing down rate of speech or the provision of an augmentative and alternative communication (AAC) system. The analysis in this chapter shows one way through which participants may utilize their own joint resources to maintain intersubjectivity. It is possible that CA may have an application in highlighting particular features in dysarthric talk for clinicians and dysarthric individuals. Awareness of such features may in turn be used to strengthen existing strategies that are shown to 'work' but to which participants may not be explicitly aware. Given that Speech and Language Therapists and their clients are already aiming to maximize effective communicative behaviour, it may be that CA principles could be utilized to enhance those therapy techniques already used – e.g. by emphasizing the joint ownership of talk between clients and family members where there is a potential belief that it is the dysarthric or the family member alone who must make adaptations (see also Murphy (2003)).

The emphasis again may be placed upon joint action rather than just the behaviour of the dysarthric speaker. This principle may then be applied to the training of health/social care professionals who may come in to contact with people with severe dysarthria but are unable to contribute to conversations in the way they might wish because of inadequate experience or knowledge of effective strategies. In this way CA findings and recorded conversations themselves could provide a useful training resource.

Concluding remarks

Demonstrating a positive clinical outcome remains a major challenge to therapists working with people with progressive speech disorders. An investigation informed by CA draws attention to joint action in a way that much dysarthria research has neglected in the past. It may also contribute to the understanding of the frequently under-defined health outcomes relating to 'participation' and the ways in which participation is being achieved through talk.

The principles of CA and its potential to demonstrate how dysarthric talk actually operates in conversation may make a significant impact upon how dysarthria is viewed. At present, the call is for more investigation not necessarily into the perceived problems of dysarthric speech, but rather the underlying mechanisms of impaired speech-in-interaction.

Notes

1 The use AAC systems or communication aids in conversation presents a number of challenges to social action through talk. See Collins *et al.* (1997).
2 'Possum' refers to the trade name of an electronic environmental control system used by John to operate his TV, bed, door etc. from one control system.
3 One type of talk that bears a surface similarity to that of spelling aloud for meaning is in the provision of telephone numbers or addresses – where one participant completes the talk of another based upon given lexical resources – see Lerner and Takagi (1999).

4
A Comparison of a Mother and a Therapist Working on Child Speech

Hilary Gardner

Introduction

Research into speech/language therapy with children has primarily focused on theories of speech development and disorder as a rationale for therapy. Therapy is an interactional process yet research has tended to overlook this aspect. In part this chapter documents how speech therapy is recognizable as a distinct form of institutional talk but has patterns redolent of both instructional and mundane adult/child interaction. Peräkylä (in press) in his work on 'Stocks of Interactional Professional Knowledge' uses Conversation Analysis (CA) to challenge therapeutic predictions and intuitions. Likewise in this chapter a combination of careful interactional analysis and linguistic (in this case 'phonetic') detail makes a very powerful clinical research tool. Quantification in the form of 'turn counts' form part of this work, an approach that Wootton (1989) and Schegloff (1993) support as long as 'coding' of turn types have been identified through detailed analysis. However, sequential placement within the interaction, the type of preceding try and what is projected in next turn, will be shown to be vital adjuncts to the numerical information.

The interaction which is this chapter's focus is that where a speech therapist or a parent seeks to bring about change in a child's speech. Speech disorders, where the child's phonological patterns are not developing typically, form a large proportion of the paediatric therapist's caseload. Children usually receive therapy weekly and parents are expected to participate in this therapeutic process through supported home practice, having observed the clinic session. In work with children with poor intelligibility, phonetic and articulatory matters become the explicit topic of interaction in a way that has rarely been found in mundane talk. Gallagher (1977), Gallagher and Darnton (1978), Gardner (1986, 1989) found phonetic repair is rarely addressed overtly in adult–child talk, unlike that dealing with lexical matters. Tarplee (1993) also described the 'disguised' and embedded nature of phonetic repair in mother/child interaction.

A theme that emerged while looking at therapists' talk was the particular influence of theoretical knowledge, especially that of phonetics, phonology and learning theories on modelling and repair of target words. The child's responses, however, can clearly display that even an experienced therapist's approach may fail to make her/him address the phonetic nature of their miscommunication. In turn the mother comes to therapy with a distinct approach and her underlying understanding of therapy issues is revealed within the talk. From a professional standpoint detailed analysis gives an informed perspective on parents' contribution to therapy and how this could be enhanced.

One broad objective of therapy is to make children aware of those aspects of their phonological system that are problematic and to execute change within their speech. In the early stages of therapy it is routine to choose sets of key words that the adult 'models' as phonetic targets through their turn design. A variety of behaviours are used including perturbation of the normal speech flow and disruption of syntactic patterns. Some of these models are 'redoings' after an error. To do a redoing . . .

> is to pick that utterance up and display it for some kind of work to be done on it. That work may be corrective, evaluative or investigative; may be immediate or delayed and may be undertaken by the redoer, the speaker of the original utterance or by both collaboratively. (Tarplee 1993: 7)

Models and redoings can additionally be differentially designed in order to engender a child repeat of the target. However, the differentiation of imitable models is not always clear cut and non-coordination of expectation between the interactants can arise. As in Schegloff's (1987) work on misunderstandings, interactants display trouble not only with possible intended referents. The child can also have trouble with the sequential import (implicativeness) of the adult turn, i.e. what action is being done by the turn and what is an appropriate next. Some particularly bizarre patterns of error are found to be linked to the prior turn design, and the use of various repeat engendering turns are of particular interest because of their effect on the trajectory of the child's repair.

This analysis concentrates on tasks aimed at verbal 'output' tasks. An assumption often made is that all production errors children make on a target word are due to 'internal' mechanisms, for instance their idiosyncratic 'phonological' system. This analysis seeks to show that a child's pronunciation errors could arise through the interaction, and how the nature of the error can be shaped by the prior talk. The phonetic data is in itself interesting as it contributes to our picture of the child's understanding of the therapeutic process.

Initially an extract of mother/child talk will identify key issues. Then a comparison of mother and therapist will ensue, often using extracts where the same words are tackled. The use of quantification, the contribution this might make to the analysis and its clinical applications will be discussed. The data is taken from five sessions, filmed at home (with the researcher present) and in a clinic over six months. The child, (Steven; 'St') was four years old at the outset of filming. Although language skills were within normal limits, his poor intelligibility had shown little improvement in the months before being taken on for therapy. His phonological system showed immaturities (e.g. fronting of velar plosives /k-t/, /g-d/) but also deviation from the expected pattern of development, such as stopping of fricatives (/s-t or ?/, /v-d/).

An initial data presentation: mother and child working together

Extract 1 is a single 'bout' taken from a practice session at home two days after attending the first working therapy session. A *bout* is a unit for later quantification and is defined as a number of turns dealing with a target word as initiated by the adult and finishing with a closing strategy or change of target/topic that is taken up by the listener. Parent and child are going through the workbook as used by the therapist in the session. The bout is initiated by the adult, a phonetic error occurs and a lengthy repair sequence ensues, finishing with a change of topic from St. accepted by his mother. The target word list illustrates final plurals [-z], here exemplified in 'frogs'. Steven labels the picture with lexical accuracy but several phonological errors occur as predicted by his phonological pattern.

Extract 1[1]

```
001  St:  ((points and looks to pic.)) bʊŋg⁽ᵗ⁾]
002  M:   not brogs, frogs.
              [((exaggerated artic.))
```

003 St: [fʊɒgtʰ]
004 M: yeh ((glance to book))
           (.2)
005 M: again look.
       (.5)((touches him))
006 M: sit up.
007 St: [[f ʊɒgᵗʰ].
008 M: well sit up.
       (0.6)
009 M: [fɹɒgᵊ z̠:ᵊ]
    < >
010 St: [fʊɒgˢ]
    [((looks to mother))
011 M: that were good were that, do it again.
012 St: [[ʃʊɒğˢ]
013 M: [fɹɒgᵊs:]
014 St: [fʊɒgtʰ] –
    ((M. moves head to seek eyecontact))
015 M: put your ser on.
      ((St. moves head away rapidly))
016 St: we have to=
017 M: =frogs::
018 St: we have to make the fishpond.
019 M: yeh, we have to make the fishpond.

(St/Mother. At home, first session, target /-z/ plural in 'frogs')

There is evidence here of the mother seeking a version of the key word that goes beyond the correct pronunciation of the actual therapy target [z], itself achieved half way through the bout. This is evidenced by the presentation of a shifting focus (by speech perturbation and verbal description) from one segment to another. The analysis details how repeat tries at the target word are achieved and closely charts the phonetic changes made by Steven.

The first repair episode occurs between lines 1 and 4, ending with a clear evaluation 'yeh'. In line 1 (the child's first try) the final [z], the target sound, is not signalled clearly. In addition the initial [f] is 'stopped' and is bilabial rather than labiodental and the second part of the /fr/ cluster is realized as [ʋ], a labiodental, liprounded approximant. At line 2 Steven's mother rejects his initial try with the overt marker 'not (brogs)', an inaccurate redoing of his errorful try as 'brogs' (he actually said [ˉbʊŋg⁽ᵗ⁾]). This rendition glosses over the poor articulation of the /z/, the focus of therapy, and of the /r/ as [ʊ], but focuses on his rendition of the initial /fr/ cluster as /br/. This redoing is then contrasted to a model of the target word 'frogs'. The focus on the initial segment, (in addition to the auditory contrast 'fr/br') is created by exaggerated articulation rather than any increase in volume/length. At line 3 Steven responds promptly to the model set up in the prior turn and successfully repairs the initial /b/ to the required /f/. Although St. is looking away during this episode this does not prevent him attending to the /f/. The final fricative /z/ is little changed.

Thus the combination of the overt rejection, contrast of the two versions and the slightly exaggerated model has prompted an appropriate repair but not of the therapy target [z]. His mother immediately confirms this repair with 'yeh' but qualifies this with a quick request to say it 'again'. Despite restlessness Steven displays interactional compliance to the 'again' request and a whole new path of repair is initiated. There is no redoing or model with the repeat request and his slightly overlapped repeat (line 7) does not differ a great deal from his prior try except that there is some voicing on the rather effortful production of the /f/ (exhibited by blowing out the cheeks in the production of air pressure). Thus he would seem still to be displaying 'doing work' on the initial phone. His interpretation is arguably that the minimal acknowledgement 'yeh' plus 'again' requires more than just a repeat but is seeking some improvement in clarity, albeit unspecified.

That this try still has segmental error as far as the mother is concerned is made transparent by the mother's next relevant turn (line 9). She does not confirm his try: the redoing/model that occurs is an implicit evaluation of his prior try as inadequate. The clear model marks the segment for attention, the final /z/. This model differs significantly from the previous one at line 2, where the stress was on the /fr/. Individual weight is given to each segment of this /gz/ through a rapid 'sforzando' on each. There is some prolongation of the final fricative but more unusually it is released with a syllabic schwa [ə']. Steven's following repeat (line 10) has a clearer element of final friction, possibly interdental. This repair is followed by praise at line 11 yet this does not function as a closing, being followed by 'do it again'. 'That were good were that' differs from the more qualified flavour of the evaluation at line 4 where the 'yeh' did not mark the status of the prior try so explicitly. Part of the nature of this sequence thus involves the withholding of appreciation following an initial appropriate repair (br-fr) until 'correct' pronunciation of the therapy target /z/ is also achieved. Thus two phonetic segments have been targeted and repaired in one sequence.

The praise at line 11 raises the question as to the purpose of the repeat request. At line 4 such a request follows a try evaluated as inadequate but here at line 11 'do it again' follows a wholly adequate token of the target word as evaluated by the mother. She seems to be trying to engineer another performance of the 'good' try. In the absence of any further model, the onus is on the child to reproduce another error free try, but in fact the result is slightly worse!

Thus the mother's request for repetition is overlapped (lines 11/12) with another try by Steven in which the final /z/ is not as good as on the previous try. Following the repeat request and overlapped try there is a further model (line 13) that once again shifts the phonetic focus. This time the final /z/ is augmented but so also is the /r/ of the initial blend. In more detail the articulation here (line 13) is unusually open with prolongation of the /r/. The plural marker is devoiced to a greater extent than would be usual following a final voiced plosive /g/ and this plosive is made almost syllabic by the release onto a schwa before the start of the /s/. Thus the final phone sounds like /s/ rather than the prescribed and discussed /z/ form of the plural, different to the models given before the rewarded child try achieved (line 10). As part of the process of encouraging the child to 'do it again', his mother has produced a version of the word that does not highlight any single element but rather has careful articulation of the whole word including the /r/ not tackled before. The request for repeat leads to a recycling of the whole process.

The mother's model does not result in an improved rendition at line 14 but in some minor change from his prior try. The alveolar plural is again stopped as a plosive but with some aspiration, reflecting the voiceless plural marker /s/ of the mother's version. The mother pursues the production of the final fricative, returning to the sought after plural with 'put your "ser" on' at line 15. This overt reference to the letter name acts as a repair request with no outward evaluation of the prior. It is Steven who signals that enough is enough and changes topic at line 16, ignoring his mother's prior request and model that interrupts his utterance at lines 16/18.

There are several features of interest here. It is evident that the length of the bout is produced not only by repair on the initial try but reinitiation of the repair process through the use of repeat requests (e.g. 'do it again') even after a positive evaluation has been forthcoming (see lines 11, 5, 15). The overt requests for repetition occur without a further model while in other cases a redoing/model projects repetition (e.g. lines 9, 13) but with shifted phonetic focus. There is thus an absence or deferment of a closing after a reasonable try at target. The lengthy bout does not result in a better version. Other data show that there are alternatives available to the adult in response to errorful and even acceptable tries. Investigation of their deployment here and in other extracts will provide evidence of contrastive and complementary use of such turns with differential sequential implicativeness for child response/repair.

A comparison of the therapist and mother in their approaches to multiple phonetic errors

It will now be shown that particular features of mother/child bouts are in contrast to therapist/child interaction. It is argued that the contrast between the two modelling styles illustrates the different motivating factors on the part of the mother and the therapist, the former aiming at generally correct speech as opposed to focused targets. The mother in Extract 1 above aims at complete 'correctness' by targeting multiple phones and further examples will show that this is a routine practice. Although the child often copes with repairing one or both phonetic segments through imitation, successful imitation is not the whole story in therapy as the global aim is to bring about permanent change in his/her phonological 'system', apparent through the child's spontaneous production and self repair. The procedures involved in implementing this aim involve the therapist in routinely addressing the target sound and glossing over other errors.

The following extract is a clear example where the therapist ignores errors that have a marked effect on intelligibility, in contrast with the mother's approach to the same problem. The therapist is tackling the word 'cars'; she augments only the target plural /z/ and the systemic error /k-t/ remains an unmarked feature with normal prosody.

Extract 2

```
001  St:   two [tʰɑdf]
002  Th:   two cars::. Again?
003  St:   two [tʰɑz:]
004  Th:   that's it.
```

(St/Therapist, 3rd session. Target /-z/ in 'cars')

Steven clearly misarticulates the /k/ as /t/ initially in the word 'cars' as well as pronouncing the plural /z/ as /f/. The therapist simply remodels the word, with the correct /k/ not highlighted in any way. However the /z/ is clearly lengthened. She requests a repeat with 'Again' following the redoing, accepts his repair to the plural and moves on with no reference to the /k/.

What is unusual about the next extract where the mother is also tackling 'cars' is that the mother's verbal description of the error and her following model do not highlight the same target. Thus two phones are highlighted through explicit description and stressed articulation in one turn.

Extract 3

```
001  St:  tʰ ɑdz/
002  M:   it's not tars it's cars, cars:
003  St:  [tʰɑz]
004  M:   yeh, but you're still saying [tʰ]. [kʰ], it's [kʰɑz:d ]
                                                     <
005  St:  tars:
```

(Mother and St, 1st session. Target -/z/ in 'cars' (picture))

What is interesting about Extract 3 is that Steven is actually signalling the target plural reasonably with /z/, even in his first try (line 1) yet this version of the target remains unevaluated. The /k/ is however said as /t/. In the next turn he receives an explication as to the source of his error that contrasts /t/ with /k/, but in the immediately following model emphasis is put on the /z/ with 'cars:'. The speech perturbation in the model (only on /z/) thus does not match either the prior description 'it's not tars it's cars', nor her following evaluation which focuses only on the t/k distinction (line 4). At no time does the initial /k/ become emphasized, the contrastive presentation of 'tars' with 'cars' is the evidence that this is a target.

Further repeat engendering turns in mother/child talk

We have seen that the child tries hard to follow the adult focus in repair and can execute positive repair, frequently through imitation. We will now consider some other requests for repetition which in themselves, unlike models, give no phonetic information for the child to follow. Skilled sequential deployment of such requests may be crucial in building a successful therapeutic interaction, both for global therapy aims and more local requirements for repair. Extract 1 shows some evidence that the child can end up in more difficulty when trying to comply with less skilfully deployed maternal requests for repetition. The next extract illustrates a similar turn of events. Here child and mother are working at length on key words with final [s]; 'horse'.

As in Extract 1, Steven's mother seeks further repetition of a reasonably successful try and crucially does so without a redoing or model that highlights the 'correct' version she requires. There is also no confirmatory comment that indicates his prior try has been successful enough. Success in terms of a repaired version of the target word 'horse' is achieved reasonably quickly (by line 7) but the child finishes (line 14) with a version that is as far away from the ideal as his original error. The latter error can be shown to be interactionally driven through the maternal use of request for repetition and redoing.

Extract 4

```
001   M:   what's that?
002   St:  'ortie.
003   M:   no, not 'orsie (0.8) 'orse:.
            (1.0)
004   M:   you do it.
005   St:  'orte.
            (1.0)
006   M:   ᵖproperlyᵖ, 'orse:
007   St:  [ 'orse,
            [ʔɔts]
008   M:   ((M. turns away to relocate book)) and again
            (0.9)
009   St:  'ors:e.
            [ ʔɔs:ˢ]
010   M:   ['ors:e
011   St:  a- 'orfsh(ers)
            [æʔ ʔɔˈʃɚʔs:]
            (1.0)
012   M:   no again, do it again.
            (4.0)((St. turns away and M pulls him round))
013   M:   sit still and do it again.
014   St:  worfse
            [wɔˈʃ]
```

015   M: ^f horse:^f
016   St: o-((looks at brother))
017   M: ((to brother Gareth)) no,(0.8) Gareth, move.

(St/Mother. At Home, second session, target [-s] in 'horse')

The initial error is 'hortie' for target 'horse'. The mother rejects this clearly and her model displays the appropriate mature lexical and phonetic version. Steven repairs the lexical but not phonetic error and this is met with a further redoing/model by his mother. Following this redoing at line 7 Steven gives a reasonable rendition of 'horse' with some signalling of the /s/ (mother and child are in unison so it is difficult to judge the accuracy. At line 8 a request for repetition occurs; 'again' alone. St. then comes in with the repeat which has only a slightly *prolonged /s/,* a minor segmental alteration. Meanwhile his mother has shadowed his turn with another redoing/model where the /s/ overruns the end of his. At line 11 Steven, after a false start, does more work on the word, producing a very distorted version with an [f] articulation appearing with the addition of another syllable; 'orfshers'. Thus he has moved further still from the correct version, apparently in response to a maternal redoing.

At line 12 this odd version is rejected by a clear 'No'(+ 'Again) but the request for a further repeat is not accompanied by a model. After the long gap in which St. has tried to disengage himself from the sequence he produces the version [wɔ^f s̩] which bears very little resemblance to the target or his original try. Not only has he made the erroneous labiodental /f/ more exaggerated but he has also substituted a phone /w/ for his original glottal stop in initial position in the word. Thus major phonetic revision follows this clear rejection of the child's try. The following model loudly targets multiple phones with an emphatic [h] (when before a glottal stop had been used by the adult) as well as prolonged final [s].

There is therefore evidence of differential treatment by the child of maternal repeat-engendering turns. In the extracts above more major segmental revision follows redoing/models than occurs following repeat requests such as 'again' when suprasegmental or articulatory features (such as manner of release or alteration in phasing) are more routinely altered. Although structures using 'again' make up a small proportion of the mother's talk, they contribute significantly to the production of lengthy sequences. Their sequential distribution is of interest in that they seem to be more narrowly distributed in comparison to other repeat instigating structures such as redoings. We have seen from the extracts above that they most commonly follow tries and repairs that show a positive trajectory. Tries with major phonological error were more routinely followed by a redoing and/or negative evaluation. These arguments will be taken up again in a comparison made to similar extracts from therapist/child data.

Comparison of length of task bouts in mother/child and therapist/child data

What stands out in the mother/child data is the way repetition requests contribute to the lengthy, seamless quality of the task bouts. Closing is deferred and repetition/repair sought on or beyond the target, even after a positively evaluated try. Indeed in Extract 1, the child initiates closing (exceptionally rare in therapist/child data). In the therapist/child extract below it will be seen that a level of targeted success (well below 'correct') is confirmed at an early point and the bout is closed. There is no use of 'again' structures and any practice on a target production is built across more than one key word, creating a series of much shorter bouts. Below, the therapist/child dyad are tackling a word that the mother has previously practised: 'horse'. Over nine turns they actually achieve two reasonable imitated renditions of the target phone.

Extract 5

```
001   Th:   an' what's this one?
002   St:   hortie.
003   Th:   horse:
004   St:   horse.
005   Th:   that's it. and what does he like to eat?
006   St:   grass
             [gæʔt].
007   Th:   grass:: did you hear the snaky sound at the end there? try it
             again
             (.)
008   St:   grass:
             [gaeʔˢ]
009   Th:   OK. and what keeps him in the field?
```

(Therapist/St. 2nd recorded session in clinic. Target [-s] in 'horse')

It can be clearly seen that the child's first improved repair at 'horse' (line 4) is accepted and then practice on the /s/ is built in to the routine through other key words (grass, fence). There is no attempt by the therapist to correct errors outside the therapy target such as [gr] simplified to [g] in 'grass'. 'Again' here is only used with a redoing plus extra phonetic information. Where several tries in a repair sequence have not resulted in a correct version then 'success' is confirmed at a point a long way short of the target as originally set.

The difference in length of maternal and therapist bouts can be summarized numerically. Table 4.1 presents the *frequency of bouts of varying length* measured by *number of turns per participant within bouts* in two complete mother/child practice sessions and the same in an equivalent number of bouts from the therapist/child data. The number of turn construction units per turn is not counted and the table excludes non work-talk such as behaviour management or preamble to a task. If the same word was practised several times it is counted in separate bouts if some intervening talk or activity occurred.

The two sections labelled A/B for each adult in Table 4.1 consist of:

A) *bouts* in the whole of the 14 minutes of the first practice session and the equivalent number of bouts in the first therapy session (excluding two episodes of auditory discrimination work).
B) *bouts* in the second filmed practice session (12 mins) and the equivalent number of bouts in the second therapy session (15 mins).

What is most striking about this table is the fact that none of the therapist/child bouts extends over more than 15 turns and a large majority falls into the 0–5 category (55–57%). In contrast the mother has a more even spread between very short bouts and some that go up to nearly 30 turns. The more leisurely pace of the therapist data, with more drawing and non-work talk, is also reflected in this table since, despite the extended length of the mother/child bouts, both dyads

Table 4.1 Frequency of bouts of varying length

No. of turns per bout		0–5	6–10	11–15	16–20	20+	Total
Mother	A)	4	4	4	4	4	20
	B)	11	16	8	2	0	37
Therapist	A)	11	6	3	0	0	20
	B)	21	13	3	0	0	37

experience 20 bouts in the same length of time in A, with only a few minutes difference in B.

A comparison of mother and therapist use of repeat initiations

Just looking at the length of the 'bouts' of therapy does not give the whole story however. Throughout the data there is a commonality in certain properties of turn types used by mother and therapist. The interactions do not look the same because the turns appear to be used at different points in the interaction and to be deployed more often by one party or the other. Some further frequency data will now be presented, based on a small section of the corpus, looking at the *proportional use* of certain turn types and assessing whether therapist and mother have any distinct *idiosyncratic* behaviours. The majority of turn types listed are those that have already been identified and discussed in the detailed data analysis of bouts in therapy talk.

Repeat initiating turn types

There are a number of options the adult can take in order to encourage a repeat try at the target word by the child and these options will be defined and then presented in table form. Some of these turns clearly give certain information to the child, as to the status of his try and/or to the type of repair that could be carried out. Others such as 'again' alone appear to give little away. The level of success of the engendered repeat is not taken into account here. All the behaviours included have been derived from the data and mostly incorporate the use of a repeat request and/or a redoing of the child's prior. Additionally the therapist uses a wider range of more descriptive repeat initiating turns than are evident from the mother and these are included as 'phonetic comments' and 'other'.

A) AGAIN ALONE i.e. with no evaluation of the prior try or any redoing.

B) POSITIVE EVALUATION + AGAIN. Positive Evaluation of the child's prior, followed by a repeat request such as 'again', e.g. Extract 1 'That were good were that, do it again.'

C) AGAIN + REDOING. The use of 'again' (often in a phrase) followed (or occasionally preceded) by a redoing of the child utterance as a model. The majority of these models follow only a micropause and are not a reaction to delay in response from the child. There may additionally be some form of positive evaluation of the child's try before the repetition request, e.g. Extract 6 'Two cars::. Again?'

D) EVALUATION + REDOING. A positive or negative evaluation of the child's try followed by a redoing as a model for imitation, e.g. Extract 3 'Yeh, but you're still saying 't','k', cars::'

E) PHONETIC COMMENT. A comment on the phonetic or articulatory structure, e.g. 'right at the back' (re tongue), or 'Put your ser on'.

F) REDOINGS ALONE. These also occur routinely as models for imitation.

G) OTHER. This includes use of self repair initiators, such as incomplete sentences for completion with the target version (It's a...) and understanding checks such as 'Pardon?' that are followed by a repeat.

The bouts labelled A and B in Table 4.1 constitute the first two complete maternal practice sessions and the equivalent from therapy. They will now be broken down into the turn types described above. The turns from the total 57 bouts have been counted together for Table 4.2 which represents the frequency and percentage proportion of turn types, excluding those that are *not* followed by a child repeat.

There are two ways of interpreting these figures. First, the *simple frequency* counts are important in revealing the sheer volume of turns in the teaching bouts while the *percentages* are critical when considering how the bouts are differently constituted for each adult.

In terms of *frequency* it is the sheer volume of *repeat engendering turns* on the mother's part that is so striking, especially when looking at the overall total of turns in the final row. In the same number of bouts, dealing with the same material, there are almost exactly twice as many of these moves by the mother. The most extreme contrast is where there are 57 cases of the mother using *redoings alone* compared with 19 therapist, and 32 maternal utterances contain *'again'* compared with 12 therapist. Additionally 41 of the mother's utterances constitute

Table 4.2 Frequency of repeat projecting turns (*turn types that successfully initiate another try at target word*)

Turn types within bouts	Mother	Therapist
AGAIN ALONE	7 (4.3%)	2 (2.4%)
POSITIVE EVALUATION + AGAIN	8 (4.9%)	1 (1.2%)
AGAIN + REDOING (+ POS/NEG EVAL.)	17 (10.4%)	9 (10.8%)
POS/NEG EVALUATION + REDOING	41 (25.2%)	7 (8.4%)
PHONETIC COMMENT + REDOING	23 (14.1%)	20 (24.1 %)
REDOING ALONE	57 (35 %)	19 (22.9%)
PHONETIC COMMENT ALONE	7 (4.3%)	16 (19.3%)
OTHER	3 (1.8%)	9 (10.8%)
TOTAL NO OF ADULT TURNS	163	83

evaluation (predominantly negative)+*redoing* compared with seven of the therapist's. In the other direction the therapist uses 16 *phonetic comments alone* while the mother produces less than half this number (seven).

Looking at the **percentages** these turns make up of the particular adult's talk gives a clearer picture of how the adults are using these turns. A type of nul hypothesis would be that despite variations in raw frequency the adults are using similar proportions of turn types, but this does not appear to be the case. The types of turn that feature predominantly with both adults are those with *redoings* as models, these making up over 80% of the maternal data and 65% of the therapist's. The majority of these, in the mother's case, occur in isolation with no other comment (35%) but also with frequent evaluation (25.2%) or phonetic comment (14.1%). This frequency may partly be explained by their serial use when an appropriate repair is not forthcoming and by the mother's concern to encourage the child to give an overall correct version (not just the target phone). The therapist normally alters her strategy more frequently in such circumstances. For her a *redoing alone* is used slightly less frequently (22.9%), a redoing being just as likely to occur with additional information such as *phonetic comment* (24.1%) or *evaluation* (8.4%). Table 4.2 also reveals some interesting individual turn choices where there are no redoings, e.g. the therapist uses more instances of *phonetic comment* than the mother does, making up a higher proportion of her turn choice.

A contrast in usage that has featured strongly in the data extracts occurs where the mother uses a small but significant number of turns that feature an explicit repeat request with 'again', in isolation and with other elements, for instance taking some opportunities to be positive, using (positive) evaluation + again, (e.g. Extract 1 lines 10–12). 'Again' turn types make up an even smaller proportion of therapist talk and they are carefully placed where the child is deemed likely to be able to repeat successfully. The therapist is more likely to add a redoing or comment, simply clarifying the nature of the repeat to follow.

These findings with both adults support the premise that all 'again' repeat turns have a role linked to positive phonetic work by the child: they can be seen to potentially permit the rehearsal of a single target word after repair has already taken place. Redoings are more rarely used like this. It is argued in contrast therefore that isolated redoings are predominantly deployed where there is a major segmental error, such as replacing one phone with another. Thus they usually follow initial phonological errors, or attempts positioned later in a sequence where no appropriate repair has been exercised or the trajectory of repair has been negative. In line with this argument *redoings with negative evaluation,* (e.g. 'No, not tee, key) make up a much greater proportion of maternal turns, being rarely coupled with positive comments.

By using a redoing the adult explicitly models the repair to be executed. Redoings are frequently followed by a phone segment substitution by the child. In contrast *'again'* is routinely treated by the child as requiring further refinement only on phonetic segments already in place. Repair to prosodic and secondary phonetic features tend to follow. However, in lengthy sequences where the child has made several attempts at repair their positive function may be lost. 'Again' without redoing does not necessarily have a positive phonetic result (Extract 4). Additionally, where there are multiple redoings with little in the way of evaluative comments the child may also begin to make more wild attempts at substitution.

Conclusions

It is clear that the child receives different instruction from the adults, at least at this early stage of therapy. The mother is stimulating a greater number of tries at target than the therapist within a given bout. Partly this is due to her seeking repair on phonetic segments that are not concerned with the therapy target. For the therapist practice on the target phone is built across tasks, rather than on one word. She gives more positive than negative evaluation and does not routinely follow the former with further requests for a repeat. Therapist talk uses a variety of structures that give more information regarding the child's prior try.

  Phonetic errors that are not directly attributable to the child's phonological system have been traced and it has been argued that these are interactionally generated by the adult's handling of repair. Other aspects of therapist talk have been shown to cause interactionally driven error, involving requests for self repair, blurring of the distinction between lexical and phonetic repair and the use of theoretically based phonetic models (see Gardner 1994, 1997, 1998). Many of the child's tries at repair show phonetic awareness and work being done but not necessarily in the direction anticipated by the adult or planned for in therapy targets. Both adults are successful in shaping the child's attempts mainly through modelling but, as stated previously, imitation is only the first step in therapy which aims to permanently change the child's phonological system. Self-monitoring and self repair at the phonetic rather than the lexical level is required. Adults must be sensitive to the child's stage of development and how a therapeutic approach needs to be structured in interactional terms in order to enhance performance. The level of phonetic sensitivity on the part of the child is of considerable interest for further investigation, for example looking at how phonetic variance is displayed at a point when he/she is considered to have grasped the wider, metalinguistic aims of therapy. There is also evidence that the child's treatment of models differs according to the interactional partner and better understanding of the interaction may give further insights into phonological development in therapy.

What is clear is that the mother in this case needed more than clinical observation and explanation to make therapy tasks a positive experience for her and the child. In this mother/child data longitudinal measures of turn type and frequency revealed there was little evidence of dramatic developments in maternal pedagogical style as compared to the therapist. The latter recognizably moved away from imitation into encouraging more spontaneous repair over ensuing sessions. In the short term there was a move away from the use of extremely long bouts by the mother (Table 4.1). It could be possible to take this line of investigation further as a clinical measure of positive change in interaction during tasks. However, this would depend on professional assessment of the nature of each dyad (long bouts might be enjoyed!). Quantification can certainly help in making outcomes of therapy more transparent and measurable but must be used alongside a level of sequential analysis and clinical judgement.

The skill of the therapist must extend to shaping the interaction of other adults working with the child if generalization of skills learnt in the clinic to other environments is to be maximized. There may be a stage when a different approach is advantageous and this could be made evident through detailed analysis with both the interactional outcome and phonetic 'success' quantified. This chapter makes a strong case for CA methodology and video training being a useful tool for helping parents support therapy and no doubt it could be equally valuable for use with other support workers and student therapists.

Note

1   Additional phonetic transcription symbols taken from the IPA international alphabet.

Part II
Professional Discourse

5

Talking an Institution into Being: the Opening Sequence in General Practice Consultations

Joseph Gafaranga and Nicky Britten[1]

Introduction

A visit to one's GP (General Practitioner) is a very common social event, at least in the British context. We (patients) visit our GPs for a variety of reasons, including reporting a new medical condition, reporting developments on an ongoing concern, renewing a prescription, and even obtaining a certificate for sick leave from work. The fact that a 'list' (Jefferson 1990) of the reasons for visiting one's GP can be attempted is an important indication of the nature of doctor–patient interaction. It is a goal-oriented activity, an instance of institutional talk (Drew and Heritage 1992b; Heritage 1997). At once these two facts, diversity of goals and goal-focus, lead to the important issue of opening, of how participants enter the interactional world of the consultation. Time constraints within which consultations are conducted (more or less ten minutes) add to the urgency to get the consultation underway as soon as possible. The ordinary everyday conversational method of introducing topics in a stepwise progression (Sacks 1992) is not likely to be helpful here. Rather, participants in a consultation overwhelmingly use the strategy of topic initial elicitors (Button and Casey 1984). Such topic initial elicitors include questions such as 'How are you?', 'What can I do for you?', 'What's the problem?', 'How are you feeling?' and even commands such as 'Fire away'. Given this diversity of *first concern elicitors*, the question arises as to whether they are equivalent, whether the choice between alternative ways of opening the consultation is random or whether it is orderly.

The issue of the opening sequence in doctor–patient interaction has long interested researchers, including medical education specialists as well as social scientists. From an educational perspective, interest in 'opening gambits' stems from the realization that initial concern elicitors may mean more than they say. Thus, educationalists advocate the use of open-ended questions in order to allow the patient to express their concerns in an unconstrained manner. On the other hand, social scientists aim to describe the orderly nature of the opening sequence in doctor–patient interaction as an activity in its own right (Bower *et al.* 2000). For example, both Heath (1981) and Robinson (forthcoming) agree that the opening sequence in doctor–patient interaction is orderly, although they differ at the level of the actual patterns they identify. Heath argued that there are two main initial concern elicitors, namely 'How are you?' and 'What can I do for you?'. According to Heath, 'How are you?' is used to open a doctor-initiated consultation while 'What can I do for you?' opens a patient-initiated consultation. As for Robinson, he identifies the following patterns: 'What can I do for you?' for a new consultation, 'How are you feeling today?' for a follow-up consultation and 'What's new?' for a routine consultation. To these three, Robinson adds a fourth category which he unspecifically refers to as not being institutional, namely 'How are you?'.

Building on this work by social scientists, our aim in this paper is to revisit the orderliness of the opening sequence in doctor–patient interaction and to foreground it firmly in the institutional character of talk. According to Drew and Heritage (1992b) and Heritage (1997), talk is context implicative and context renewing. That is, the context in which talk occurs provides for its orderliness and, at the same time, through orderly talk, the very same context is renewed afresh, is talked into being. Schegloff (1992b) nicely captures this reflexive relationship between talk and its social context by means of two key principles, namely the principle of *procedural consequentiality* and the principle of *relevance*. By procedural consequentiality, Schegloff means the fact that the context impacts on talk organization, and of course a particular organization of talk can be related to a particular aspect of the context in which it occurs. The principle of relevance starts from the fact that the same context can be correctly described in very many ways depending on occasions. Therefore, it becomes necessary to specify which aspect(s) of the context participants are orientated to on each occasion of talk. These two principles have important implications as regards the orderliness of the opening sequence in doctor–patient interaction. For example, the principle of procedural consequentiality implies that patterns such as those referred to above are context specific. A pattern may be typical of General Practice and unusual in hospital medicine, for example. The principle of relevance means that identified patterns must be related to specific aspects of the institution at hand that would have occasioned them. In this chapter, we will look at the orderliness of the

Context   talk organization

opening sequence in a specific institutional context, that of General Practice, and will seek to answer three specific questions: (1) what order regulates the opening sequence in GP consultations?; (2) what aspect(s) of the institution of General Practice account(s) for the orderliness of the opening sequence?; and (3) to what extent is the institution of General Practice talked into being through orderly openings?

The data we will use in this chapter come from a study of 62 General Practice consultations collected in the Midlands and Southeast of England. Ethical approval was obtained from 11 local health authority ethics committees. Each patient was interviewed before and after the consultation, ideally in their own homes and, in a small number of cases, at the general practitioners' surgeries. Consultations were recorded and transcribed and doctors were interviewed about each consultation they had had with each of the patients recruited in our sample. In analysing these data, we proceeded as follows. For each consultation, the opening sequence was analysed *sequentially*. More specifically, a display of a first medically relevant concern in a particular turn by the patient allowed us to locate the strategy, used by the doctor in immediately preceding talk, that had 'occasioned' it. We also looked at the doctor's talk immediately after the patient's display of a concern in order to ascertain that our understanding of a particular sequence corresponded to participants' own understandings. Finally, for each consultation, we went beyond sequentiality and checked every opening sequence against participants' previous mutual knowledge, interpersonal relationship and the reason they were consulting as these were reported in the relevant pre- and post-consultation interviews (triangulation).

Contextualizing the issue

To begin to address the issue of the orderliness of the opening sequence in GP consultations, it is necessary to have a broad picture of the various devices participants may draw on. As a starting point, consider the following extract from a GP consultation:

Extract 1

D: = Doctor
P: = Patient

001 D: come in please
002 P: hello

003	D:	take a seat. I won't be a moment. (pause) Mr Nixon is it?
004	P:	yes
005	D:	oh, I recognize you. haven't seen you for a long time. ((laughs))
006	P:	how are you?
007	D:	pretty well, thanks.
008	P:	are you? good. splendid.
009 →	D:	eh, I shouldn't say 'how are you?' should I? ((laughs)) I should say 'what can I do for you?'
010	P:	well, what I've come around about, doctor, on and off from time to time I seem to get like a leg aggravation. it, eh, it seems to be like a smarting type of feeling and eh, it aggravates like, itches.
011	D:	itches, does it?

(Tuckett *et al.* 1985: 60)

In this extract, a number of observations can be made, but we will focus only on talk in turn (9) and its immediate sequential environment. Before this turn, participants had been engaged in some relational talk. Turn (8) is particularly interesting for it is closing implicative, indicative of participants' readiness to move from the greeting sequence to topical talk (Schegloff 1968). In turn (9), the doctor engaged in a metalinguistic activity whereby the expressions 'How are you?' and 'What can I do for you?' were said to be both usable at this particular juncture. The issue here is: what is it that both expressions can do at this point in the inter-action? A look at turn (10) reveals precisely what it is that these two expressions accomplish in this environment. Here, the patient started displaying her reasons for consulting. In turn (11), the doctor confirmed the normativeness of the patient's acts. Thus, both participants confirmed to each other, and to the analyst, that the two expressions can be, and indeed were, used as first concern elicitors.

Two more observations can be made on the basis of the extract above. First, as the transcript shows, the doctor hesitated between the use of 'How are you?' and 'What can I do for you?'. Through this hesitation, the doctor seemed to indicate that the two are not equivalent, that their use is rule-governed, that there are contexts in which one, and not the other, can be used. Therefore, our concern is: when is 'How are you?' appropriate and when is 'What can I do for you?' more adequate? That is to say, what selection rule governs the choice between these two? Secondly, the fact that the doctor hesitated between 'How are you?' and

Table 5.1 Some patient concern elicitors

L/09/28c:	so, what are we going to do for you today?
L/01/01c:	what are we talking about ?
L/04/07c:	there we are
B/05/14c:	how are you getting on?
L/01/05c:	fire away = begin
L/06/12c:	what brings you in today?
B/02/07c:	carry on
L/08/32c:	so what am I doing for ((first name)) today?
B/06/21c:	what's been the trouble?
L/01/04c:	so

'What can I do for you?' raises the issue of whether these were the only two options available. Observation of our data revealed that a number of other devices are actually available to participants, some of which are listed in Table 5.1.

Since many possibilities were available, how do we account for the doctor's decision to contrast 'How are you?' and 'What can I do for you?' rather than any other pair? The particular behaviour seems to confirm Heath's (1981) argument that 'How are you?' and 'What can I do for you?' are the two main first concern elicitors. Indeed, a perusal of the above list shows that, with few exceptions, each entry is either a variant of 'How are you?' or of 'What can I do for you?'. Therefore, in the following, we will trust doctors and patients and investigate the rule governing the choice between 'How are you?' and 'What can I do for you?', although we are quite aware that, in actual interaction, there may be variations on the theme. Indeed, a section of the chapter will focus on some of the reasons why doctors and patients may decide to adopt a non-standard first concern elicitor such as 'Fire away!'.

Developing a scheme of interpretation

Sacks made the interesting remark that conversation is a 'self-explicating colloquy'. That is to say, evidence/explanation of the orderliness of talk must be found, not outside the interaction, but in the talk itself. Examination of GP consultations reveals that they come in a series (Freeling 1983). A current consultation projects a next consultation and, where appropriate, implicates a previous one. That is to say, each consultation is a historical moment, is part of a series of consultations: each consultation is either a first in a series or a non-first in a series. Consider the following episode of talk that occurred towards the end of a consultation.

Extract 2

```
001  P:   most people do that in one night (0.1) (of drinking). but (0.1)
          they don't have problems. well not that I know of anyway
002  D:   well some people can get away with it but other people can't
          (0.3) Anyway
  →       try those and er if it's not getting any better come back and
          see me again.
003  P:   right. okay then
004  D:   cheerio
005  P:   okay
```

(L/06/11c)

Before closing down this consultation, participants jointly agreed on the relevance of a next visit. Therefore, given this agreement, if a next visit does indeed take place, it will be interpreted as a follow-up from the current one. Extract 3 below illustrates how a next visit is interactionally defined as a follow-up from a previous one.

Extract 3

```
001  D:   hello Mr W. how are you doing?
002  P:   well- well not too bad really. I can still get these symptoms
          but I don't they're – I don't know whether they're not
          quite so bad,   [but
003  D:                   [mm
004  P:   I still get this blanching of the fa – it's round- it's round the
          mouth area you know
```

(L/07/22c)

The patient's talk clearly indicates that current interaction followed a previous one. An assumption is made that the doctor is aware of the 'symptoms' and the 'blanching' the patient is talking about. On the linguistic level, deictic devices such as 'still', 'this', 'these' and 'so', working as 'retrospective tying references' (Firth 1995: 188), connect the current consultation to some previous one.

This view of each consultation as a member of a series is so strong that participants use it to anticipate each other's acts. Consider Extract 4 below.

Extract 4

001		D:	come in
			((door opens))
002		D:	hello Mr G
003		P:	hello
004		D:	come and sit yourself down
			((door closes))
005	→	P:	nothing to do with the heart this time
006		D:	is it not? ((laughs))
007		P:	lower back
008		D:	sit yourself down
009		P:	okay
010		D:	what's been the trouble?

(B/06/21c)

The patient's talk in the extract (turn 5) indicates that, on previous occasions, he had been consulting about heart problems. This time however, he had come for an unrelated concern. Because of that history of consulting about heart problems, he anticipated that, unless something was done, the doctor would by default see the current consultation as yet another member of the series. Thus, even before any concern elicitor was produced, the patient undertook to block the default definition of this consultation.

This view of each consultation as a member of a series of consultations on the same concern allows the resolution of the entry issue. Each consultation either follows a previous consultation or it doesn't. That is, there is a 'scheme of interpretation' (Garfinkel 1967). Parallel to this content-related scheme is a language-related scheme, namely 'How are you?' vs. 'What can I do for you?'. That is to say, when a particular consultation is a non-first in a series, doctors use 'How are you?' as a strategy for eliciting the first medically relevant concern. Alternatively, when a consultation is a first in a series, doctors use 'What can I do for you?'. Consider Extract 5 below.

Extract 5

001	→	D:	that's fine. well how are you?
002		P:	my cold's much better
003		D:	your cold's [much better
004		P:	[much better

(L/04/08a)

This is a rather unproblematic entry into the consultation. There had been a previous consultation about 'my cold'. This new consultation followed on from that previous one to report on the progress made. 'How are you?' was smoothly used. Tying devices used include possessives (my/your) and the comparative form 'better'. Also consider Extract 6 below.

Extract 6

```
001 → D:  now sit down ((turns pages)) how are you?
002   P:  er still surviving
003   D:  has it    [got any better?
004   P:            [surviving. that's right. well this thing I had on
                    my leg you remember
```

(L/10/21c)

The doctor opened the encounter with 'How are you?'. The patient's oriented to this opening as a greeting and responded with 'still surviving'. However, the doctor had actually meant it to be a first concern elicitor. He therefore produced a 'subsequent version' (Davidson 1984) by way of 'pursuing a response' (Pomerantz 1984a). In so doing he used three retrospective tying devices, namely the present perfect tense (has got), the pronoun (it) and the comparative form (better). Even though a misunderstanding had developed in the extract, participants attributed it, not to the inadequacy of 'How are you?' as a first concern elicitor, but rather to its ambiguity (see Schegloff (1984a) for a discussion on ambiguity in conversation). Because this is a follow-up consultation, the adequacy of 'How are you?' is upheld.

By contrast, consider Extract 7 below.

Extract 7

```
001 → D:  okay. what can I do for you L?
002   P:  oh (0.1) well I was in the other week with tonsillitis
003   D:  right
004   P:  and it's – it's better but I just still don't feel a hundred
          percent.
```

(B/10/34c)

In the extract, the doctor opened the consultation with 'What can I do for you?'. As the patient was consulting for the same concern (tonsillitis) as the week before, she indexed the irregularity of this first concern elicitor (oh, pause) and then went on to put it on record that she was actually follow-up-consulting (I was here the other week with tonsillitis). In other words, she indicated, without stating it in so many words, that 'What can I do for you?' is inappropriate in this context. Even more explicit is Extract 8 below.

Extract 8

```
001  →  D:  right. okay. and what can I do for you today?
002     P:  you – my blood test er from er my gout ((laughs))
003     D:  right. yes. yes. yes. th:e uric acid is – is high
004     P:  is it. yeah
```

(B/03/11c)

In opening this consultation, the doctor used 'What can I do for you today?' as if this were a first consultation in a series. In turn 2, the patient rejected this definition. Some of the strategies she used to signal the inadequacy of the doctor's opening are hesitation (you-my, er) and the troubles telling laughter (Jefferson 1984b). In turn 3, the doctor acknowledged his error rather emphatically (Right. Yes. Yes. Yes).

Along the same lines, consider Extract 9 below.

Extract 9

```
001     D:  sorry to keep you waiting so long
002     P:  that's all right
003  →  D:  behind this afternoon (0.2) how are you?
004     P:  okay. erm (could see) a couple of things
005     D:  mm
006     P:  and about my knee again but mainly erm I've been getting
                really bad headaches [basically
007     D:                         [right
008     P:  couple of weeks ago I banged my head and gave myself
                concussion
009     D:  right
```

(L/10/20c)

The doctor opened this consultation with 'How are you?', thereby indicating that he saw it as a follow-up. As indicated in the patient's talk in turn 6, participants had previously consulted on the object of 'my knee' (see deictics 'my' and 'again'). However, the patient had a different agenda for current consultation. On this occasion, he was consulting 'mainly (because he'd) been getting really bad headaches basically'. Therefore, an interactional clash arose between the doctor's definition of the consultation and the patient's own. In order to navigate around this difficulty, the patient acknowledged the doctor's definition by mentioning an ongoing concern (my knee again), immediately bracketed it off and moved to his own new agenda. Through this interactional work, participants confirmed that, in GP consultations, 'How are you?' is not universally adequate.

As a final piece of evidence, consider Extract 10 below.

Extract 10

```
001    D:  hello there
002    P:  hello there
003    D:  sorry to keep you. [had a
004    P:                     [oh that's all right
005    D:  interesting afternoon (0.2) have a chair (0.3) now that
           thyroid test I did in March April was normal, wasn't it?
006    P:  yeah
007 →  D:  what can I do for you today?
008    P:  erm (0.1) couple of things (0.2) (talk goes on)
```

(L07/24/c)

In this extract, both the choice of the concern elicitor and its placement may at first seem odd. As can be seen in turns 5 and 6, participants had already met on medical grounds, so 'How are you?' would seem more appropriate. Furthermore, since participants have already dealt with a medically relevant issue, 'What can I do for you today?' in turn 7 would seem to be out of place. However, a close inspection of the extract shows that this piece of talk is actually orderly. Normally, the structure of the opening episode is: elicitation by the doctor + first concern by the patient + evaluation/continuer by the doctor (see a similar three-step sequence in educational discourse in Sinclair and Coulthard 1975). In this case, no elicitation was produced and the issue was introduced by the doctor rather than by the patient. In turn 6, the patient revealed his/ her agreement with the doctor's talk. Through this interactional work, participants jointly reached the consensus that the previous consultation series had been concluded. Because the previous series had been concluded, the present visit could be seen as the beginning of a new medical history, as a new consultation, hence the unproblematic use of 'What can I do for you today?'. On the other hand, because of a previous history, participants could not normatively open the consultation with 'What can I do for you today?'. Some interactional work (turns 5 and 6) was necessary to establish the relevance of this specific opening device, hence its delay. In other words, just like "How are you?', 'What can I do for you?' is not universally adequate.

All in all, a selection rule exists for the choice between 'How are you?' and 'What can I do for you?' in GP consultations. The first is used in follow-up consultations and the second in new consultations. However, it must be stressed that the nature of a consultation as a follow-up or as a new consultation cannot be taken for granted, because the actual nature of a particular consultation is an interactional accomplishment. Participants jointly establish *in situ* whether they are follow-up-consulting or seeing each other for a new problem. In this sense, the use of first concern elicitors such as 'How are you?' and 'What can I do for you?' is best understood as a proposal made by the doctor to the patient as to how to view their interaction. This proposal may or may not be confirmed in interaction. In GP consult-ations, the choice of a first concern elicitor is a 'discourse strategy' (Gumperz 1982).

Using the scheme of interpretation

In the section above, we have been deliberately using the ethno-methodological notion of 'scheme of interpretation' without defining it (see Garfinkel 1967 and Heritage 1984b for a discussion). The point about schemes of interpretation in practical social action is that they do not allow 'any time out'. Either they are followed or they are deviated from. In the latter case, deviance is either repairable or it is strategic, i.e. func-tional. Two of these three possibilities have already been discussed in the section above, namely normative use of the scheme and repairable deviance from it. In this section, we turn to strategic uses of the scheme.

Instances of strategic deviance from the selection rule can generally be understood as attempts by the doctor to emphasize or else de-emphasize some aspect(s) of his/her relationship with a particular patient. In turn, strategic deviance may take either of two forms: a standard form may be used in a context where it is not immediately relevant or a non-standard form may be used where a standard one would be expected. For lack of space, we will use only two examples to illustrate these possibilities. Consider Extract 11 below.

Extract 11

001	D:	hello
002	P:	hi
		((door closed))
003	D:	thanks. take a seat. (. . .)
004 →	D:	what er (0.1) can I do for you
005	P:	the pain in my belly (0.2) er i:t's not going away. no matter
		what I'm doing even I can't eat properly now
006	D:	right

(L/06/11c)

This consultation brought together participants who knew each other
very well. As the doctor reported in the post-consultation interview
(L/06/11d), he had been with this patient, now aged 19, ever since he
was a child. The doctor knew the patient's family and their social
background and he had long been aware of the patient's condition.
Against this shared background knowledge, the mismatch between
the two parties' conduct becomes obvious. In the opening sequence,
the doctor used 'What can I do for you?' as if this were a new consultation.
In turn 5, the patient packaged his concern display in a manner that
indicates that he had seen this doctor before about the same problem.
The issue therefore is: Why this misalignment? In the post-consultation
interview, it appeared that, for the doctor, the patient was a 'very
tricky one', someone who was 'a bit of a challenge really' and 'very
difficult to relate with in a meaningful way really'. Among other problems
with this patient, according to the doctor, was the fact that he had abused
the health system 'to the extent that the ambulance services refuse to go
to him anymore'. Therefore, the doctor may have used 'What can I do for
you?', in a context where it at first looks inappropriate, as a deliberate
move to distance himself from this 'difficult patient' (Steinmetz and
Tabenkin 2001). The doctor was flouting the rule strategically.

Alternatively, strategic deviance from the selection rule may be
meant to emphasize solidarity and mutual alignment. Some doctors
go to great lengths, such as using colloquial expressions, to claim a
solidarity relationship with their patients. In discourse analytic terms,
this is known as 'positive politeness strategies' (Brown and Levinson
1987). An example of such strategic deviance from the norm is Extract
12 below.

Extract 12

((talk while setting up the recording equipment with lots of laughter))

001		D:	fine [((laughs))
002		P:	[((laughs))
003		D:	erm ah I get myself lost a bit here
004		P:	(laughs)
005	→	D:	dee der er. right (0.3) right ho. fire away
006		P:	right. I'll show you what it is. er I've got a very sore foot which I've had for about a year on and off.
			and I [haven't sort of
007		D:	[on off
008		P:	yes
009		D:	[on
010		P:	[((laughs))
011		D:	off
012		P:	well I have been on and [off my feet [to be honest ((laughs))
013		D:	[on [off

(L/01/05c)

The quality of the relationship between the two parties in this consultation is best summed up in their own words. The patient had this to say about their relationship:

Pretty good, on the whole, pretty good. He (the doctor)'s quite communicative, he seems quite knowledgeable about things that you might propose to him, you might ask him details of something and he's quite open about discussing things with you giving you the benefit of his knowledge. (. . .) But generally I would say he's pretty good, yes. (L/01/05b)

The same feelings are echoed by the doctor as follows:

Oh again we go back, I've sort of looked after mum (patient) since sort of 1980 . . . seen her daughter growing up . . . and again they're just . . . Mrs A (patient) is one of these delightful people, one just sort of gets on with. . . . she's just got a nice open sort of face, ... (L/01/05d)

In terms of medical history, this patient is not a regular at the surgery. She 'has come in over the years with very standard things every so often ... comes in maybe once, twice a year for standard things like contraception ... cervical smears and things like this foot problem.' (L/01/05d). Therefore, her present visit at the surgery can be seen as a new consultation and the standard way of eliciting her concern would have been 'What can I do for you?'. Instead, the doctor used 'Fire away' and, as the transcript shows, in subsequent talk, no indication is given that this rather unusual opening needs repairing. A clue to the reason for the doctor's choice is gained if one takes the whole context into account, particularly the fact that participants laughed and teased each other (repetition of 'on/off'). The choice of 'Fire away' as a first concern elicitor was designed to contribute to the informality of the consultation. As Ragan (2000) shows, humour and verbal play is one of the strategies that participants in a medical encounter use to maintain a sense of mutuality. In the post-consultation interview, the doctor confirmed this interpretation saying: 'I think we had some fun in this consultation, if I remember'.

The institutional character of opening sequences

So far we have considered the orderliness of the opening sequence in GP consultations. We now turn to the issue of where that orderliness comes from. Is the particular order random or is it contextual? That is to say, is the particular order context-free or is it specific to the institution of General Practice? Available evidence points to the context-boundedness of the particular order. For example, in ordinary everyday conversation, 'How are you?' is not understood as an elicitation of a medical concern. Similarly, 'What can I do for you?' is understood differently depending on the type of service encounter at hand. In Heritage's words, this is an issue of 'inferential frameworks and procedures that are typical to specific institutional contexts' (1997: 164). If such is the case, the above question can be rephrased as follows: is there anything in the institution of General Practice that would account for the orderliness we have described?

Three key features of General Practice (see Fry 1993) account for the orderliness of the opening sequence as we have described it. First of all, General Practice works as a first port of entry into the care system. At this level, a patient who enters a GP surgery could be seeing the doctor for any one out of a hundred possible reasons. In this case, the only thing the doctor can safely do is to offer a general readiness to help. This is precisely the job the first concern elicitor 'What can I do for you?' accomplishes. According to Heath (1981), 'What can I do for you?' is a generalized offer of help which, at the same time, displays the doctor's lack of knowledge of the reason for the visit.

The second most important feature of General Practice is known as continuity of care. In this respect, Boddy (1975: 1) writes:

> The most significant factor of all is that of continuity of care; the doctor in General Practice cannot be concerned with single episodes of illness. He [*sic*] will continue to see his patients (. . .) He cannot readily discharge his patient to the care of someone else (. . .).

This idea of continuity is directly reflected by the notion of consultation-in-a-series. As we have seen, in General Practice, there is a strong assumption that the doctor will see the patient more than once, that a next consultation will follow a present one and, when relevant, that a present consultation is a follow-up from a previous one. This idea of continuity is indexed by the use of 'How are you?'.

A third important feature of General Practice is that of doctor–patient relationship. Because doctors and patients see one another many times over a long period of time, a relationship develops between them. Ideally, that relationship is positive, but it may also be negative, and the quality of this relationship is thought to affect positively the nature of medical care (Britten *et al.* 2000). Instances of strategic deviance from the selection rule reflect participants' own orientation to this feature of General Practice. As we have seen, doctors go to great lengths to claim solidarity with patients through the use of non-standard openings such as 'Fire away', but, as illustrated by Extract 11, they may also deviate from standard uses in order to index a difficult relationship.

Conclusion

The opening sequence in GP consultation is an orderly activity. Participants systematically draw on an identifiable rule in order to enter the interactional world of the consultation. Put simply, the rule is that, for a new consultation, 'What can I do for you?' is used and, for a follow-up consultation 'How are you?' is used. However, the nature of a consultation as new or as a follow-up does not precede the use of these openings. Rather, through the use of these openings, participants negotiate that very same nature. Part of the rule-governedness of the opening sequence in GP consultation is the possibility for participants to deviate from the norm strategically. Doctors deviate strategically from the norm either to distance themselves from particular patients or to claim solidarity with particular other patients. The orderliness of the opening sequence as observed in talk is not free-standing. Rather it is contextual;

it reflects the reality of the institution of General Practice and is context-shaped and context-shaping. The institution of General Practice is consequential for the organization of talk between GPs and their patients. Reflexively, each instance of an orderly opening is a 'document' of the institution of General Practice (see Garfinkel 1967 for the notion of *documentary method*) through which the context is created for 'yet another first time'. It is through orderly openings that doctors and patients talk the institution of General Practice into being.

Note

1   Dr Gafaranga was supported by Sir Siegmund Warburg's Voluntary Settlement. Dr Britten was supported by a senior research fellowship from the British Academy and Leverhulme Trust. The study on which this paper is based was funded by the Department of Health as part of the Prescribing Research Initiative. The views expressed in this paper are those of the authors and not the Department of Health. The other members of the study team were Nick Barber, Christine Barry, Colin Bradley and Fiona Stevenson.

6

Would You Like to Do it Yourself? Service Requests and Their Non-granting Responses

Erik Vinkhuyzen and Margaret H. Szymanski[1]

Introduction

Many organizations have inherently conflicting goals when it comes to customer service. On the one hand, they must provide their customers with the service they desire to ensure a large, loyal patronage. On the other hand, the cost of providing those services can become very expensive and thus curtail an organization's profitability. In order to remain solvent, organizations must keep the cost of providing customer service within bounds. Almost inevitably, this will result in a circumscription of services; some customer requests simply cannot be granted.

In business, responding to a customer's request with anything less than a granting is a delicate matter. Economic analysis has shown that the negative consequences of dissatisfying a customer can be much costlier than the positive consequences of satisfying a customer (Hart *et al.* 1990). Customers may revoke their patronage; they may even become upset and create a scene (so that the negative experience of one customer can then affect others). Yet, not all customers who are recipients of some kind of 'non-granting' response become upset or even express displeasure. While different responses to non-grantings could be attributed to any number of psychological and/or general sociological factors (e.g., age or gender) that apply to the customer, this chapter investigates possible interactional grounds that contribute to the outcome. From an applied research perspective this is a fruitful approach, as one cannot intervene to change the psychological and/or sociological traits of customers, whereas the interactional 'moves' of employees can be more easily targeted by an intervention.

To address this problem we studied interactions between employees of a local reprographics business and customers who request service at the store's 'drop-off' counter – usually to have copies made of their documents. In some instances, instead of granting the customers' request by accepting the job to be completed by the store's employees, the counter employees redirect the customer to the do-it-yourself (DIY) area, proposing that they use the self-service machines to produce the copies themselves.

In examining these instances, we became interested in how employees' non-granting responses to requests were shaped by the ways in which customers produced their requests in the first place. In particular, we noted that the grammatical formatting of the customer requests constrains how employees construct their non-granting responses; the grammar of the request determines whether the non-granting can be done in an affiliative or disaffiliative way.

Requests in action

'Requests' have provided a rich domain of inquiry for analysts interested in the study of the intersection of language, action and interaction (Garvey 1975; Ervin-Tripp 1979; Goodwin 1980; Ervin-Tripp 1982; Levinson 1983; Gordon and Ervin-Tripp 1984; Ervin-Tripp *et al.* 1987; Wootton 1981, 1984). In part, this is due to the plentiful interactional, personal and social contingencies that are managed in request sequences. As Ervin-Tripp (1981: 195) has remarked, requests 'do more than one thing at a time. They affect the activities of the partner. At the same time, inevitably, they convey a social interpretation which defines the relation of the speaker and hearer.'

One of the reasons requests have been the subject of much research in linguistics (Garvey 1975; Ervin-Tripp 1982; Levinson 1983; Gordon and Ervin-Tripp 1984; Ervin-Tripp *et al.* 1987) is that an utterance which is pragmatically easily identifiable as a request can occur in many different syntactic forms. This aspect of requests led some to argue that access to the social situation or context in which an utterance is made is critical to understanding its pragmatic import (Gordon and Ervin-Tripp 1984; Levinson 1983).

Indeed, from this view grammar is not a self-contained linguistic system but rather part of a broader array of systems that lie behind the organization of social life. Consequently, linguistic theories and methods are too limited for investigating the impact of the grammatical formatting of customer requests and their responses in service encounters (Levinson

1983; Drew and Heritage 1992b; Schegloff 1992c). Their limitations in this regard can perhaps best be illustrated by speech act theory, where the grammatical format of an utterance is seen as separate from its illocutionary force (Levinson 1983: 236). In contrast, sociologically-oriented researchers in the field of conversation analysis (CA) have demonstrated that the grammatical format of turns can have definite interactional consequences. Turns can be constructed out of lexical items, phrasal or clausal units or sentences, and hearers attend to the utterance in progress for possible pragmatic, intonational, and grammatical completion (Sacks *et al.* 1974; Ford *et al.* 1996). Moreover, Raymond (2000) has shown that the grammatical format of a sequence-initiating turn, specifically 'yes–no type interrogatives', can interactionally constrain the grammatical format of the response, and that the preference organization at the level of grammar is independent of the one at work at the level of action.

Another limitation of linguistic research is that the traditional focus on a single utterance ignores the most important context for understanding turns at talk. Research using naturalistic conversational data has shown that the primary social context for any utterance is the utterances that immediately precede it; i.e., 'context' is 'most proximately and consequentially temporal and sequential' (Schegloff 1992d: 195). It is the temporal/sequential context that supplies the foundation on which the whole edifice of human action is built.

From a sequence organizational perspective, requests are sequence-initiating actions, the first part of a paired set, which make relevant either granting (acceptance) or a non-granting (declination) responses. However, requests are unusually delicate social actions in that they constitute a dispreferred first pair part (Schegloff forthcoming); speakers will often hint that a request is forthcoming by first making a pre-request instead of launching an overt request. Not only are issues of face and solidarity at stake in the responses to requests (Goffman 1967; Holtgraves 1992; Lerner 1996); subtle issues of social obligation and indebtedness are also involved in their launching.

In business settings, of course, the very purpose of many interactions is a customer's request and the organization's fulfilment of that request (Merritt 1975; M. Whalen and Zimmerman 1987; J. Whalen *et al.* 1988). In these commercial contexts, customers are expected to produce their requests as the first order of business. The organizational context thus mitigates the dispreference for launching requests seen in everyday conduct, but where the customer's request cannot be granted the employees' situation is delicate, because they must now produce a non-granting response to an overt request. Employees thus do not usually get the opportunity to respond to a pre-request to indicate that the forthcoming customer request cannot be granted.

Methods, data and setting

The data for this chapter were collected as part of a three-year ethnographic study of service organizations conducted in a local copy centre, 'Eastside Reprographics', and is part of a research programme in workscape analysis (M. Whalen *et al.* in press; J. Whalen and Vinkhuyzen 2000). The research team collected the data in three phases:

1) ethnographic observations, shadowing and interviewing employees while they worked;
2) extensive video recordings in the store; multiple cameras used simultaneously in over 100 hours of interaction produced over 400 hours of video data;
3) participant observation, working as employees, serving customers and operating the printing and copying equipment.

Our data corpus contains more than 500 interactions between customers and employees, more than half of them order-taking interactions in which a customer makes a request to print or copy some files or documents. In most instances, the employee grants the request. The excerpts presented in this paper deviate from this pattern; instead of granting the request, the employee redirects the customer to the DIY area of the store.

The organization of Eastside Reprographics

Eastside Reprographics owns and operates three local copy shops (the name is a pseudonym; Eastside is a competitor to franchise operations such as Copy Max). Eastside's customers possess a wide variety of document reproduction needs. The store offers customers two types of service: 1) employees can take the customer's order and production employees will produce the copies on the machines behind the counter, or 2) customers can use the machines in the DIY area and produce their own copies.

From the customer's perspective, each service offers distinct advantages. With DIY, customers need not wait; they have full control over their documents and can leave with the finished product. When the organization produces the order, customers need not operate complicated copier equipment, nor must they pay for defective copies.

From a business perspective, however, there are distinct advantages to having customers make their own copies. Most importantly, when customers use the machines in DIY, Eastside effectively capitalizes on their labour. The economic incentive to direct customers with smaller or labour-intensive projects to DIY is especially strong as business margins do not allow them to be done profitably by employees.

However, it must be noted that Eastside has no official policy that states that it will not accept orders below a certain size for full-service. Moreover, the price difference between copies made in DIY and those made in full-service is negligible. It is perhaps not surprising, therefore, that a substantial number of customers with small jobs come to the counter and request that the copy centre make their copies. It is then up to the front counter employees to direct these customers to the machines in the DIY area. Persuading customers to accept an alternative service to the one they requested can be a delicate activity both interactionally and organizationally. In successfully complying with one organizational goal (sending customers with smaller projects to DIY), employees jeopardize another organizational goal: satisfying their customers.

To address the delicate issues of redirecting customers to DIY, we now turn to an analysis of actual instances of customer requests and employee responses.

Requests and responses: sequential placement and turn design

Order taking interactions commonly start with a greetings exchange after which the customers produce a request. This section will focus on that request and the subsequent turns. In our data, requests take two predominant forms: customers format their requests as self-oriented declaratives stating a customer's desire or need (e.g., 'I'd like (I need) to make three copies of this'), or they format their requests as other-oriented interrogatives that inquire about the organization's willingness or capability to produce a document followed by a job description (e.g., 'Can you make two copies of this document?').

Self-oriented declarative requests

In Extract 1 a customer (C) walks up to the 'drop-off' counter, and the employee (E), who was sharing a joke with another employee, turns towards her.

Extract 1: Self-oriented declarative

```
001  E:   hi(hh) he he
002  C:   hi:.
003       (4.4)((C removes pictures from envelope))
004  C:   I wanna get uhm some quality copies of this
005       (1.9)((C lifts picture then sets it down))
006  C:   this (0.5) this part
007       (1.5)
008  E:   okay, for the best quality they're six ninety nine and
009       they're done out in do-it-yourself
010       (0.8)
011  E:   they're six ninety nine a copy and they're done on that
012       Ac[me machine.
013  C:   [oh okay
014  C:   okay
015  E:   that's the best quality
016  C:   okay
017       (0.2)
018  C:   and (0.5) uhm, can I get a heavier paper?
019  E:   what's it's come on the=uh
020  E2:  it [comes on a paper like that
021  E:      [the Acme pa- it's just like this
022  C:   ohkay (.) cool
023  E:   it's six ninety nine a copy.
024  C:   awright
025       (0.8)
026  C:   so I just make it myself?
027  E:   hm↑hm
028  C:   alrighty
```

The customer uses the anchor position, the first slot after the greeting sequence, to formulate a declarative request 'I wanna get some quality copies of this' (lines 4–6).[2] The declarative format displays the customer to be epistemically disadvantaged; she knows what she wants but not how to get it and thus leaves it to the employee to tell her how she can attain the quality copies. This allows the employee to treat the customer's utterance not as a request to place a full-service order, but as a request for advice (see Drew 1984: 136 for a similar observation).

The employee responds with a turn-initial acknowledgement token (line 8); she acknowledges the customer's request as complete and coherent, without yet accepting or rejecting it (Beach 1993). The employee continues her turn by telling the customer where the best quality copies are 'done' (lines 8–9). By using the passive rather than active voice the employee indeed treats the customer's request as a request for advice and explains to her the organization of the centre and the capabilities of the machines as well as the price of the service. The passive voice also obfuscates just who would be making the copies.

The customer does not immediately respond to the employee's suggestion (lines 10–24), but finally produces an upshot of the employee's initial response to her request: 'so I just make it myself'. Note, then, that the grammatical format of the customer's request allows the employee to send her to the DIY area as a preferred response to the customer's initial request.

A similar response to a declaratively formatted request can be observed in Extract 2, which involves a customer who has come to the counter holding a small stack of papers.

Extract 2: Self-oriented declarative

```
001  E:   hi!
002       (0.4)
003  C:   hi, I have these things that are two sided printing,
004       so what- uhm = I need (.) eleven of each of these pages
005  E:   ohkay, you have a choice, you can do 'em yourself I
006       have a young man out there that can assist you,
007  C:   assist me?
008  E:   show you how to do it?
009       (0.6)
010  C:   okay
```

The employee responds to the customer's declarative request 'I need eleven of each of these pages', by explaining that the customer has a choice. Again, we can see how the employee treats the customer's request as an inquiry into the services of the copy centre, not as a request to have the organization make the copies. She does not provide another option, which may be due to the customer's positive reaction to the DIY option (the customer immediately turns to look at the DIY area when the employee points to it). As in Extract 1, the grammatical formatting of the customer's request allows the employee to explain the organization of Eastside and send the customer off to the DIY without misalignment.

The self-oriented declarative format of the customers' requests in Extracts 1 and 2 enable the employee to suggest the DIY area as a way to fulfil their requests. However, not all customers who format their request in such a manner are necessarily asking for advice; some intend to place an order to have copies made. Consider Extract 3, in which a man directly approaches an employee at the register, which is not the 'correct' spot to place an order.

Extract 3: Self-oriented declarative

```
001  C:   hello, [how are yuh?
002  E:          [hi!
003  E:   how [can I help
004  C:        [I've gotta make a copy of=uh this document.
005  E:   okay would you like to do that yourself in do-it-
006       yourself?
```

In this case, the customer's declarative request is formatted as an urgent need, 'I've gotta make a copy of this document'. The declarative format (reinforced by the fact that he approaches the wrong part of the counter) shows that the customer is unfamiliar with Eastside's operations. In this case, the employee does not explain the choices the customer has, but instead offers the DIY machines to the customer by formatting her response as a yes–no type interrogative, asking whether that would be to his liking (line 5–6). The question is produced as an unproblematic response to the customer's request, delivered without a moment hesitation and with friendly intonation. Although the question implies that there may be more options, the employee refrains from mentioning what they might be. And the options the customer now has with respect to the employee's question are not neutral; answering with the preferred 'yes' would constitute an acceptance of doing the job himself, whereas the customer must implement the dispreferred next action to indicate that he wants Eastside to make the copy.

   Here is the customer's response:

Extract 3 (continued)

```
005  E:   okay would you like to do that yourself in do-it-
006       yourself?
007  C:   I guess I could, yeah, can you- >how much more< does
008       it cost if you just [do it?
009                           [(((CUS extends document
010       toward EMP))
```

The customer at first reluctantly accepts the offer but then inserts a question inquiring how much more it would cost if the employee would make the copies. He thus makes his acceptance of the offer contingent on the price; he may be willing to pay more to have the copies made to order by Eastside. Despite his initial acceptance, the customer thus indicates that he might (actually) prefer the copy shop to make the copies (which is further reinforced by the repeated but failed attempts to 'hand over' the manuscript, lines 9–10).

Again, the grammatical formatting of the customer's initial request allows the employee to produce a response that offers the customer the DIY area. The 'packaging' of the employee's offer into an inquiry smoothly manages the possibility that the customer wanted the store to make the copies for him; it does not presume that the customer wants to make the copies himself, but nevertheless makes that option the preferred one. With the employee's offer on the table, the only way the customer can insist on having the organization make the copies would be to reject the offer that the very formatting of his request made relevant.

These examples therefore illustrate that the formatting of the request as a self-oriented declarative statement, expressing the customer's desire provides the employee with more opportunities than just accepting or rejecting the request; it allows employees to treat the request as a request for advice and thus to explain that the DIY area is the appropriate place where the customer can get their job completed.

Interrogative requests

The second main way in which customers format requests is by using other-oriented interrogatives, explicitly requesting the employee to produce the documents for them. Consider Extract 4.

Extract 4: Other-oriented interrogative

```
001  E:   hi
002  C:   hi
003       (.)
004  C:   I just want to know if you could make a photocopy of
005       this, a color one?
006       (1.9) ((C searches bag))
007  C:   it's a passport. I don't wanna be carry'it with me
008       (0.9)
```

009 E: okay, ye[ah] actually that's made out in do-it-
             yourself=
010 C: [( )]
011 E: =I have someone that will <u>help</u> you to make that
012   (0.7)
013 C: just like that in color?
014 E: it will be just like that, but it will be a color copy.
015 C: ohkay

In this extract, the customer formulates his request (lines 4–5) as an interrogative inquiring about the copy centre's (or the employee's) willingness or capability to make a photocopy. The turn-initial 'I just wanted to know if' packages the request as an information-seeking inquiry[3] that subordinates the request itself and minimizes its imposition (Brown and Levinson 1978). Additionally, it shows the customer to be inexperienced, someone unfamiliar with Eastside's services and perhaps not yet fully committed to having the copies made.

The employee responds to the interrogative request with an acknowledgement 'okay,' and a type-confirming response 'yeah' that answers the implicit question in the customer's request regarding the organization's capacity to do the work. The employee continues with 'actually that's made out in the quick copy area.' 'Actually' marks what follows as disjunctive with the expectation that was implicit in the customer's turn (Clift 2001). In this case, the contrast concerns just who would be making the copies; the customer's formulation implies that the organization will make the copies, while the employee's response implies that Eastside's services are such that the customer must make them himself.

The interrogative formatting of this request – a yes–no type inquiry about the organization's capabilities – does not allow the employee to respond with a confirming answer to the question, because such a response would imply that the centre accepts the order. In order to send the customer to DIY, the employee must implement a dispreferred response using the disjunction marker 'actually' and additional TCUs (i.e., 'I have someone that will help you to make that') that serve to make the suggested course of action more enticing and pre-emptively counter potential objections to it. Note especially that even though this customer demonstrates himself to be a novice, the employee's response is constrained by the grammatical format of the requests.

Customers can format their other-oriented interrogative requests so that they more overtly request that the employee accept the job as an order. In Extract 5, the customer has walked up to the counter and has organized some papers and opened a box containing blank paper stock.

Extract 5: Other-oriented interrogative

```
001  E:   hi, what dya have for us to[day?,
002  C:                             [hi,
003        can you (.) can you ta:: (.)print up (0.2)
004        on this paper five copies of each of these for me=on
005        one of your good printers, ((points to the printers))
006        (0.4)
007  E:   well, it=to be honest with you, ((hand hits counter on
008        'honest')) we ha:ve ((points to DIY area)) two of
009        our better printers are out now ((hand hits counter on
010        'in')) in do-it-yourself,
011        (0.1)
012  E:   they're just like ((E points to DIY printers, C
013        turns, looks to DIY area)) the ones we'd run 'em in here
014        if you want to try: doing that I have two people
015        ((points with pen to DIY on 'two')) out in
016        do-it-yourself that can help you out with that,
017        (0.2)
018  C:   we[:ll((gathers his things from counter))
019  E:      [be a lot quicker for ya an:
020        (0.2)
021  E:   they could help you get it done right now, (taps pen on
022        counter twice on 'right now'))
023        (0.4) ((C opens lid of paper box, looks, closes it))
024  C:   o:hkay ((lifts papers from counter, turns towards
025        DIY))
026  E:   alright? uhm (.) let me let me (get-/giv-) ((turns to
027        walk to DIY))
028  C:   ((walking to DIY)) I've had bad luck with these
029        in the past,
```

In this extract, the customer formats his request as a yes–no type interrogative, inquiring into the organization's ability/willingness to make some copies (lines 3–5). The preferred, type-conforming response to the request would be 'yes, we can' or something similar. The employee uses a dispreferred response format, however, delaying his response after the customer's request is possibly complete and starting his turn with the disjunctive 'well' (Pomerantz 1984b), and a bad-news marker: 'to be honest with you' (lines 7–10). Subsequently, he contradicts the customer's proposal concerning the location of quality equipment; some of the better printers are in now in DIY. While not an overt non-granting of the request, it clearly refrains from accepting the job and further undermines the argument for the organization to make the copies.

Extracts 4 and 5 illustrate how interrogative requests create a more challenging sequential environment for employees who want to redirect customers to the DIY area. In Extract 4, the employee successfully sends the customer to DIY by exploiting the customer's displayed lack of knowledge about Eastside's operations and explaining that his project can be accomplished in DIY. However, in Extract 5, the formatting of the customer's request asking specifically that the 'good printers' behind the counter be used to produce his order constrains the employee even further as the customer displays some understanding of the organization's operations in his request. To send this customer to DIY, the employee first undermines the account for the customer's request to place an order (better machines are behind the counter), and then induces the customer with assistance and a shorter turn-around time.

Producing a non-granting response to an interrogative is much more delicate than not granting a declarative request as the grammatical formatting of the yes–no type inquiry constrains the employees' response and leaves them no option but to format their response as a dispreferred next action. By grammatically formatting the initial request as an interrogative about the organization's capabilities, the customer creates a sequential environment where the preferred response is for the employee to accept the order. In this regard, it is interesting to consider that customers who were sent to the DIY area in previous visits to Eastside may choose to format their requests as an interrogative with the aim to sequentially constrain the range of possible next actions the employee can produce in response. Evidence for this can be seen in the customer's last turn of Extract 5, when he refers to the machines in DIY: 'I've had bad luck with these in the past.'

Just how the grammatical format of customer requests constrains the employees' response is further illustrated in Extract 6. Here the customer self-repairs his request, upgrading it from a declarative statement that expresses a personal need to a more overt request that specifically nominates the employee/organization to make the copies.

Extract 6: Repaired request

```
001  E:   hi
002  C:   hi, I would like to:: (0.4) you to (0.3) enlarge
003       (0.4) this article
004       (0.5)
005  E:   to >what si[ze<=
006  C:         [closest to thisz:: size this is the size of
007       the (0.3) front door
008  E:   okay ((cheerful))
009  C:   and then laminate it
010  E:   uhm:::::::::::::: >okay< [.hh the machine ]=
011  C:                           [and then make = uh]
012  E:   = that you can copy this on?
013       (0.7)
014  E:   .tch ((tongue click)) is out in do-it-yourself.
015       (0.1)
016  E:   we can laminate it back here for you, but it
017       be quicker (.) and it would be, you know, i-it
018       would just be a lot quicker to do it yourself,
019       and also, I think we have somebody (..) out
020       yeah there's a co-worker out in do-it-yourself, he's
021       wearing the same thing I'm wearing and = uhm just
022       let him know what you need to do and he can
023       help you on the machine.
024       (0.3)
025  C:   what about = uh this size, I need like twen-
026       twenny eight of this: size also
027       (0.8)
028  E:   [yeah that's-
029  C:   [( this )
030  E:   yeah
031       (0.4)
032  E:   you can still: (.) you- yeah you can do
033       that ou- you can do that out there also
```

Here the customer changes the formatting of his request from a self-oriented declarative statement to an other-oriented directive that requests that the organization make the enlargement. Initially, the employee does not respond with the preferred granting of the request, but delays her response by inserting a question (line 5). The question suggests that enlarging to certain sizes would result in a non-granting of the request, but does not reveal the sizes Eastside can produce. After the customer responds to the insertion and adds an increment to the order (lines 6–7, 9) a response to the (now-modified) initial request is pending. The employee begins her turn with a very long 'uhm' as if in thought, delaying her response, followed by an acknowledgement (indicating that the pondering is over; she has come up with a plan), and continues with a clause 'the machine that you can copy this on?' (lines 10 and 12). Although not a grammatically complete TCU, the questioning intonation contour and the pause that follows appear designed to leave space for the customer to produce a continuer. Note that, in contrast to the customer's repaired request, the clause suggests that the customer make the copies. Hence, if the customer were to provide a go-ahead response he would be agreeing to this change in agency. Not surprisingly, then, the customer withholds a response. The employee completes her TCU by adding the location of the DIY machine.

Observe that the employee's eventual response to the customer's repaired request in Extract 6 is more typical of a response to a self-oriented declarative, that is, to the un-repaired version of the customer's request. Her explanation of the location of the machine treats the customer's request as a request for information, not as a request to place an order; it would constitute an appropriate response to a customer-oriented request such as the one in Extract 1, and would be fitted to the customer's request had it not been repaired (i.e., if his request had been 'I would like to enlarge this article'). The employee thus effectively ignores the customer's self-repair.

In the absence of the customer's response, the employee continues (lines 16–23) by offering to do the lamination (a partial granting mitigates the previous non-granting). She then re-evokes her offer for DIY by providing two inducements: DIY is a lot quicker, and there is someone in the DIY area to help (see Extract 5 for a similar strategy). Despite these inducements, the customer resists the course of action so diametrically opposed to his initial (repaired) request. To further his case he shows that he has even more business, perhaps hoping that the size of the overall job will persuade the employee to accept his initial request as a full-service order (lines 25–6). However, this request is denied too (line 33), and eventually he leaves the counter without properly closing the interaction, obviously very displeased.

We have shown some examples that demonstrate how the grammatical format of customer requests constrains employee responses. Customers appeal to the normative organization using the preference structure of interaction, which promotes social cohesion, to further their own objectives. Similarly, we have seen how Eastside employees can (and do) resist these attempts, often by explaining the normative organization of the copy centre's services.

Conclusion

same belief
different normative organization

In order to profitably serve the copying and printing needs of its highly diverse customer base Eastside Reprographics has created two distinct operations: self-service for customers with small jobs, full-service for those with larger orders. When customers come in and present their work at the counter, the employees make an assessment as to the kind of job the customer has and offer the appropriate service.

However, to Eastside's customers the way in which the copy centre assigns jobs to different areas can appear quite arbitrary. Customers quickly learn that there are two tiers of service on offer, and that they may not be offered both services as a matter of choice. Not surprisingly, many customers will attempt to influence the counter employees who decide on the level of service.

Our research has shown that one of the most commonly used levers customers manipulate to increase their chances of attaining full-service is the grammatical format of their request. Relying on the normative organization of talk-in-interaction, they formulate their request so that denying them full-service must be done as a dis-affiliative response. Often, these interactions at the counter result in a verbal tug-of-war in which customers resist being directed to the DIY area and employees entice the customers to the DIY area ever more strongly.[4]

By letting the front counter employees implement the organizational policy that determines the service Eastside Reprographics is willing to offer to what type of customer, the organization has put these counter employees in a difficult position. To redirect customers to DIY without upsetting them, counter employees must use interactional finesse for which they were not trained by Eastside. The copy centre may well be better off by increasing the charges for full-service and letting the customers decide what service they desire, rather than letting its reputation for service depend on the skill with which its front counter employees can handle a delicate interactional moment.

Notes

1 The data for this paper was collected in a research project conducted by a group of social scientists at the Palo Alto Research Center. The following researchers were part of this project and contributed to this chapter: Robert J. Moore, Geoffrey Raymond, Jack Whalen and Marilyn R. Whalen.
2 These encounters are not unlike phone call openings (Schegloff 1968, 1986); in our case, as the customers walk into the store, there is a greeting exchange after which a slot is created for the customers to announce the reason they came in.
3 We take this and the account for his request (lines 7–8) as evidence that the dispreference for requests in ordinary conversation affects the way in which requests are designed in institutional settings.
4 Our own experience of working in Eastside taught us that employees often feel like customers are being unreasonable, that they are trying to ignore the operational protocol of the copy centre.

7
Social Identity and Language Choice in Bilingual Service Talk
Maria-Carme Torras

Introduction

The aim of this study is to provide an identity-related account of how *service*, as a form of institutional talk, is 'talked into being' (Heritage 1984b) in settings where more than one language can be used. In the existing body of research on service interaction (e.g. Halliday and Hasan 1980; Ventola 1987; Aston (ed.) 1988; Coupland and Ylänne-McEwen 2000), the issue of bi/multilingualism seems to have attracted little attention. Bi/multilingual service talk-in-interaction is undoubtedly a relevant researchable matter in the context of our current western society, which is becoming increasingly more service-based and multilingual as a result of globalized communication.

Ethnomethodologically based studies of social identity (e.g. Antaki and Widdicombe (eds) 1998) claim that participants can adopt multiple social identities. From this perspective, Drew and Heritage (1992b) characterize talk-in-interaction as institutional insofar as participants orient to their professional or institutional identities. Drawing upon Membership Categorization Analysis, this article reveals that the institutional nature of the service encounters under analysis lies not only in the participants' enacting of institutional identities but also in their *navigation* (Gafaranga 2001) between these institutional identities and others made relevant in the course of the interaction. In bi/multilingual service talk-in-interaction, one such set of identities is that of *linguistic* identities (Gafaranga 2001; Torras 2002; Torras and Gafaranga 2002).

This study is based on a corpus of Castilian/Catalan/English service encounters audio-recorded in a number of service settings in Barcelona, where the use of any of the three languages is possible. Catalan and Castilian constitute equally legitimate choices on account of their co-official status in Catalonia. Because of the foreign/international nature of the settings, a third possible language choice is English, although occasionally another foreign language may be used.[1]

The chapter first introduces some basic theoretical notions and claims on which this study draws, then discusses the participants' negotiation of social identities in the opening turns of their interaction. This concentrates on the three main *categorization devices* to which participants in my data evoke occasioned membership, namely *service parties, acquaintanceship* and *language preference*. Subsequently I show how participants strategically resort to renegotiation of their social identities to achieve successful service. Identity *navigation* reveals the participants' orientation to an underlying service norm which functions as a *scheme of interpretation* (Garfinkel 1967). Finally, the conclusion brings together the main findings and suggests possible practical applications in the service sector.

Some key concepts and ideas

Following Wilson (1991), this study seeks to explain how institutions are 'talked into being' by directing explicit attention to the relationship between the sequential organization of talk-in-interaction and the participants' orientation to the social-structural context of their inter-action, i.e. the participants' orientation to their relevant identities in a particular situation.

Torras (2002) characterizes the 'service talk' occurring in the data under study as one type of 'institutional talk' associated with *non-formal institutional settings* (Drew and Heritage 1992b). Through the study of participants' behaviour, an underlying service norm is inferred that can be characterized as a *practice-based* preference (Schegloff 1988b) for successful compliance with the service seeker's request(s). This norm functions as a *scheme of interpretation* accounting for the overall *order* of service. The service providers are seen to orient to compliance with the service seeker not only in terms of the service goal, but also in the management of interactional pace and of relational talk episodes as well as in the selection of *medium*. The orientation to this underlying norm causes participants to react in cases of unsuccessful compliance (i.e. deviance): compliance becomes 'noticeably absent' and its absence becomes the object of remedial efforts.

From an organizational perspective, Gafaranga (1999, 2000) shows that, in bilingual talk-in-interaction, language choice is 'a significant aspect of talk organization'. His conversation-analytic approach accounts for order in bilingual talk through the notion of *medium*, the linguistic code to which participants show orientation in their talk. Gafaranga argues that bilingual talk is informed by the principle of *preference for same medium talk*.

As upheld by Membership Categorization Analysis (hereafter MCA), social identity is understood here as categorization. Members cast themselves and others into *membership categorization devices* (MCD) and a participant's identity is to be understood as their 'display of, or ascription to, membership of some feature-rich category' (Antaki and Widdicombe 1998: 2). Each MCD consists of a set of identities and is associated with a number of category-bound activities in a co-selective way. Social identity is of paramount importance to the study of institutional talk as participants' orientation to identity provides the analyst with a link between interaction and the encompassing social orders.

The negotiation of social identities

This section examines the negotiation of social identities belonging to the following MCDs: *service parties, acquaintanceship* and *language preference*. These are the main MCDs to which participants in the data evoke occasioned membership. This section focuses on service openings. The opening turns of any encounter are sites where a 'multiplicity of jobs' (Schegloff 1986: 113) are done which will be relevant to the subsequent interaction. One of these jobs is the negotiation of the participants' *alignment*, that is, their mutual orientation to the set of articulated identities projected or assumed locally for the purposes of the present interaction (Zimmerman 1992: 44). Interestingly, Gafaranga (this volume) also focuses on the interactional relevance of openings in the context of medical consultations.

Doing 'being service parties': the negotiation of institutional identities

Studies of institutional talk characterize talk-in-interaction as institutional insofar as participants orient to their professional or institutional identitities (Drew and Heritage 1992b: 25). In what follows, I show how service, as a social-structural context, is effectively brought into being and sustained by the participants' engagement in category-bound activities that display an orientation to the MCD 'service parties'.

In the *prebeginning* (Schegloff 1979b: 27) of any face-to-face encounter, there is an identity *pre-alignment* (Zimmerman 1998) between the participants. In service encounters, the party that reaches the setting is categorized as 'service seeker' by the party working at the setting, who in turn is categorized as 'service provider' by the other party. One is accountable for having some service purpose in mind, whereas the other is accountable for being qualified to provide service.

The pre-alignment is subject to ratification (or modification) by the service parties in the opening turns of the upcoming interaction. Extract 1 exemplifies how mutual display and confirmation of any *situated* identity (Zimmerman 1998) is done through the category-bound activities associated with it.

Extract 1[2]

At a pub.

001 A: **dime**
         what would you like
002 Z: **una de Kilkenny**[3]
         a Kilkenny

In turn 01, A places a service bid, a category-bound activity that makes relevant for this participant the situated (i.e. institutional) identity of 'service provider'. The institutional identity 'service provider' projects for Z the institutional identity 'service seeker' by virtue of the *consistency rule* (Sacks 1974: 219). In turn 02, Z ratifies A's categorization as 'service provider' and confirms his own as 'service seeker' through a category-bound activity associated with the latter, namely the service request.

In short, participants establish, through their first turns, a mutually oriented-to set of identities implicative for what is to follow. The 'continuity of relevancies' (Wilson 1991: 25) of the initially negotiated service context is then reconfirmed turn by turn through subsequent activities bound to the MCD 'service parties'. Knowledge about the MCD 'service parties' and its category-bound activities represents a shared basis on which participants can demonstrate their common grasp of what is going on in the interaction.

Another interesting aspect of service talk as a form of institutional talk concerns access routines. Schegloff and Sacks (1973) argue that, in ordinary talk-in-interaction, openings and closings are the two only compulsory parts of the overall structural organization of conversations. In the data examined, and as also documented in other studies (e.g. Halliday and Hasan 1989; Aston (ed.) 1988), service openings (i.e. greetings) and closings may be absent (or incomplete). As Extract 1 illustrates, such absence makes interactionally relevant the placement of the service bid or request right at the first turn at talk. It demonstrates the participants' orientation to their institutional identities and to the service occasion in which they find themselves.[4]

Doing acquaintanceship

Participants' multiplicity of identities is witnessed in service encounters in that they may choose to interact, for parts of their encounter, under identities other than those in the MCD 'service parties'. For example, in categorizing participants as members of the MCD 'acquaintanceship' in the data, they make their personal identities relevant to the here and now of their interaction. Following Schenkein (1978a: 58), 'personal identities' are understood here as those non-institutional identities that participants negotiate from their separate or joint biographies into the unfolding of their encounter. This section argues that, although 'acquaintanceship' is non-institutional, the negotiation of this MCD in the opening turns of the service encounter reveals the participants' sensitivity to the institutional occasion.

Participants evoke 'acquaintanceship' through the accomplishment of a number of category-bound activities. Participants may initiate an encounter with the use of recognitionals such as calling each other by their names, or may engage routinely in the exchange of 'howareyous'. 'Howareyou' sequences can be used as access displays, thereby signalling availability for interaction under the social identity of acquaintances, or may occur after a greeting sequence. A further category-bound activity is *relational talk*, which frequently occurs after the 'howareyou' sequence. 'Acquaintanceship' is negotiated in the following encounter.

Extract 2

This is the opening of an encounter at an airline office. A comes into the main office, where Z has been waiting for him. Z has been talking to B in the meanwhile.

001	A:	Jaswinder![5]
002	Z:	**qué hay señor Antonio?**
		how are you doing Mr. Antonio?
003	A:	what's the excess weight?
004	Z:	I don't know - **yo:- yo:- yo:**
		- I:- I:- I:
005	A:	one hundred kilos!
006	B:	your weight your weight!

007 Z: **no** ((laughs)) !
           no

008 B: your excess weight!

009 Z: **yo eh: el mía sí - ciento diez kilos**
           me uh: mine yes - one hundred and ten kilos

010 B: ((laughs))

011 Z: what is your excess weight?

012 B: ((laughs))

013 Z: er: forty-seven kilos

014 A: forty-seven kilos?

015 Z: **si tenía que pesar yo sesenta y ocho y peso ciento seis kilos**
           my weight should be sixty-eight and it's one hundred and six
           kilos

016 A: **QUÉ BESTIA** – what are you eating?
           GROSS

017 Z: **gambas!**
           shrimps!

018 A: **GAMBAS** ((laughs))!
           SHRIMPS

019 B: **GAMBAS** ((laughs))!
           SHRIMPS

020 A: **pero hombre!**
           hey man!

021 Z: **siempre estoy viajando en - por fuera – vino y eso** (0.3) **vas**
           a venir tú al aeropuerto?
           I'm always travelling in - abroad - wine and that stuff (0.3) *are*
           you going to meet us at the airport?

In the previous section, I examined encounters where the participants categorize each other in the opening sequences as anonymous
local versions of the institutional MCD 'service seeker-service provider'.
By contrast, the ascription of 'acquaintanceship' is based on personal
identification. The process of categorization that participants accomplish
in the opening sequence consists of two phases, namely *identification
displays* and *access displays* (Schiffrin 1977: 680). In Extract 2, participants'
recognition of each other is signalled through the identification displays in
turns 01 and 02, which in this case consist of calling each other's names.
Identification displays are followed by access displays, which have the
function of establishing co-presence and communicating readiness to
initiate an engagement (Goffman 1971). Typical access displays are
greetings but, as Schegloff (1986) points out, 'howareyous' can be used

as greeting substitutes and work as access displays,[6] as in Extract 2. The 'howareyou' sequence is incomplete and gives way to a relational talk episode from turn 03 mainly consisting of bantering. The service transaction as such is not tackled until turn 21.[7]

In the data, relational talk episodes frequently consist of bantering, understood as trading of jokes and playful insults between the participants.[8] In Extract 2, service providers A and B team up to tease service seeker Z about his overweight. The relational talk episode starts in turn 03 with a play on social identities. A's request 'what's the excess weight?' is a routine request in the compliance episode of the services at the airline office, one of the issues that the participants need to address in the process of selling/buying a ticket. The request can thus be seen as a category-bound activity to the identity of service provider, which in turns projects for Z the identity of service seeker. This is the alignment taken up by Z in turn 04, where he says that he does not know. In fact, the effectiveness of turn 03 as a tease depends entirely on the inferential framework invoked by its institutionality, hence Z's response in turn 04. In turn 06, B makes it clear whose weight A is referring to, namely Z's. Z accepts the alignment as revealed by his laughter in turn 07 and by proffering the information in turn 09. In the subsequent talk, A and B carry on teasing Z about his weight and his diet through increased loudness, laughter and remarks such as 'qué bestia' (literally, 'what a beast').

The negotiation of acquaintanceship in the opening of the service encounter has a bearing on the way the institutional context is locally constituted. The display of acquaintanceship in the opening turns makes the encounter one 'in-a-series' (Button 1991). The encounter in question is constituted as one in the series devoted to the provision of one specific service. Evoking acquaintanceship 'oils the wheels' (Laver 1975) to initiate the service interaction. This is especially relevant to the management of encounters where the service request has been formulated in an earlier encounter and thus the service is resumed *in media res* in the current encounter. In Extract 2, Z's first institutional interpretation of turn 03 can be put down to the acquaintanceship evoked in the first turns, which has made this encounter one 'in-a-series'. The ascription of acquaintanceship enables the participants to set their talk on track in a way that their service can be resumed at the very point where they left it in their last encounter. In this connection, Gafaranga (this volume) argues that the categorization of a medical consultation as a new consultation or as one 'in-a-series' lies in the specific formulation of the opening turn.

Negotiating linguistic identities

The service settings selected for this study are especially interesting for the study of social identities and institutional talk on account of their multilingual dimension. Participants can conduct their interaction in three possible languages (i.e. Catalan, Castilian or English). A large number of the encounters consist of first-time encounters. Participants, who may come from different sociolinguistic backgrounds, do not know each other and thus they are not necessarily aware of each other's *language preference* (Auer 1984). Therefore, they need to negotiate on the spot a *medium* for their interaction and this is done in the opening turns of the encounter (Torras 1998, 2002).

Gafaranga (2001) accounts for the orderliness of bilingual talk-in-interaction by considering *language preference* as a MCD whereby participants categorize themselves and each other as having a monolingual or bilingual identity, and in which language(s). *Medium selection*, which is one of the activities bound to *language preference*, is made possible in bilingual talk-in-interaction by participants' locally negotiated linguistic identities (Gafaranga 2001; Torras and Gafaranga 2002). To illustrate this point, consider the local negotiation of linguistic identities in the following extract.

Extract 3

This is the beginning of a service encounter at a pub. Z and Y are talking to each other at the bar while waiting to be served. Eventually A approaches them.

```
001  Z:   copa de whisky i: endavant ( (laughs) )!
            a glass of whisky and: let's carry on
002  Y:   ( (laughs) )
003  A:   què vols?
            what would you like?
004  Z:   erm uh one chupito of Jameson and some water please
                         shot
005  A:   sure - thanks
```

A opens the encounter in turn 03 with the service bid. He has overheard Z and Y using Catalan and thus adopts the linguistic identity under which the two customers are interacting, namely 'monolingual Catalan'. A is in fact British and only has basic command of Catalan. For the purposes of the service he initiates, he fits himself into the same togethering as Z and Y. However, in turn 04, Z does not take 'monolingual Catalan' as an *adequate reference* to conduct the service. He reveals his language preference by placing his service request in English. In the following turn, A adopts a 'monolingual English' identity, which is established as the participants' linguistic identity for the rest of the service encounter.

Summing up, through the initial display and subsequent consensus on a given language identity, the participants select a medium for carrying out their service encounter successfully. Participants' orientation to *preference for same medium talk* leads them to engage in medium negotiation processes. The negotiation of linguistic identity offers an interesting insight into how the institutional character of bilingual service talk-in-interaction is talked into being. The participants' language preference is displayed sequentially through a series of divergent talk turns, which Auer (1984) identifies as a *language negotiation sequence*. In the data, the service provider (A in Extract 3) routinely converges to the service seeker's (Z's) displayed language preference as soon as it is revealed. The underlying service norm of compliance with the service seeker's request(s) also governs the participants' conduct at the level of medium selection.

The study of bilingual service interaction reveals that part of the identity negotiation work that participants accomplish corresponds to their categorization into the MCD 'language preference'. This categorization process occurs alongside with categorization into MCDs like 'service parties' and 'acquaintanceship' in the opening turns of the service encounter. Whether they agree to do 'being service parties' or 'acquaintances', participants must negotiate the linguistic identity under which they are to interact. Language preference can thus be seen as a platform for the display of other identity sets, institutional or otherwise, relevant to the interaction. In other words, without the display of a linguistic identity, participants would lack the vehicle to articulate other identities and the category-bound activities of which their interaction is made.

Renegotiating identities for the accomplishment of successful service

Research on social identity has widely shown that participants can use and attribute to each a variety of identities as their interaction progresses. Identity ascription is in every case occasioned by the dynamics of the interaction. In this section, I discuss how order in bilingual service talk-in-interaction can be explained through the participants' juggling of social identities. In particular, I concentrate on how participants *navigate* among identities in order to repair conduct that is deviant with respect to the service norm of successful compliance with the service provider's request(s).

The study of deviance is useful methodologically speaking because it is through the participants' deviant behaviour that the analyst can infer what the norm is as perceived by the participants themselves (see *deviant case analysis* in Heritage 1984a). Extract 4 below illustrates an instance of unsuccessful service compliance (i.e. deviant behaviour) managed through a shift of both non-linguistic and linguistic identities.

Extract 4

This telephone interaction takes place at a chamber of commerce. Z has called the chamber to complain about a cheque he has not received yet.

```
001  B:   yeah well - she told me that uh: the cheque is sent - eh is sent
          by mail and
002  Z:   but when - Josep?
03   B:   sorry?
004  Z:   when?
005  B:   uh: well uh: ( (laughs) ) m- my news is that the cheque uh has
          been sent - I: suppose er: last week or:
006  Z:   OK but OK but I wa- I was told that it had been sent
007  B:   yeah
008  Z:   er: I was told this er: four weeks ago
009  B:   four weeks ago
010  Z:   yeah - obviously you tell me now it was sent last week
011  B:   yeah
012  Z:   then obviously - the first message - wasn't correct
013  B:   well no no actually I don't know exactly the date when this
          has been sent - but well er: - the ne- - er [what they know is ( ) ]
014  Z:                    [no no no OK OK    ] let's OK - vamos a ser profesionales
                                                        - let's be professional
015  B:   yeah
016  Z:   y: necesito: ↑
          a:nd I nee:d ↑
017  B:   sí
          yeah
```

018   Z: **una carta:** ↑
             a letter: ↑

019   B: **sí**
             yeah

The participants have negotiated both an institutional identity ('service seeker-service provider') and a 'monolingual English' linguistic identity in the opening turns of the interaction. Z has been trying to find out to no avail when a certain cheque was sent out (e.g. turn 02 and 04). Eventually, in turn 14, Z explicitly formulates the need to renegotiate their institutional identity through the use of an *identity category* (Greatbatch and Dingwall 1998), namely 'professional'. He urges B to be 'professional', thus implying that his performance as a service provider so far has been deviant. In this extract, the shift thus concerns a redefinition of 'service provider', which, as perceived by Z, has lacked the category-bound feature 'professional'.

The redefinition of 'service provider' co-occurs with a renegotiation of linguistic identity from English to Castilian. The shift is conversationally flagged by pausing and retracing in turn 14. B displays the requested 'professionalism' not only by dutifully complying with Z's new request for a letter (turn 18) but also by adopting (turn 17) the new linguistic identity displayed by Z. This extract illustrates that linguistic identity, as any other type of social identity, is not something static but something that participants 'do' and which might be shifted to meet the needs of the ongoing interaction. In Extract 4, in shifting to Castilian, Z seems to be orienting to the 'foreignness' (Torras 2002) of A's English identity.[9] From Z's perspective, 'English' is not an *adequate reference* for the local version of 'service provider' he wishes.

Finally, Extract 5 illustrates how the display of the MCD 'acquaintanceship' in the course of the service transaction is occasioned by the dynamics of the institutional interaction. The shift strategically ensures that behaviour is not deviant with respect to the service norm.

Extract 5

The conversation takes place at a butcher's market stall. A is serving L (Lola) while at the same time taking the order placed by Y.

001   A: *Lola què més vols* ((to L)) - *ja m'ho diràs ja em diràs* ( )
             ((to Y))
             Lola would you like anything else ((to L)) - *just let me know just let me know* ( ) ((to Y))

002 Y: **ja torn- ara tornaré**
         I'll b- I'll be right back

003 A: **vale reina**
         OK love

004 Y: **avui està obert a la tarda**
         today it's open in the afternoon

005 A: **sí tot el dia**
         yes all day

006 L: **tot el dia avui**
         all day today

007 A: **LOLA QUE HAY GENTE AQUÍ ESPERANDO**
         LOLA THERE ARE PEOPLE WAITING HERE

008 L: ( )

009 A: **espabila no?**
         hurry up will you?

010 L: **ya está nada más**
         that's it nothing else

011 A: **ya está y para eso tanto:**
         is that it and just for that such a:

012 L: **para eso tanto follón**
         such a fuss just for that

013 A: **QUÉ BARBARIDAD** – yo digo yo digo vendrá hoy a portarse
         como una mujer
         MY GOODNESS – I say I say she's come today to behave like a
         woman

014 L: **no ( )**

015 A: **mil cent noranta-dos Lola.**
         one thousand one hundred and ninety-two Lola.

016 L: **quant?**
         how much?

A and L (Lola) have negotiated a Catalan linguistic identity and the institutional identities 'service seeker-service provider' in the first turns of the encounter. In turn 01 in the extract, A invites L to formulate a new service request and subsequently addresses Y, with whom she is sorting out an order for the following day. In turn 06, L becomes a participant in A and Y's service interaction, rather than a bystander deciding on a new service request. Turns 07 and 09 reveal that, in A's view, the service pace at the busy stall is being slowed down by L. A resorts to identity navigation to deal with this transactional problem. A starts a bantering episode, first teasing L on her slowness and asking her to hurry up (turns 07 and 09), raising her voice, then teasing L on her small purchase (turns 11 and 13). Bantering evokes a new set of identities for the participants, namely 'acquaintanceship', further evoked through the use of L's name 'Lola'. Turn 12 shows that L goes along with A's banter by completing her previous unfinished turn, thus confirming the 'acquaintanceship' they are enacting.

Extract 5 is also interesting because, in one and the same encounter, the shift from institutional identities to acquaintanceship and the subsequent shift back to institutional correspond in each case with a shift of linguistic identity. A different linguistic identity (i.e. Castilian) is adopted for the whole of this bantering episode (turns 07–13). The participants then shift back to their institutional identities from turn 15, where A initiates the next activity bound to 'service provider', namely stating the amount due. From this turn too, they go back to the initial Catalan identity they had adopted for the service transaction. Participants do 'being acquaintances' and 'being service parties' under different linguistic identities.

To sum up, 'acquaintanceship' is evoked here by the dynamics of the institutional interaction. A needs to speed up the pace of the service but, under the 'service provider' identity she has been ascribing so far, she cannot nag her customers. Compliance with the service seeker's request is an essential category-bound activity of a service giver which also involves accommodation to the service seeker's pace. For this reason, A fits herself into another MCD under which nagging the other party can be seen as a legitimate activity. Her ultimate goal, however, is institutional in nature, namely to sell as many goods as possible.

Conclusion

This chapter has provided an identity-related account of how *service*, as a form of institutional talk, is 'talked into being' (Heritage 1984a) in settings where more than one language can be used. Encounters are constituted as service (i.e. institutional) occasions through the participants' negotiation of social identities and navigation between them in the course of their encounter. I have argued here that the participants' accomplishment of category-bound activities in the first turns at talk ratify their pre-alignment as 'service seeker-service provider' and project a particular line of interaction as well as an agenda aimed at the achievement of a service goal. In line with other conversation-analytic studies, it has been shown that it is the participants' orientation to their professional/institutional identities that makes their talk institutional. It has further been shown that the institutional character of the encounters lies not only in the participants' ascription of the MCD 'service parties', but also in their display of other identity sets in the course of their interaction. The display of other identities is occasioned precisely by the dynamics of the institutional interaction. Here I have concentrated on the MCDs 'acquaintanceship' and 'language preference'.

The participants' initial categorization into the MCD 'acquaintanceship' through category-bound activities such as recognitionals and relational talk constitutes the current encounter as one 'in-a-series'. Evoking this MCD serves an 'oiling' function (Laver 1975) in the opening of encounters where a given service is resumed *in media res*. The ascription of 'acquaintanceship' enables the participants to set their talk on track in a way that their service can be resumed at the very point where they left it in their last encounter. Further, it defines the service seeker as 'regular', as opposed to 'anonymous'.

I have argued that the MCD 'language preference' must be treated as a key aspect in the study of institutional talk, which so far has been mainly concerned with monolingual interaction. Without the negotiation of a linguistic identity, participants would lack the vehicle to articulate other identities and the category-bound activities of which their inter-action is made. In turn, the negotiation of linguistic identity shows the participants' orientation to the institutionality of the occasion. Service providers routinely adopt the linguistic identity enacted by the service seeker, thus showing orientation to an underlying service norm whereby the service provider complies with the service seeker's request(s) at a number of levels, among them, *medium* selection.

Unsuccessful service compliance constitutes deviant behaviour with respect to the service norm and calls for remedial action. In the data, participants resort to renegotiation of both non-linguistic and linguistic identities to tackle actual (or potential) unsuccessful compliance. This multiple ascription is exploited strategically in service. In the course of an encounter, participants enact different (non-)institutional identities under different linguistic identities with the aim of repairing (or preventing) deviant service behaviour.

The conversation-analytic/MCA approach adopted in this article throws new light on a number of service phenomena such as the nature of greetings and the occurrence of relational talk, which have been largely disregarded in traditional systemic linguistic-based studies of service encounters such as Halliday and Hasan (1980, 1989). The identity-related account provides us with a deeper understanding of the richness of activities, bound to both institutional and non-institutional identities, which actually occurs in service interaction and their institutional relevance.

This study suggests a number of practical applications for training in the service sector, especially in our age of increasing international and intercultural communication. The service provider must be made sensitive to the fact that linguistic identities are not something static to be taken for granted; they are a negotiable matter requiring some conversational work. One obvious issue that needs to be emphasized is the importance of negotiating a medium in the very first turns of the interaction. Early medium negotiation will ensure successful communication and avoid potential 'language barrier' problems in the course of the interaction.

The service provider's immediate convergence to the service seeker's displayed linguistic identity improves service quality because it shows systematic compliance with the service seeker at all levels and this has interesting implications for training in multilingual service settings. Situations often arise where the service seeker proposes a medium of interaction in which he or she is not really proficient. A prototypical case is that of the visitor at a tourist resort who wants to use the local language interacting with a service provider who is proficient in the visitor's first language. The service provider needs to be made aware that good service may lie in accepting the service seeker's medium at the cost of smooth communication rather than in choosing the most 'effective' medium.

The *personalization* of service has been much advocated by businesses and organizations in our so-called 'macdonaldized' service- and information-based society. In multilingual service interaction, the service provider's convergence to the service seeker's displayed language preference may be regarded as one way to contribute to this personalization. In 'one-in-a-series' service encounters, the service provider's awareness/display in the service opening of the service seeker's language preference – as established in previous encounters – is one effective way of constructing the service seeker as a familiar face at the institutional setting, that is, as a 'regular' service seeker.

Another aspect that requires consciousness-raising in training programmes is participants' multiplicity of identities and, more specifically, how this multiplicity may be exploited strategically in actual interaction to accomplish successful service. There are occasions when the service process may benefit from evoking social identities other than the institutional set 'service provider–seeker'. The data have revealed that the participants' use of recognitionals as well as the initiation of 'howareyou' sequences and relational talk episodes can contribute to giving a more personalized service, especially in service extending over a number of encounters. Engaging in activities bound to the non-institutional MCD 'acquaintanceship' within the service framework makes the participants' personal identities relevant to the interaction.

Training programmes should likewise address identity renegotiation or shift as a strategic resource to tackle potential or actual unsuccessful service compliance. The data shows that shifts of identity prove useful in easing up or preventing conflict in service interaction. Further research on globalized multi-cultural/-lingual service interaction is needed and this study has illustrated some of the many practical contributions that the CA/MCA approach to institutional talk-in-interaction can make to the areas of design and intervention in the service sector.

Notes

1   See Torras (2002) for an in-depth description of the sociolinguistic context in which the data were gathered.
2   Transcription conventions for language contrast in extracts in this chapter only are as follows:

Catalan	*Catalan is written in bold-italic type*
Castilian	**Castilian is written in bold type**
English	*English translation is written in italic type*
English	Utterances in English are written in normal type
Unidentified	Utterances where it is unclear which language is being used are underlined in dotted type

3   The phonetics of this utterance is Catalan: 'una de' is pronounced /unədə/.
4   If greeting parts occur in the service opening, they serve a service-oriented specific function. Consider the following extract.

(This is the beginning of an encounter at a pub)

```
001 A:  hola
        hi
002 Z:  pint of McEwan's
```

The greeting in turn 01 actually corresponds to the service provider's second part in a summons–answer adjacency pair, where the summons has been accomplished non-verbally by the mere presence of the service seeker (Torras 2002). But see the function of greetings in the negotiation of 'acquaintanceship' in the corresponding section.

5   Pseudonyms have been used for the proper names appearing in the transcripts.

6   Note that there is *compression* (Schiffrin 1977) of the identification and access display phases in the opening sequence. The second part of the recognitional ('señor Antonio') and the first part of the 'howareyou' are compressed into turn 02. Compression in this sequential context is common in the data. Schiffrin also documents it in other kinds of social encounters.

7   Insofar as there is a service goal to be attained in the encounter, an identity shift from 'acquaintanceship' to 'service parties' needs to occur in the course of the interaction. I will not deal with this type of shift here. See Torras (2002) for discussion.

8   Bantering is characterized by Lindenfeld (1990) and Torras (1998) as a frequent feature of their respective service corpora.

9   Grammatical, lexical and phonetic features in A's speech clearly reveal that English is not his first language.

8
University Students Resisting Academic Identity

Bethan Benwell and Elizabeth H. Stokoe

Introduction

A commonly documented phenomenon in educational settings in the UK has been students' resistance to academic tasks and identity (e.g. Felder and Brent 1996; Francis, 1999, 2000; Willis 1977). This resistance tends to take the form of challenging the teacher, joking and doing the minimum amount of work necessary. It has chiefly been researched within the compulsory sector and tends to assert an association between resistance and masculinity, although recent studies suggest a similar pattern among girls (Pichler 2002). In an interview-based study of London schoolboys, Phoenix and Frosh (2001) suggested that antagonism to school-based learning was influential in determining pupil popularity. In a similar study carried out with Australian pupils, Martino (2000: 102) suggested that pupils resisted the teacher's task and the institutional agenda by preferring to 'muck around' in class, 'give crap' and 'act cool'.

This research, focusing as it does on compulsory education contexts, has neglected potential patterns of resistance in the post-compulsory sector. This is possibly because an assumption exists that once students are voluntarily invested in post-compulsory education, resistance will not be a valid or desirable form of expression. Limited support for this comes from Redman and Mac an Ghaill (1997), who interviewed sixth formers about their attitudes to work. Contrary to their younger counter-parts, these students expressed an investment in being good at academic work and working hard. The authors concluded that the move into tertiary education 'marks a key cultural transition that involves young people in new social relations (in particular those of the labour market) and requires new forms of identity to handle these' (p.169). In other words, a hard-working, competitive identity becomes a form of cultural capital within this domain.

Conversely, a small literature aimed at improving teaching methods points to continued patterns of resistance in the university setting, particularly to student-centred tasks. For instance, Felder and Brent (1996) discuss the hostility and lack of co-operation that frequently accompanies active learning, and Butts (2000: 80) describes the 'grunts and groans' that greet the prospect of group work. However, this research, like the research on attitudes of pupils in the compulsory sector, is based on ethnographic *accounts* of classroom experience and disposition rather than on systematic analyses of actual tutorial interaction. For example, in Phoenix and Frosh's (2001: 31) interview-based research, the authors ask the questions: 'Do any boys get teased who do very well?' and 'what makes boys popular in your school?' Such questions implicitly hold the assumption that the criteria for 'popularity' is linked to resisting being seen to do well. Similarly, Francis (1999) asked pupils what they thought of the idea that pupils' underachievement is linked to 'laddish' forms of behaviour. Unsurprisingly, their responses reveal considerable support for the statement, yet reveal very little about whether such behaviour is actually enacted discursively within a school setting and, if so, what it 'looks like' empirically.

One of the major limitations of the ethnographic interview, conducted without recourse to observation of naturally occurring interaction, is the potential disparity between elicited, self-reflexive accounts of identity and the accounts of identity that *emerge* from discursive interaction. As Sacks (1992: 27) argues:

> the trouble with [ethnography based on interviewing] is that they're using informants; that is, they're asking questions of their subjects. That means that they're studying the categories that Members use, to be sure, except at this point they are not investigating their categories by attempting to find them in the activities in which they're employed.

Although asking participants about particular topics can tell researchers about the culturally circulating discourses that are invoked in producing answers, it is important to examine the potential operation of such discourses as meaning-making resources in actual interaction. Sacks's analytic approach requires analysts to investigate categories such as resistance 'by attempting to find them in the activities in which they're employed'.

In this chapter, therefore, we analysed naturally occurring data in order to focus on actual interaction in tutorials, rather than on participants' accounts of their tutorial experience. This ethnomethodological frame-work enabled us to study the methods and strategies by which the students made sense of their tutorial interactions. In explicating social life, including talk's procedures, ethnomethodologists observe interactions and focus on what participants are attending to, using conversation analysis (CA) to analyse the regular patterns in turn-taking sequences and the endogenous orientations of speakers (Sacks 1992).

We used CA to explore the sequential organization of tutorial talk and how participants mutually orient to and achieve orderly conversation as they accomplish their interactional business. Although the notion of 'resistance' remains an analysts' rather than participants' category, we aim to establish an emic, rather than etic, perspective on tutorial talk by exploring students' own orientations to their task and performance within it. The category 'resistance' provides a useful gloss for indicating, in broad terms, how students might be constructing and assessing their disposition, performance and activities (see Cuff 1994). We argue, therefore, that conversation analytic methodology is ideally suited to the exploration of classroom discourse because education is a 'language-saturated institution' (Watson 1992). As students interact with each other and the tutor they reveal, to each other and the analyst, the cultural order of the tutorial: what is normative and non-normative in such a discursive environment.

Methodology

This chapter extends previous work by both authors on aspects of tutorial talk in university contexts (see Benwell 1996, 1999; Benwell and Stokoe 2002; Stokoe 1995, 1997, 1998, 2000). We drew together data sets of tutorial talk from three higher education institutions all located in the UK. The first set came from two British universities, a 'new' university (formerly polytechnic) and a traditional campus university. Eight undergraduate tutorials, each lasting one hour and representing a range of disciplines (Electrical Engineering, Physics, Politics and English Studies) were audio-recorded. The tutorials were tutor-led and involved either discussion of issues or texts (Politics and English), problem solving or revision of homework (Engineering and Physics). The size of the group ranged from three to ten.

The second set came from another British university (formerly a higher education college). Undergraduate students were drawn from different disciplines (Education, Psychology and Behavioural Sciences). A total of 30 classes took part in the study including seven from a post-graduate class of teacher trainers (PGCE: Postgraduate Certificate of Education students). All of the groups had the format of the class in common: the sessions involved small group work rather than tutor-led discussion. Typically, students would talk in groups for 45 minutes with a plenary at the end. Within the larger group of 15–20 students, one small group (between three and six participants) was video-recorded while talking about the day's task. The tutor, who gave students discipline-specific material to read and a list of questions to guide their subsequent discussion, provided the structure of task. Across both data sets, all of the students had English as their first language, a small proportion was classified as mature (aged 21 or older) and the data represented students from each academic year.

The recorded data were transcribed in detail using conventions adapted from Jefferson (1984a). We analysed the data by tracking sequences in the interactions where students oriented to their tutorial task or their effort and performance within it. We also examined segments where students displayed an orientation to their own or each other's academic knowledge.

Analysis

Across our data, there were numerous instances in which students oriented to their task, their own performance of the task or their academic knowledge. Overwhelmingly, in each of these instances, students marked their task, their performance or their knowledge in terms of a resistance to, or distancing from, the academic endeavour.[1] This resistance or distancing was realized in two main ways. First, we found that students constructed disengagement with their task (1) by invoking their lack of preparation in order to avoid engaging or to appear disengaged, or (2) by challenging the parameters of the task itself. Second, we found that students regularly revealed a reluctance to display their academic knowledge by policing each other's contributions and by disclaiming and prefacing their contributions with distancing devices. We consider each pattern in turn.

Negotiating (dis)engagement with the tutorial task
Disengagement strategy (1): minimising preparation
The first extract in this section comes from a second-year psychology tutorial in which four students are discussing their task: the students

have to produce, collaboratively as a group, an essay plan for a particular question.

Extract 1

```
001  A:   I can't remember any of this.
002       ( . )
003  D:   look there it is look, ((points at paper on desk))
004       ( . )
005  A:   you typed it up!
006  D:   what? ((points again at the paper))
007  A:   oh: I thought- I thought you'd typed your ( . ) your outline
008       [up this morning! heh heh heh]
009  D:   [o h  n o  : :. heh heh heh]
```

(EHS Psychology tutorial data)

In this extract, the students are discussing the content of their essay plan. Diana treats Ann's comment that she 'can't remember any of this', the material they are supposed to be including, as a request for information. She points at the instructions that the tutor has provided for the group. However, it is clear from Ann's response that she thinks Diana has already prepared some work. She states 'you typed it up' (line 5). In Diana's next turn, she points again at the instruction sheet that the students have and Ann repairs her interpretation (line 7): that these were notes that Diana had prepared 'this morning'. Note Diana's emphasized denial (line 9) and the students' laughter which follows, both of which manage Ann's potential criticism of Diana. The denial functions to resist the implication that she may have done some early preparation for the tutorial. This interpretation is supported by other instances across the data, where doing some work ahead of the tutorial is treated as an accountable matter: students like Diana display work's accountable nature in their descriptions, as do the other students in their subsequent laughter. It appears that doing work is a negative activity, something that does not pass by unmarked in conversation.

Extract 2 comes from an English tutorial, in which the tutor is attempting to get the discussion started:

Extract 2

```
001  T:   Fay ( . ) have you have you got a copy?
002  F:   ↓no.=
```

```
003  T:   =did you get a chance to read it?
004       ( . )
005  F:   no.
006       (0.7)
007  T:   ↑oh=
008  F:   =sorry.
009  T:   right.
010       (0.5)
011  T:   why?
012       ( . )
013  F:   I've just been preoccupied with other essays at the moment.
014       (0.9)
015  T:   .hhh right,
016  F:   okay,
017  T:   right.
018       (2.0)
019  T:   >what an interesting way of putting it.<
020       (0.5)
021  T:   ↑if you look at the Ode to a Nightingale
```

(BMB English tutorial data)

In the opening 'task-setting' sequences of tutorials, we found that students' turns often challenged or were in some way disruptive to the task execution (Benwell and Stokoe 2002). The extract starts with two question–answer adjacency pairs. First, the tutor asks Fay if she has 'got a copy' of the book they are discussing and then whether she had 'a chance to read it' (lines 1 and 3). Fay's responses to the tutor's questions (lines 2 and 5) are both 'dispreferred' second pair parts (Pomerantz 1984). The preferred responses, given the context of the questions, would be 'yes' on both occasions. What makes Fay's responses seem rather rude is that they are unmitigated dispreferreds. Conversation analysts have found that, when giving a dispreferred response, speakers usually mitigate it in some way. So whereas answering 'yes' to 'would you like to come for lunch?' is straightforward, answering 'no' requires further work, usually in the form of an account: 'oh, I'm sorry, I'd love to come but I'm a bit tied up'. Giving dispreferred responses without an account breaks normative conversational patterns. In these two sequences, Fay's turns display a disregard for normative institutional practices in educational talk. In particular, her behaviour flouts the maxims of educational business in which turning up having done some preparation is expectable for students.

At line 8, Fay's 'Sorry', which might preface an account, is not developed further. The tutor's 'right' (line 9) is an acknowledgement token, which suggests that she expects further accounting from Fay and the 0.5 second pause on line 10 indicates a transition relevance place that is not taken up. The tutor then explicitly requests an account at line 11: 'Why?', which is provided by Fay at line 13: 'I've just been preoccupied with other essays at the moment'. The upshot of this turn is to signal that she cannot be involved in this discussion: she doesn't have a book, she hasn't read the book and she is preoccupied. The tutor displays some dissatisfaction with this interchange with her ironic comment: 'what an interesting way of putting it' (line 19). However, she moves on to address the rest of the group and Fay has effectively established her non-participation.

What is particularly interesting about this sequence is the breakdown in the usual rights and obligations associated with the membership categories 'tutor' and 'student'. The activities normatively associated with being a student might include reading and preparing for class. The absence of these activities results in the interactional trouble seen in this exchange. Moreover, not doing work is something that students should account for, particularly after an initial question about it. Fay's turns suggest her membership of the category 'student', and the obligations and entitlements associated with it, are somewhat at odds with normative institutional arrangements (see also Markee, this volume).

Distancing strategy (2): challenging the parameters of the task

We conclude the first half of our analysis by examining another strategy used by students to disengage from their task. Extract 3 comes from a group of four first-year psychology students, discussing content for their essay plan:

Extract 3

```
001  B:   could put- ( . ) could put,
002       (3.0)
003  B:   put that in paragraph one couldn't we?
004       (1.5)
005  J:   could do.
006       (1.9)
007  J:   °crap question.°
```

(EHS Psychology tutorial data)

This sequence, in which the students begin to discuss content for their essay plan, contains several long pauses, which indicate some trouble around carrying out the task. Brad's suggestion is heavily mitigated and hesitant. Although Jason responds to Brad's suggestion to include a particular piece of information in 'paragraph one', this comes after a long pause and maintains the low modal status of Brad's initial suggestion. In other words, Jason's 'could do' (line 5) does not seem to be a future-action oriented agreement; it does not offer the expectable endorsement (e.g. 'yes, do that!') that would propel the task forward. Following a second pause, Jason then provides a negative assessment of the question around which they are constructing their plan: '°crap question°' (line 7). This evaluation might function to account for his lack of enthusiasm in response to Brad's suggestion. Furthermore, it is uttered in a whispered tone that displays his orientation to the camera and potential for the tutor to hear this comment: the students are being recorded so their talk is potentially in the public domain. The whispered delivery of the assessment reveals an understanding of normative educational goals and agendas, and that criticism of the tutor/task is not part of the institutional business. Thus Jason's turn encapsulates the conflict between institutional norms and student resistance to these norms.

In the next example, the students again challenge their task, but for a different reason:

Extract 4

```
001  L:   I don't see the point in doing this at all personally.=
002  P:   =yeah let's go heh [heh heh heh]
003  L:                      [heh heh heh]
004  F:                      [heh heh heh]
005  C:                      [heh heh heh]
006       (3.0)
007  C:   it's got to be done,=
008  P:   =if you don't do it you fail the course,=
009  C:   =yeah [y o u  f a i l] the course (0.2) [no]
010  F:        [you're joking!]
011  P:                                           [no]
012       (0.5)
013  F:   that's ridiculous
014       (2.0)
015  F:   well if you're not gonna use it then ( . ) I mean °what's the
016       point of doing it°
```

017   (0.4)
018 J: °just seems useless to me.° (.) you wouldn't write an essay plan
019   in a group anyway.

(EHS Psychology tutorial data)

The students' assessments of their task reveal an orientation to an instrumental approach to learning, in which work is only valuable and worthwhile if it is assessed. In Extract 4, from a group of second-year psychology students, the task is to produce an essay plan as a group, which must be attached to their individual essays in order to pass the essay itself. First, note Penny and Lucy's first turns in which 'resistance' is formulated. However, laughter in response to Penny's suggestion 'let's go' evaluates the suggestion of resistance to the task as non-serious, yet allows it to be uttered nonetheless. The students therefore manage two interactional goals simultaneously: that they have to do the task but also display their detachment from it. The grounds for their negative task evaluation is that it is not marked officially, revealing an instrumental orientation to education. This instrumentality is elaborated in Frances and Jennifer's turns at lines 15–16 and 18. Frances suggests that there is no point in producing a piece of work that does not get used; Jennifer suggests that working in a group is the flaw in the task. The whispered delivery of these assessments again demonstrates their orientation to the potentially overhearing tutor, thus revealing their simultaneous acceptance of the authority of the tutor to set the educational agenda alongside resistance to this agenda (see Felder and Brent 1996; Butts 2000).

In the final extract, we explore a similar challenge to the task in a tutor-led session. The students in Extract 5, from an engineering tutor, are responding to a request from the tutor to work out mathematically some wavelengths:

Extract 5

001 J: wouldn't- wouldn't you have a ↑ book [t o   ] look
002 T: [pardon?]
003 J: something like that up from,=
004 T: =well=
005 J: =' cos would you be ex↑pected to know the wavelengths of
006   light [of colours.]
007 T: [w e l l] not in an exam (.) not in exam when you're
008   conditions but preparing the work at home

009 V: mm.
010 J: oh yeah.

(BMB Engineering tutorial data)

Here, Jack challenges (albeit in a hedged manner) the basis of the tutor's question, suggesting that such information can be accessed from a book, and therefore does not need to be calculated by hand (lines 1–3). The tutor produces an account for her question (lines 7–8), arguing that 'in exam conditions', something students need to be prepared for, the calculations would have to be made. This is accepted by Vincent and Jack (lines 9–10). Rather than accepting the tutor's entitlement as a member of that professional category to set the task, the student formulates a challenge to the nature of the task, which the tutor accommodates by treating it as an accountable matter.

In this section, we have shown that, in a variety of ways, students routinely display disengagement with, or an instrumental approach to their task. We argue that this reveals a resistance to or distancing from academic identity such that students do not want to be positioned as 'clever', 'keen', 'prepared' or enthusiastically engaged in their tasks. In the post-compulsory sector, a culture of distance and lack of interest appears normative and permeates students' activities in the university tutorial. It also reveals a misaligning between institutional objectives (tutors set tasks, students prepare for classes and engage in tasks) and the construction of 'student' as a categorial identity: being a student seems to involve displaying resistance to these objectives. We consider further interactions that reveal this emerging culture in the next section.

The interactional management of knowledge displays

The second section of analysis addresses instances of talk in which students orient to 'knowledge displays': sequences of talk in which a student constructs a piece of information, evaluation or theory. We found that students regularly policed each other's and their own knowledge displays. In other words, students would treat such displays as accountable matters, and this accountability was revealed in a variety of ways: in censorious, ironic, disclaimed or otherwise troubled responses to 'cleverness', either self- or other-initiated. In the same way that speakers will often repair errors in conversation (see Schegloff, Jefferson and Sacks 1977), by correcting themselves (self-initiated self-repair) or by responding to another speaker's correction (other-initiated self-repair), we found regular patterns across the data. We start with 'self-initiated' accounts before moving on to 'other-initiated' devices for downgrading or distancing from knowledge displays.

Accountable knowledge displays: self-initiated

In Extract 6, which comes from a tutor-led electrical engineering tutorial, the group is revising a principle from engineering theory and illustrating examples by drawing diagrams on a board:

Extract 6

```
001  M:   I said blue, ( . ) that wasn't far out.
002       (0.4)
003  M:   at least I got the right end of the spectrum here.
004  D:   yeah.
005  T:   yes. ( . ) heh heh ( . ) the thing to remember is that
006       erm=
007  M:   =that's- ( . ) that's unusual for me actually.
```

(BMB Engineering tutorial data)

In this fragment, we can track the sequential organization of Mike's knowledge display 'I said blue' and his subsequent accounting strategies. The knowledge display is followed by a sequence of three comments reflexively oriented to the display: 'that wasn't far out', 'at least I got the right end of the spectrum' and 'that's unusual for me actually' (lines 1, 3 and 7). In particular, the final comment functions to distance Mike from his earlier correct answer, or in some way downgrade and mitigate his knowledge of the subject.

Extract 7 is from another tutor-led English tutorial:

Extract 7

```
001  T:    now ( . ) what you're suggesting Jane is that there,
002        (.) that there is ano:ther envy as well ( . ) which is
003        to do with the birds somehow having ( . ) erm a more
004        direct access to beauty which I think is wo:ndrously
005        spot on in terms of Keats ( . ) but I want to know how
006        you got there.
007        ( . )
008  J:    so do I! h[eh heh
009  All:           [heh heh heh heh heh
```

(BMB English tutorial data)

Here, the tutor formulates Jane's knowledge display (lines 1–4) and assesses it as 'wondrously spot on' (lines 4–5). This praise contains the extreme case formulation 'wondrously', thus positioning Jane as 'clever' in front of the rest of the group. In response to a request for a more detailed explanation, Jane responds with a distancing device and laughter (line 8), which is echoed by the rest of the group. Jane's disclaimer 'so do I' functions to evaluate her 'wondrously spot on' answer as an accident or one-off: something that is unusual for her.

In these first two extracts, the accounting device follows knowledge display or engagement. The pattern is reversed in the next fragment:

Extract 8

```
001  T:   would you like to just read us the stanza=
002  R:   =heh heh heh er I don't know if I can read it
003       very well heh heh=
004  T:   =have a go. (.) we're not going to be critical.
005  R:   ((reads first words of stanza))
```

(BMB English tutorial data)

In Extract 8, Rachel prefaces her reading with a disclaimer: 'I don't know if I can read it very well' as well as laughter (lines 2–3). Such prefaced disclaimers have possibly multiple functions: distancing students from their engagement with the task, orienting to the tutor's potential disapproval, deflecting potential criticism as well as managing their academic identity and position as 'novice' academics. Prefaced disclaimers were also found in the small-group tutorials as well as tutor-led sessions and we discuss these elsewhere (Benwell and Stokoe 2002). We move on now to consider a second type of accounting.

Accountable knowledge displays: other-initiated

In Extract 9, four first-year students are also engaged in an essay plan task, this time discussing classic social psychological obedience studies. In contrast to the prefaced knowledge display we saw above, here we can see what can happen if knowledge displays are not accounted for in some way:

Extract 9

```
001  (1)  →  J:  well for number one it was at ( . ) Yale which is
002             ( . ) prestigious as well so [that's one yeah.]
003         C:                                [at Yale which ]
```

004 (2)   →   B: d'you get that out your head heh heh heh
005 (3)   →   J: no (.) in here. ((points at the task materials))
006   B: ah that's okay then.

(EHS Psychology tutorial data)

At line 1, Jason starts to provide an answer to a question on their task
sheet. At line 4, Brad asks if Jason got the information 'out your head',
suggesting that Jason might own or possess some task-relevant knowledge. This turn marks Brad's knowledge display and foregrounds it in
the interaction: the content is no longer as relevant as Brad's knowledgeable status. The laughter that accompanies this turn mitigates
the potential challenge levelled at Jason that he is being 'too clever'.
Jason treats Brad's turn as a prompt for an account, and produces the
disclaimer 'no (.) in here', meaning that he has seen the answer in the
materials they have to work with – this is a preferred knowledge
source rather than admitting to any prior knowledge. Thus the following
sequential pattern could be seen in these instances of 'other-initiated'
disclaimers:

(1) →   Unmarked knowledge display
(2) →   Marking of/challenge to knowledge display
(3) →   Account/disclaimer

From our perspective as tutors, Brad's treatment of Jason seems over-
stated: Jason's description of the psychological topic is quite basic.
However, this response to unmarked/unmitigated knowledge displays
occurred routinely across the small-group data. The next extract comes
from a group of second-year psychology students:

Extract 10

001 (1)   →   L: and is it the context in which an attitude was
002   expressed that was all important,=
003 (2)   →   F: =how do you remember all this?
004 (3)   →   L: cos I've just looked it up heh heh heh.

(EHS Psychology tutorial data)

Lucy provides a knowledge display (1) which is challenged by
Frances (2). Lucy draws on the same disclaiming device as Jason does in

Extract 10: she has read the answer in the materials available to all the students and does not 'know' things *a priori* (3).

Throughout these examples of 'other-initiated disclaimers', we have seen that the episodes are punctuated by laughter and the development of a humorous context for challenges. Thus humour functions to downplay the seriousness of the challenges but also allows them to occur. In the final two extracts, we can see further examples of the way humour is built into the three-part 'other-initiated disclaimer' sequence. Extract 11a comes from a group of four first-year female psychology students engaged in the essay plan task. Extract 11b comes from a group of PGCE students whose task is to fill in missing words from a piece of educational writing:

Extract 11a

```
001  (1)  →   T:  does rehearsal (.) help (.) retain the stimulus.
002           (1.0)
003  (2)  →   A:  oohh! [heh heh heh]
004           N:        [heh heh heh]
005           H:        [heh heh heh]=
006  (3)  →   T:  =heh heh ( . ) phew ( . ) where did that come from?
007           heh heh
```

(EHS Behavioural Sciences tutorial data)

Extract 11b

```
001           R:  ((reading)) first schools and teachers should be ( . ) we
002               didn't do number one=
003  (1)  →   C:  =diversity ((the correct answer))
004  (2)  →   P:  aayyyyy!! [heh heh heh ]
005  (2)  →   B:            [wo:w! heh heh]
006  (2)  →   R:  heh heh heh Chris! [you sta::r! heh heh]
007  (2)  →   B:                     [Chri::s!! heh heh ]
008  (2)  →   B:  what a sta::r! heh heh
009  (3)  →   C:  see I put my glasses on now so I've turned clever.
```

(EHS PGCE tutorial data)

In 11a, Taz produces a sentence for the group's essay plan (see Benwell and Stokoe 2002 for a longer analysis of this extract). Anita's response at (2) functions to mark or challenge the knowledge display, which is then oriented to in Taz's disclaimer at (3). The disclaimer, 'where did that come from', functions to distance herself from ownership of the knowledge display: the language belongs to someone else rather than herself.

It is interesting to observe that this pattern was also found in the postgraduate data. In Extract 11b, Christopher provides the correct answer to one of the missing word items in their task. At position (2), we can see how Pat, Rebecca and Barney jointly produce an exaggerated teasing response which marks Christopher's knowledge display. Although their assessment could be treated as praise ('wow', 'you star', 'what a star'), Christopher's response at (3) suggests that it is more of a 'heckle' or 'tease': he accounts for his knowledge in an interesting way by suggesting that his glasses have made him 'turn clever', thus constructing and perpetuating a particular type of 'swotty' student identity.

Our analyses have revealed that students regularly mitigate or account for their own knowledge displays, mark out and challenge others if they appear 'too clever', and produce conversational devices that function to distance themselves from knowledge, effort or engagement with their tutorial work. Their interactions work to produce a particular culture in these tutorial sessions in which 'being a student' involves appearing detached from the academic endeavour. This culture comprises a system of norms regulating the boundaries around normative tutorial behaviour. Students co-construct the discursive limits in which being 'too clever' is problematic: being a student seems to necessitate being 'average' and not standing out.

Discussion

In this chapter, we have explored issues of academic identity, student resistance and the negotiation of institutional goals, in university tutorial talk. We asked whether the resistance commonly reported in the compulsory sector could be found within the post-compulsory university setting, or whether achievement, knowledge and effort was preferred once students entered education voluntarily. Secondly, if such resistance was still evident in higher education, we wanted to examine how students in their tutorial settings might articulate such resistance: what does it 'look like' empirically? We have argued that a conversation analytic approach is best able to explicate the interactional procedures that operate in students' talk-in-interaction. Through a fine-grained analysis of the turn-by-turn organization of tutorial talk, we are able to examine the cultural order of the tutorial as participants work up and manage their membership of the category 'student'.

Our analysis of the data revealed a number of interesting findings. First, we found that university students routinely oriented to what we gloss as resistance to or distancing from academic identity. Two broad strategies were identified: one in which students minimized or challenged their task, and another in which they policed their own and each other's knowledge displays. These strategies functioned to create distance between the student and their knowledge or effort, thus constructing a particular type of student identity in which appearing to work hard was to be resisted and mitigated. We found numerous instances in which students jointly constructed an instrumental approach to learning in which group work was explicitly criticized. This was just one in a spectrum of strategies of resistance, in which expressing knowledge and doing work *per se* could be problematic.

We would like to conclude this chapter by suggesting some possible applications of our findings for pedagogical practice. There is a wealth of literature, for example, that explores methods of induction for new students and staff in both school and university contexts (e.g. Carter and McNeill 1998; Norrie and Middleton 2002). This body of work is dedicated to finding ways of helping students make the transition from school to university and become members of the university culture. We suggest that such educational programmes might benefit from an understanding of the social and cultural context of tutorial and other types of learning environments, which we have revealed in our conversation analysis of such interactions. Acknowledging that students are not only 'doing education' but also 'doing being students' in ways that sometimes appear resistant, contradictory or ambivalent may prove valuable in the development of materials to facilitate their induction into higher education. New staff members, in their own induction programmes, might also benefit from treating the tutorial as more than a simple transaction of knowledge, but as a subtle negotiation of a range of sometimes-conflicting identities.

Notes

1 We are currently engaged in further analyses of our data corpus in which we focus on *unmarked* knowledge displays: instances of tutorial talk in which the students do not mark each others' contributions with censorious or praising orientations. We also found that, in a minority of cases, being 'too stupid' was also oriented to and marked by students. These deviant cases are the subject of another paper (see Benwell and Stokoe forthcoming).

Part III

Native Speaker and Non-Native Speaker Interaction

9
Different Orientations to Grammatical Correctness
Salla Kurhila

Introduction

This chapter explores the interaction between native (NS) and non-native speakers (NNS) of Finnish. Linguistic asymmetry between the participants can result in linguistic difficulties that may impede successful communication. This chapter focuses on one phenomenon that tends to impede the progress of NS–NNS interaction: a difference in the participants' orientation towards grammatical correctness.

Turns that focus on grammatical details are unequally distributed in the data, being readily initiated by the NNSs and only rarely by the NSs. Moreover, in the cases where the NNSs produce turns that orient to grammatical correctness, the NSs can refuse to align with this orientation in their responses. Thus, a discrepancy seems to appear in the participants' 'eagerness' to orient to grammar and grammatical details in NS–NNS interaction. The aim of this chapter is to shed light on this discrepancy, its interactional consequences and its relation to the participants' identities as 'native' and 'non-native' speakers.

Authentic NS–NNS interaction with its characteristics and problems has been studied relatively little and only very recently (see e.g. Firth 1996; Carroll 2000; Hosoda 2000; Kidwell 2000; Wong 2000a and b; Kurhila 2001). Research on this kind of interaction is, how-ever, called for: because of globalization, both the volume of NS–NNS interaction and the variety of languages involved have increased exponentially over recent decades. Members of divergent societies are increasingly involved in interactional situations, both publicly and privately, where participants do not share linguistic resources. In the public domain, knowledge of potential interactional trouble sources is crucial for many institutional bodies that perform their professional activities mostly in and through second language conversations.

Therefore, a need exists to find out if and how the asymmetric linguistic positions of the participants can impede interaction, so that these difficulties can be accounted for. Conversation analysis (CA) supports this purpose well, since it can treat the participants' nativeness or non-nativeness as a dynamic factor and can tie the relevance of these categories to different interactional phenomena.

The starting point of this paper is the participants' perspective, their orientations and activities. By looking at how the participants orient to their nativeness and non-nativeness, this chapter seeks to achieve two aims. First, it articulates and examines an interactional phenomenon that can impede the progress of NS–NNS conversation – a discrepancy in the participants' orientation towards grammatical correctness. Second, by uncovering the discrepancy from and through the details of interaction, this chapter demonstrates that CA is a valid and fruitful method of studying NS–NNS interaction. The ways in which the participants orient to their speaker identities as native or non-native speakers will be shown to be consequential to the construction of the interaction.

Turns that focus on grammatical correctness are initiated mostly by the NNSs in my data. This chapter is organized according to the NSs' responses to these initiations. The NSs can either align with or refuse the NNSs' orientation. First, I will discuss cases where the NSs accept the NNSs' orientation to grammar and engage in the activity begun by the NNSs; then I present and discuss sequences where the NSs ignore the NNSs' attempts to focus on grammatical details and avoid being involved in the activity initiated by the NNS. On the basis of the NSs' responses, a discrepancy in the orientations of the participants is discerned, and the reasons for this and its implications are described. In the last section, it is argued that the discrepancy is related to the participants' speaker identities as a 'native' or 'non-native' speaker.

Data, transcription and translation

The data of this study consist of approximately 14 hours of naturally occurring conversation within a range of everyday and institutional situations in Finland. The institutional conversations have been video-taped in the offices of three educational institutions offering courses on the Finnish language for non-native speakers. In these dyadic conversations, the participants are the secretaries and the clients who either study or are planning to begin studying Finnish at the respective institution. The data include also everyday conversations between friends. The participants conducted their normal conversation freely; no instructions were given. There are approximately 100 non-native speakers in the data, from all over the world, and their knowledge of Finnish varies greatly. There are approximately 20 native Finnish speakers, five of whom are secretaries.

The turns in the examples are in most cases represented with three lines: the first line is the original Finnish utterance, the second is the gloss line and the line in italics is an idiomatic English translation. The gloss line is removed in the cases where it is not considered to provide any relevant information. An orientation towards grammar in the speech of the NNSs usually surfaces at the morphological level, concerning, for example, case endings. This is somewhat problematic in the translation provided here, as Finnish and English are typologically very different. Finnish is an inflective language that expresses grammatical functions, dependency relations and locations mostly with various word-final morphemes. Nouns, adjectives and verbs are inflected, and the inflectional morphemes are attached to the end of words as suffixes. Grammatical modifications by the NNSs often focus on these word-final suffixes and on the variations caused to the stem of the word. The gloss line provides information on the different alternatives produced by the NNS if possible; the differences in typology and pronunciation between Finnish and English restrict idiomatic translation. The abbreviations used in the gloss line are explained in the notes.[1]

The NNS orients to grammatical details – the NS accepts the orientation

An orientation towards grammatical correctness can surface in grammatical repair – in sequences in which the speakers correct or modify grammatical details in their own or other speakers' utterances. It is much more common in the data that the speakers modify grammatical details in their own speech than in the speech of the recipient (about the preference for self-correction, see Schegloff *et al.* 1977). No instances occur in the database where the NNS corrects the grammar of the NSs, and the NSs correct the NNSs' grammar only in restricted environments and in ways which make possible other interpretations than that of correcting (Kurhila 2001; see Jefferson 1987 on 'embedded correction', and Wong (this volume) on sidestepping grammar).

Instances in which the speaker focuses on a grammatical element in her own speech are easier to find, especially in NNS talk. Moreover, the

NNSs are involved in 'extended' self-repairs where, instead of simply replacing an element with another, they produce various forms of a linguistic unit or otherwise expose their 'mental path' towards some target word or utterance. This phenomenon is also known as 'forward-oriented repair' and 'word search' (Carroll this volume). The NSs do not produce such turns. The following excerpt illustrates a situation unilaterally typical of the NNSs in my data: focusing on a grammatical element within a word while formulating a turn.

Extract 1

NNS has been telling a story about two babies who were mixed up in a birth clinic.

```
001  NNS:  .hhhh Sitte he    (0.2) huomaa huomu- huom-huoma=*
                  then they         notice + PRS + 3
  →              .hhhh Then they  (0.2) notice notid- noti- notic=
002  NS:   =Jo [o  huomas ]
                ye [s  notice + PST + 3
             =Ye [s  noticed  ]
                 [          ]
003  NNS:        [huomat   ] °huomas°
                 [          ] notice + PST + 3
                 [ notic    ] °noticed°
004  NS:   °Joo°
           °Yes°
005        (0.4)
006  NS:   Mitäs siinä tapahtu  sitte
           What       happened then
```

*Variations of stem of the verb.

(Friends I)

While describing an event to the NS, the NNS uses the verb *huomata* 'notice' (line 1), and begins to search for the correct form. He first produces the third person present tense form (*huomaa*), after which he repeats modified versions of the beginning of the word. The NS completes the already-begun word (line 2) after the NNS's third modification. The completion is the past tense form of the verb, which can be assumed to be the target form, since the NNS has mostly used the past tense in his narrative. The NNS accepts the completion by repeating it (line 3).

In this excerpt, the NS aligns himself with the orientation of the NNS: after the NNS has displayed that he was searching for a particular form of a word, the NS responds by providing the target form. Situations where the NS provides the target word and so accepts the grammatical orientation put forward by the NNS share a range of features illustrated in the example above, of which three will be highlighted. First, the repair turn (i.e. the completion, line 2) contains not only the new version but also an affirmative particle (*joo*), which is systematic in the data. The particle *joo* can receive the prior talk as understood (Sorjonen 2001); hence, it can indicate that, despite the uncertainty displayed by the NNS, the level of intersubjectivity between the participants has not been shaken and that mutual understanding still prevails, thus encouraging the NNS to move forward from the search sequence. This aligns with what has been reported about *joo* as a confirming device: if the turn to which *joo* responds forms a departure of some main line of talk that the speaker is developing, then *joo* suggests a closure of the departure (Sorjonen 2001: 86).

Second, the NNS accepts the new version by displaying uptake through repetition (line 3). When the search is brought to completion by the NSs, the NNSs often repeat the new form. In Extract 1, the repetition could also be related to the fact that the completion is produced in overlap with the NNS's alternatives, but repetitions are recurrent even if there is no overlap.

Third, the repair is offered and accepted straightforwardly, without hedging either in the NS's completion or in the NNS's repetition. The NS does not 'downgrade the repair (i.e. the new form) on a "confidence/uncertainty" scale' (cf. Schegloff *et al.* 1977: 378), and the NNS does not challenge the repair. No explanations for the new form are requested or given. The sequence remains minimal with two brief turns, the repair by the NS and its acceptance by the NNS, both consisting of the plain target word; the only other element in the turns can be the affirmative particle. The participants return to the talk in progress without further comment on possible alternatives.

These features can be shown to be a reflection of the participants' orientation toward their speaker identities. When displaying hesitancy about the inflection, the NNSs are orienting to the linguistic asymmetry between the participants, portraying themselves as not-yet-competent speakers of the language, as the uncertainty concerns morphological rules that are usually internalized by the NSs. This orientation is continued in the NS's response, in the cases in which they provide the target form. They utter the form from a 'knowledgeable position', asserting it rather than offering it as negotiable (see Drew (1991) on authoritative access to knowledge). The repair turns by the NSs (as line 2 in Extract 1) are not modulated; for example, no interrogative elements or particles (e.g. *siis, ai* 'y'mean') frame the turn as being the recipient's interpretation of the prior which needs to be confirmed by the speaker. Rather, the NS produces the confirmation himself when he provides the affirmative particle (line 2). Since the particle *joo* can be closing-implicative (cf. Sorjonen 2001), it implies that the repair sequence is not worth more attention. While continuing the NNS's orientation towards grammatical details (by providing the target form), the NSs simultaneously suggest closure of the repair sequence. Thus, the NS neither displays hesitancy while doing the repair nor expects a response (an acceptance of the new form) from the NNSs. The fact that the NS suggests closure of the repair sequence even before the NNS has reacted to the repair displays his epistemic authority over the issue.

In sum, the NNS's hesitations about inflecting the verb in Extract 1 seem to activate the linguistic asymmetry between the participants. The subsequent turns are produced and received from the positions of 'linguistically knowledgeable participant' and 'non-knowledgeable participant'. As a consequence, the sequence remains brief; the repair (i.e. the completion) is not challenged or explained or justified. The following example illustrates further how the speaker identities of the participants can be consequential in the sequences with regard to orienting to grammatical correctness:

Extract 2

NS is planning to study a year in France as an exchange student. NNS (who is French) is telling about his study experiences in French universities.

```
001 NNS:  Äämmh olin (.)    opiskele- äoo olin       opiskelluthh
                            had + 1sg  study-        had + 1 sg study + PPC
          #öömm# .hh
          Ehmm I had (.)    study- eoh I had studiedhh  #ehmm# .hh
002       ja:## mmh asia    oli #ee##ttä mt .hh #mm# semm## tämä
          and       thing was that               it         this
          and:## mmh the thing was #th##at mt .hh #mm# that## this
003       (.) ää kurssi ä[äm## mt .hh ää kes- ääh <kes-
                    course [            las-      las-
   →      (.) eh course e[hm## mt .hh eh last- ehm <last-
                        [
```

```
004  NS:              [Mm:?,
005        (1.0)
006  NS:   °Ke[s°(t)°°
           °La[s°(t)°°
           [
007  NNS:  [toi*?> ° ke[stoi °
→          [id?>   ° la[stid °
                     [
008  NS:             [Kestää,
                     [last + PRS + 3
→                    [Lasts,
009  NNS:  Kestää, .hh ää kaks vuottah?
           Lasts,  .hh eh two  years h?
010  NS:   Joo:
           Ye:s
```

*Past tense morpheme; cannot be attached to the verb *kestää*

(Friends II)

In Extract 2, the NNS displays having difficulty with the conjugation of the verb *kestää* 'last'. He produces the first, invariant syllable of the verb, cuts it off, hesitates and repeats the syllable in a slow tempo (line 3). After a one-second pause (line 5), he produces a morpheme (*toi*), which is a regular past tense form for a particular verb type in Finnish. The NNS attaches the morpheme to the stem of the verb (line 7), ending up with the word *kestoi*, which is a hybrid form and ungrammatical according to the norms of standard Finnish.

The hybrid form is very likely to represent the past tense of the verb *kestää*, i.e. *kesti*. The NNS has made an effort to tell the story in the past tense, evidence of which is a self-repair concerning the tense at the beginning of his turn. He corrects the verb *opiskele-* to a past participle form (*opiskellut*). The next verb (*oli* 'was'; line 2) is in the past tense as well. It is therefore expected that the following verb should also be in accordance with the two previous ones.

As in the previous example, the NS joins the search and produces the target form (line 8). It should be noted, however, that the completion is not the past tense, for which the NNS has been searching and has tried to formulate, but the present tense. What happens then is, quite surprisingly, similar to the previous example. The NNS accepts the form given by the NS by repeating it (line 9), although he was clearly looking for another form.

This example illustrates how strongly the participants' orientation towards their speaker identities can influence the conversation. The

NNS is involved in a search in which he attempts to construct a particular verb form. When he finds the form, however, he presents it only as a candidate that needs to be validated by the NS. The morpheme *toi* (line 7) is pronounced cautiously, with a rising intonation and the resultant hybrid form with a soft voice. Moreover, when the NS then gives him a different form, he accepts it as the 'correct' form. The NS, for her part, does the completion (line 8) from the position of the knowledgeable participant: she produces the completion immediately after having heard the candidate morpheme by the NNS, without hedging it or framing it as tentative. Thus, the sequence remains as minimal as in Extract 1, consisting of a repair (line 8) and a repeat of the repair (line 9), after which the talk in progress is continued. The NS 'informs' the NNS of the target form, and the NNS registers the new form by repeating it, even though the repair provided him with a different form from that of his own search.

However, the NSs do not always follow the grammatical orientation of the NNSs. In the following section, I will discuss cases where the NS does not adopt the role of the linguistically knowledgeable participant.

The NNS orients to the grammatical details – the NS ignores the orientation

The previous section illustrated one possible way the NS can respond to the linguistic problems of the NNS, which was to supply the correct form as a by-the-way occurrence. The NSs can treat the grammatical modifications of the NNSs either as a self-repair or as a self-initiation of repair (see Schegloff *et al.* 1977). In the former case, the speaker is assumed to be carrying out the repair herself, whereas in the latter case, as in Extracts 1 and 2, the modifications are treated as repair initiations, in order to prompt repair from the recipient. The crucial factor in whether or not the recipient is invited to join the activity is the speaker's gaze. As noted in earlier studies, the gaze shift to the recipient during a search turn invites her to participate in the search (cf. Goodwin and Goodwin 1986; Goodwin 1987; Laakso 1997). Thus, grammatical modifications by the NNS invite the NS to respond, provided that the NNS simultaneously gazes at (or shifts her gaze to) the NS.

However, the NS can participate in the repair in a number of different ways. The various ways of managing the problems are consequential for the salience of the asymmetry. At one extreme, the NSs could focus heavily on linguistic correctness and display their knowledgeable position e.g. by doing exposed correction (cf. Jefferson 1987) and giving grammatical rules and explanations. Such instances do not exist in my data. Another alternative was illustrated in the examples in the previous section in which the NSs provide the correct form but do so *en passant*. These responses by the NSs are less salient with respect to the linguistic asymmetry (cf. Wong in this volume). In this section, I will focus on a third, still less salient alternative – responses where the NSs ignore the NNSs' attempts to focus on grammatical correctness. The following extract is a case in point:

Extract 3

NNS and NS have been talking about studying. NNS is telling NS about his current studies in Finland. (NNS's gazes are marked in the transcript, NS is gazing at NNS throughout the whole extract.)

```
              NNS___,                                  NNS:____
001  NNS:  <Mutta: nythh> ääm mä luulen      että    #ööm# (1.0) kielet
            but      now      I    think+1sg that              languages
            <But:  nowhh> ehm I   think  that  #ehm#  (1.0)  languages
         NNS:___,,         ._____
002         ovat ääm (0.5) tärkeim-
            are            important+SUP+PL
→           are ehm  (0.5) the most impor-
003  NS:    Mhm.= ((nods))
         NNS:____
         NNS:_____
004  NNS:  =Tärkeimmät
            important+SUP+PL+NOM
→           =The most important
005  NS:    Joo.
            Yes.
         NNS:___,
         NNS:_____
006  NNS:  Tärk [eimpiä
            impo[rtant+SUP+PL+PAR
→           Most [ important
                 [
007  NS:         [.joo
                 [.yes ((nods))
         NNS:___,       :_____,        .._____
008  NNS:  Hheh .hh ☺°tärkeimpiä°☺           ja:  nyt mm=
                     important+SUP+PL+PAR and  now
            Hheh .hh ☺°most  important°☺     an:d now mm=
009  NS:    =Eli sul        on  nyt niinku sit (.) suomi
            PRT you+ADE have now PRT  then     Finnish
            =So  you   have now  like    (.) Finnish Swedish
         NNS:_____
```

```
010         ruotsi   ja   venäjä.
            Swedish  and  Russian
            and Russian then.
      NNS: _____
```

(Friends II)

In this extract, the NNS gives considerable attention to producing the correct inflectional morphemes. He starts the word *tärkeim-* (line 2) but does not inflect it. The search is directed to the recipient: the NNS shifts his gaze to the NS when he starts producing the beginning of the word (the end of line 2), and he keeps gazing at her during the entire search until he repeats the form he has previously produced (line 8).

The grammatical repair in Extract 3 is similar to the ones in the previous section. However, it is only the NNS's participation which is similar in his display of uncertainty about the inflectional morphemes within a word (lines 2, 4, 6, 8). The NS, in contrast, does not substantially participate in the search by completing or correcting the target word; instead, the NS indicates with acknowledgement tokens (lines 3, 5 and 7) and head nods (lines 3 and 7) that she has understood what the NNS was saying. Her acknowledgement tokens and nods display an orientation towards an aim beyond the actual search, to mutual understanding and the progress of conversation. The NS's orientation towards a broader aim of conversational progress is particularly well reflected in her acknowledgement in line 7, which is produced in overlap with one of the versions by the NNS (line 6). The NS receives the prior talk as understood even before she has heard the form that the NNS produces, and so the case ending is not relevant from her point of view.

The NNS, however, has a more local aim than maintaining interaction. For him it is not enough that the recipient recognizes the word; he also wants to find the target form and produce it correctly. Therefore, despite the indications of recognition and understanding (lines 3, 5 and 7), the NNS concentrates on the missing element: first he produces the word in nominative case (line 4), then he changes the case to partitive (line 6) and finally, having generated a final version, he topicalizes it by repeating it (line 8).

In sum, it seems clear that both participants attempt to close the repair sequence. However, the ways in which they try to achieve this closure do not coincide. The NNS's recipe for completing the search is to find the target word, and he addresses the NS through gaze in order to achieve this aim. The NS, in contrast, attempts to close the search by displaying understanding; she has already recognized the word that the

NNS is trying to formulate and hence there is no need to focus on the inflection of the word. That is, the NS's recipe for ending the repair sequence is to demonstrate that it is interactionally unnecessary to continue with the search. The discrepancy between the NNS's orientation to the repair's linguistic aspect and the NS's orientation to the interactional aspect prolongs the sequence as the NNS attempts to find the target form and to involve the NS in the search process, while the NS tries to show that she already understands what the NNS means and so tries to disengage both herself and the NNS from the search process.

Such discrepant positions are common in the office conversations in my data. The NSs, i.e. the secretaries, do not usually correct or comment on the linguistic details of the turns by the NNSs (the clients), even if the NNSs had focused on these details, as illustrated in the following example:

Extract 4

The secretary and the client are filling in the client's application form for the student allowance. The secretary has just asked whether the client has been studying in Finland before.

```
           NNS:_____,,,,
001  NNS:  Juu minä: (.) olen     >opiskellut< (2.0) työvoima- toimis::
           yes I         have+1sg study+PPC    employment- offi::
  →        Yes I: (.) have >studied< (2.0) the employment- offi::
           NS:_____,,                  ._____
           NNS:_____         _____  _____
002        (0.8) ts- (1.0) <työvoima   toimis ton   järjes::tämässä>
           ?off-   employment offi   ce+GEN organize+INF+INE
  →        (0.8) off- (1.0) <a course organized by the employ ment>
     NS:   _____
     NS:   _____
003  NS:   Mm:?=
     NNS:  _____
     NNS:  _____,,,
004  NNS:  = kursi. (.)    [hehhh
           course+NOM [
  →        = office. (.)   [hehhh
     NS:   _____,,,,,,,   [
005  NS:                   [Mm:?
```

006 NS: Joo?=
         Yes?=
007 NNS: =Heh .h kurssissa   ja.=
              course+INE and
→   =*Heh .h in the course and.*=
008 NS: =°(Ihan)°. (.) se v̲armaan pitäisi tähän   laittaa.
         =°*(Quite)°. (.) it should probably be put down here.*
                                          NNS:————,
009 NNS: Ah̲aa .
         I see.

In this example, the NNS is not just trying to find a single case ending, but instead he is struggling to formulate a relatively complicated construction with an agentive participle form (*työvoimatoimiston järjestämässä kurssissa* 'a course organized by the employment office'). The effort the NNS uses in the formulation of the utterance is exhibited in the slow tempo of pronunciation, with pauses, re-starts and sound stretches (lines 1–2). The atypical stress on the last syllable of the construction (line 2) increases the impression of a 'hard-fought struggle'. While constructing the utterance syllable by syllable (line 2), the NNS shifts his gaze to the NS and holds his gaze (lines 3–4). The NS takes the turn but, as in the previous example, does not produce a substantial response with any comment on the efforts by the NNS or the correctness of the version he has formulated. Instead, she produces a minimal response token (line 3), thereby giving the NNS an opportunity to continue.

A further discrepancy lies in the orientations of the participants in this example: the NNS's orientation is linguistic whereas the NS's orientation is institutional. The difference between their perspectives becomes evident in subsequent turns in which the NNS continues to focus on the grammatical details, while the NS responds to the turns on the basis of their institutional relevance. The NNS first completes the agentive participle construction by producing a head of the noun phrase (*kurssi* 'course' line 7). The NS does not comment on the completion but only produces continuation-relevant particles (lines 5–6). The NNS then performs a morphological self-correction. He replaces the former case ending of the head noun (nominative; line 4) by the inessive (line 7), making the head agree with the modifiers. After this self-repair, the NS produces a more substantial turn. Instead of commenting on the correctness of the alternative versions by the NNS, the secretary verbalizes the institutional aim of completing a blank for 'previous studies' in the form (line 8). The utterance 'it should probably be put down here' reflects the secretary's institutional interest. The secretary verbalizes the practical applications of the (institutionally relevant) piece of information, thereby implying, since no new information on the issue is presented, that the topic of 'previous studies' can be closed and the conversation can be continued.

In the examples in this section, the NNSs oriented to their role as non-fluent speakers by displaying their effort in formulating a word or an utterance correctly. The NSs did not, however, adopt the role of linguistic experts; instead of topicalizing the problematic word forms, the NSs produced continuation-relevant particles that encouraged the NNSs to proceed with the conversation. The activity by the NSs can be seen as serving interactional purposes, as an attempt to carry the conversation forward instead of stalling on a detail. This orientation towards the progress of the conversation can also serve institutional purposes. The institutional role of the NS may 'override' the role of the linguistically knowledgeable participant; even if the NNS displays hesitancy with a construction, the NS does not topicalize the construction or orient to the linguistic aspects in the turn.

An interesting aspect of this study is that where the speaker identities are brought into interactional focus, it is a result of the NNSs' activity. I will discuss this 'hierarchy' or discrepancy in the participants' orientations in the concluding section of this paper.

Discussion: the discrepancy in the participants' orientation to grammatical correctness

It seems evident on the basis of the data that the NSs are less 'eager' to orient to grammatical correctness than the NNSs. The data show that the NSs' responses to the grammatical modifications by the NNSs are at the non-salient end of the continuum of responses according to relative focus on form. No instances exist where the NSs orient to the sought-for form by topicalizing or explaining it; if they provide the target form, they do it as a by-the-way occurrence, keeping the repair sequence as minimal as possible (cf. Extracts 1 and 2).

What is behind such a discrepancy? Why do the NSs not reciprocate the NNSs' interest in grammatical details? The answer can be found in the interactional consequences of different responses – each response talks a different set of identities and relationships into being. By producing responses that would focus on achieving linguistic correctness, the NSs emphasize their role as the 'linguistic expert' and make salient the asymmetry between the participants. This situation partially resembles language teaching, in which the participants' orientation to their roles as an expert and a novice shape the interaction (cf. e.g. McHoul 1990; Seedhouse 1996). However, the data of this study consist of non-pedagogic conversations, and in the cases where the NSs have an institutional role, it is 'secretary' and not 'teacher'. Since the secretaries are responsible for conducting the encounters according to the rules of the institution, they orient to the turns by the NNSs with reference to their institutional relevance and not to their grammatical correctness, as demonstrated in Extract 4. That is, by only minimally orienting to the form of the NNSs' utterances, the NSs avoid 'doing being second language teachers' and maintain the relevance of their role as a secretary or a friend.

For the NNSs, to a certain extent, the situation differs. In institutional encounters, the NNSs are a particular type of client. They are clients in institutions that offer courses in the Finnish language for foreigners in Finland. Therefore, they might find it profitable to portray themselves as 'good learners' who are interested in the details of the language and are trying to produce language that is as error-free as possible. This, in turn, can lead to a heightened attention towards grammar.

A more general version of this idea can also be applied to the non-institutional conversations: by focusing on the linguistic details, the NNSs can display the knowledge they already have about the language, portraying themselves as careful and committed speakers (or learners) of the target language. This view is supported by the fact that in the search sequences where the NSs do produce the completion, the NNSs usually repeat it, thus displaying uptake of the correct form.[2]

By orienting to grammatical details and correctness, the NNSs do 'being a second language learner'; their grammatically-oriented turns portray them as someone who is struggling with linguistic details but who is an active learner and keen to do well. These turns do not impose constraints on the NSs' next turn but effectively cloud the issue of whether they were self-repairs or self-initiations of other-repair. It is left to the NSs to respond as substantially or minimally as they want. By choosing a minimal orientation, the NSs display an interest beyond the level of linguistic forms. Hence, they avoid emphasizing linguistic asymmetry and avoid creating a pedagogical context in which language would be the focus of interaction instead of a vehicle for it.

Yet another possible explanation for the discrepancy in the participants' orientations can be shown, which may also have implications for teaching Finnish as a second language. Namely, it seems likely on the basis of the latter set of Extracts 3 and 4 that the NNSs treat grammatical correctness as being a more important factor for understanding than the NSs. As illustrated in Extracts 3 and 4, the NNSs use considerable time and energy in constructing grammatically correct utterances, even though the NSs encouraged them to continue with the subject matter. If it is the case that the speakers have different conceptions of the interactional importance of grammatical correctness, then it sets up a challenge for second-language teaching: how should Finnish grammar (especially morphology) be taught so that it helps rather than hinders successful interaction with native speakers?

A related possibility is that the NNSs use the interaction as a learning environment. If this is the case, the persistent focus on linguistic elements results from the speaker's aim to discover or learn a particular linguistic detail. Consequently, the interactional orientation of the NS contradicts the aim of the NNS and causes more difficulties in closing the search sequence: a claim of understanding from the NS is not enough for the NNS to close the search sequence if she wants to discover a particular word form. Although both participants aim at mutual understanding and progress in the interaction, the NSs seem to attempt to reach the aim by focusing on the recognition of lexical items (i.e. sufficient information) while the NNSs focus on grammatical correctness. This discrepancy may impede successful communication and result in misunderstanding or even negative stereotyping. From the NSs' point of view, the NNSs may appear to be incompetent as interactants because they halt the progress of conversation by being ensnared in unnecessary details. From the NNSs' point of view, the NSs may appear unhelpful and uncooperative when they ignore the NNSs' efforts to produce the suffixes correctly.

Understanding NS–NNS interaction (and discovering potential problems and discrepancies in such interaction) is important in terms of consciousness-raising for parties who are involved in, or perform their activities through second-language conversations. Information on communication difficulties is essential for developing programmes that aim to educate or integrate immigrants or train members of the majority culture (cf. Egbert this volume). In language pedagogy, such information can be exploited when teaching methods and curriculum are developed to better respond to the challenges posed by real-life interaction. A detailed analysis of instances where the progress of NS–NNS conversation is impeded and the participants must remedy the situation sheds light on the mechanisms through which the participants negotiate the relevance of their speaker identities. This analysis shows how language, grammar and social interaction are interrelated (cf. Wong this volume), and how grammar and grammatical details can be used as a resource in talking different identities or relationships into being.

Notes

1   The abbreviations used in the gloss lines are the following:

[Case endings]		*[Others]*	
NOM	nominative (subject)	CLI	clitic
GEN	genitive (possession)	INF	infinitive
PAR	partitive (partitiveness)	PL	plural
INE	inessive ('in')	PPC	past participle
ILL	illative ('into')	PRS	present tense
ADE	adessive ('at, on')	PRT	particle
		PST	past tense
		SG	singular
		SUP	superlative
		1	1st person ending
		2	2nd person ending
		3	3rd person ending

2   This is a possibility that calls for a comparative study. As mentioned, when exposing their difficulty in utterance formulation, the NNSs in my data focus on morphology, particularly on inflectional morphemes. Brouwer (2000), in her study about everyday conversations between native and non-native speakers of Danish, found similar instances where the NNSs made an effort to produce correct language, but the domain that the NNSs focused on was pronunciation. The mother tongue of the NNSs in Brouwer's study was Dutch, which is typologically similar to Danish. In this chapter, the mother tongues of the NNSs in the examples are Japanese, French and Russian, which are all typologically different from Finnish. It seems that there might be a phenomenon, 'doing linguistic orientation', i.e. the NNSs' exposed attempt to produce correct talk, which can be found in different NS–NNS conversations, regardless of the source or target languages. However, the target and/or the source language can shape the characteristics of the phenomenon, so that it can be realized in interaction e.g. in 'doing morphology' or 'doing pronunciation'. Examining NS–NNS interaction in a variety of languages could help uncover which aspects of a particular language are vital and not vital to spoken communication.

10
Sidestepping Grammar[1]

Jean Wong

Introduction

The notion of colligation (Jefferson 1988) refers to ways in which participants focus on a troublesource (or troublesources) of another speaker in the talk without explicitly 'doing correcting'. Interactants may be seen to be 'tying together a wrong item and the item which puts it right, such that the wrong item is *added to* by the right item, rather than discarded and replaced' (Jefferson 1988: 6). This notion finds resonance in the work on exposed and embedded correction (Jefferson 1987). In this regard, Jefferson (1987) observes that recipients of other-correction sometimes accept or incorporate a correction into their own utterance or turn at talk, and at other times reject it.

The importance of practices of conversation such as those briefly alluded to above lies in their recipient design character, their turn by turn *achievement* by participants. Interactants monitor one another's talk in the course of its production in a manner far more subtle, fine-grained, or fine-tuned than one might imagine using the naked ear and eye. As Jefferson confirms:

> The interchanges do not simply run off that way; it is not automatic. Rather, not only is it to be worked out, here and now, step by step, whether a correction will be accepted or rejected ... but it is a matter of collaborative, step by step construction that a correction will be an interactional business in its own right, with attendant activities addressing issues of competence and/or conduct, or that correction will occur in such a way as to provide no room for an accounting. (Jefferson 1987: 99)

The issues of competence and conduct as they relate to the practices of colligation and exposed and embedded correction are worthwhile exploring in the context of native–nonnative (NS–NNS) speaker talk because repair or correction also possibly serves as a special vehicle for language learning (Schegloff *et al.* 1977; Norrick 1991). Recent literature has been encouraging in terms of bringing stakeholders from the academic fields of conversation analysis (CA) and applied linguistics (AL), turning over old and new stones in search of greater interdisciplinary connection and understanding (e.g., Carroll 2000, 2004; Hosoda 2000; Kasper and Ross 2001; Kurhila 2001; Schegloff 2000a; Schegloff *et al.* 2002; Wagner 1996; Wong 1984, 1994, 2000a, 2000b, 2000c, 2002, 2004; Wong and Olsher 2000). Research on the uses of repair or correction in the institutional context of the language classroom and in tutorial sessions (e.g., Koshik 1999; van Lier 1988; Seedhouse 2004) points to the special nature of repair or correction as a pedagogical tool facilitating a learner's gradual mastery of the target language. However, the 'context' of everyday conversation may pave the way for social constraints or linguistic practices that may be slightly different from that found in classroom settings. The theme of this chapter, based on a discussion of single case analyses grounded in NS–NNS naturally occurring conversation, is that native speakers, as producers of other-initiated repair (OI), may sidestep or disattend to a nonnative speaker's grammatical errors, emphasizing meaning rather than form or accuracy.

Here I offer single case analyses of four exemplars from my corpus, three of which involve NS–NNS conversation and a fourth which involves NNS classroom discourse, as an exercise in order to see what light can be shed on how NSs and NNSs deploy and orient to other-initiated repairs and corrections, and whether their use reflects matters that pertain to the linguistic competence of the latter. What lies at the heart of this study is whether NNSs have available and use the resources of the language in similar ways as NSs do, and whether NSs use the resources of the language with NNSs in ways that they would when interacting with NS.

In the three instances from naturally occurring conversation, there is seemingly no linguistic 'asymmetry' since NS appears to sidestep or disattend to NNS's ungrammatical troublesource. On the other hand, in the instance extracted from classroom discourse, the teacher and the nonnative speakers jointly orient to and build the talk in a different manner, constructing their identities as linguistic expert and novice, native and nonnative speakers of the language of classroom interaction.

Repair in native–nonnative speaker interaction

When a native speaker responds to the talk of a nonnative speaker, s/he may do so in a manner that sidesteps or disattends to an error that a nonnative speaker produced, as signalled by the arrow at line 014 below.

Extract 1

R: = Ruan (NNS)
L: = Liz (NS)

```
001    R:  okay uh:: do you know (.) anyone else whaat:: what they're
            gonna
002        bring? (0.2) to the picnic?
003    L:  .h yeah I do .h
004    R:  you do?
005    L:  um:: let's see d- hot
006    L:  [dogs
007    R:  [gi- so give me some ideas uh yeah
008    L:  oh (.) um:: hot dogs .h
009    R:  uh huh (h)(h)
010    L:  potato chipss um:: hh tch fruit (.) sa::lads:: (0.2) all kind
            of different
011        salads (0.2) cookiess
012    R:  is anyone bring drinks?
013        (0.2)
014  → L:  drinks?
015    R:  yeah
016    L:  [um:: .h yeah you- why 'on't you-
017    L:  [that'll be something
018    R:  [if- if- no one (.) if no one bring I can bring drinks that's
            easy for
019        me
020    L:  yeah okay
021        (0.2)
022    L:  drinks would be (h)(h) (0.2) a good idea
023        (0.2)
024    R:  okay so::
025    R:  [so:: can I change mine so I bring drinks an' then .h so I-
026    L:  [fine (drinks?) yeah sure
027    R:  so:: I don't have to:: go an' buy
```

```
028  R:   [some eggrolls
029  L:   [yeah okay
030  R:   because that's (0.2) harder (h)u(h)-(h)u(h)
031  L:   yeah okay
032  L:   [whatever's easier yeah
033  R:   [so how- how many:: (0.2) fifteen people okay let me see...
```

(Wong 1994. Ruan/Liz 4:18)

In the troublesource turn at line 012, Ruan omits the 'ing' morpheme from the verb 'bring.' In Ruan's native Mandarin, tense and aspect are signalled by adverbial expressions and particles; therefore, the acquisition of tense and aspect in English may be more challenging for a nonnative speaker whose native language is Mandarin. It could be that Ruan has not fully mastered how to form questions or that he does not hear clearly enough the 'ing' morpheme in a native speaker's production of the word 'bringing' because the base verb 'bring' already contains an 'ing' sound.[2] After NNS produces the question, 'Is anyone bring drinks?', which is intended as a proffer to bring this item to the potluck party, there is a delay of two-tenths of a second before NS responds with the question 'Drinks?' Liz's utterance is a slightly delayed other-initiated repair (OI),[3] (Pomerantz 1984b; Schegloff 2000a; Wong 2000a; Kasper and Ross 2001), but not of the sort discussed by Schegloff (2000) that are produced by NS in NS–NS conversation.

Although Ruan's turn constructional unit (TCU) at line 012 is one that is projectably complete and draws the turn to a closure, at the silence of two-tenths of a second, NS may be providing NNS with an opportunity to do a transition space repair, providing him with an opportunity to correct the verb form to 'bringing' (Wong 2004). However, the opportunity for NNS to initiate self-repair (Schegloff *et al.* 1977) is foregone at the moment of silence, after which in the next turn NS initiates other-repair, producing the item 'drinks?'. By repeating the item 'drinks' in NNS's just prior turn, Liz produces a stronger as opposed to a weaker form of OI (Schegloff *et al.* 1977; Drew 1997), exhibiting a problem only with the last item of Ruan's turn at talk ('drinks?') and not any other segment of it.

Done as a repetition of the turn terminal lexical item, Liz's OI does not expose or embed correction (Jefferson 1987, 1988) of NNS's incorrect grammatical utterance, but it offers repair on her own hearing or understanding of what Ruan offers to bring to the potluck party. It is possible that her OI passes up an opportunity to set Ruan's inaccurate grammar aright. For example, she might have produced a longer rather than a shorter re-check on her hearing or understanding: 'Is anyone bringing drinks?' or 'bringing drinks?'. OIs such as those might serve a double agenda, namely, re-check Ruan's proffer to bring drinks and simultaneously embed a correction of his ungrammatical utterance, but NS sidesteps or disattends to a grammatical issue. It is also arguable that what is of interactional concern, as displayed at the slight delay in Liz's uptake of Ruan's proffer to bring drinks, is not a matter of grammatical incompetence (or error). It may be that Liz is not pleased with Ruan's suggestion to change his mind from bringing eggrolls or 'barbecue port' (i.e. barbecue pork), which he had said earlier in the talk that he would bring to the party (not shown on the transcript).

Liz's responses to Ruan's suggestion to bring drinks may reflect a dispreferred action[4] (Pomerantz 1984b). She gives the impression that bringing drinks is acceptable but not of high priority: 'Um:: .h yeah you- why don't you- that'll be something'. Note the delay markers and aborted, cutoff segments constituting that utterance. In response, Ruan reformulates and upgrades his offer to bring drinks, now adding that he prefers to bring drinks because it involves the least amount of effort ('if- if- no one(.) if no one bring I can bring drinks that's <u>easy</u> for me'). Again, Liz's subsequent responses possibly orient to a dispreferred status, for example, the 'yeah okay' which is followed by a delay of two-tenths of a second after which she utters 'drinks would be (h)(h) (0.2) a good idea'. The interactional space and distance that separates her saying of the initial segment of the utterance from her uttering of the post-predicate segment, which is punctuated in between by outbreaths and a pause, contribute to a hearing that Liz regards Ruan's offer to bring drinks as *not* a good idea but only a satisfactory one.

The above analyses of Ruan's troublesource turn and the OI that it precipitates have taken two slightly differing tracks. One track concerns NNS's being a nonnative speaker or user of the language, that is, NNS's passing up of an opportunity to do a transition space repair, repairing his grammatical error. Another track attends to the interactional business at hand, more specifically, making decisions regarding what to bring to the potluck party. In NS–NNS conversation, it is possible that these two tracks or orientations run parallel or simultaneously for participants in ways that may be slightly different from that in NS–NS conversation because the notion of grammatical error or the usage of 'correct' English may loom larger in a nonnative speaker's interlanguage than it does in native speaker talk, just as it may in child first language talk. In choosing to make relevant repair of the talk rather than correction of the (NNS) grammar, Liz is perhaps pursuing her own agenda, namely, focusing on

Ruan's picnic contribution. Had she chosen to do both repair and correction, which is of course possible using embedded repair for the grammar, Ruan would have had the option of disattending to the talk, i.e. his picnic contribution, and focusing on the grammatical problem. By ignoring this, Liz displays orientation to achieving a social goal rather than a 'grammatical' one.

Ruan's grammatical 'error' is not exposed or embedded as a correction (Jefferson 1987, 1988). It is not displayed as a problem for either participant; it is not an observably relevant error (Jefferson 1988). This may be one form of syntax-for-conversation (Schegloff 1979b) in second language talk, a way in which NS sidesteps NNS's grammatical infelicity by doing other-repair but not other-correction. However, Schegloff *et al.* (1977) have noted that in NS–NS conversation, speakers sometimes do allow errors to pass uncorrected or unrepaired, for example, response tokens such as 'uh huh' may specifically do the interactional job of passing up an opportunity to initiate other-repair or correction (Schegloff 1982; Wong and Olsher 2000). But in this case, it is possible that Ruan produces a linguistic error of which he may not necessarily be (entirely) aware. Hence, he would not be able to self-repair in an emergent turn-so-far or at a transition space, and so may not be passing up an opportunity to do self-repair.[5] This is in contrast with native speakers who, even if they pass up an opportunity to self-repair a grammatical error, would almost certainly be able to do so.

Negotiating what to bring to a potluck party is a practice of ordinary conversation. Liz incorporates other-repair of *the talk* but not other-correction of *the grammar*. This is to be appreciated as an interactional achievement of the participants in the joint construction of the talk, one that displays the power of the notion of recipient design (Sacks *et al.* 1974; Wong and Olsher 2000), and how that vehicle shapes and informs our grammar *in* interaction (Ochs *et al.* 1996), our discourse *and* context (Celce-Murcia and Olshtain 2000), and, in the final analysis, the ways in which participants interact, both constructing and reflecting their social and linguistic identities as NS and NNS for one another.

One interactional design and effect is that the talk is produced, oriented to, and repaired in ways that seemingly or superficially exhibit NNS as a *competent* user of the language of interaction despite his grammatical infelicity or, at least, that the issue of NNS's conversational 'incompetence' at that particular moment in the discourse remains an unspoken matter. This is in contrast with classroom discourse, as later illustrated in Extract 4, in which an instructor offers overt correction or other-initiated repair as a strategy for getting the language learner to focus on his or her error(s).

When interaction is constructed in that manner, the identities of the participants as language learner and teacher, linguistic novice and expert, are more clearly delineated and emboldened in the structures of talk and action.

In the next instance, NS produces two OIs that target NNS's phonological error.

Extract 2

V: = 　Vera (NS)
H: = 　Huang (NNS)

001	V:	what (.) is baby's <u>name</u>?
002	H	OH:: yeah: his name is <u>Steveen</u>
003		(0.2)
004	H:	.h he got um mm:: (0.2) English name Engli- English first name is
005		Steveen
006 →	V:	Stewing?
007	H:	STeveen
008 →	V:	Steven?
009	H:	mm hmm
010	V:	oh:: that's a <u>very</u> <u>good</u> name
011	H:	you think so?
012	V:	y-yes:
013	H:	thank you
014	V:	=because um .h Steven (.) was a man in the bible

(Wong 1994)

In response to Vera's query concerning the name of Huang's baby, Huang replies that the English first name is 'Steveen.' Huang displays an inability to pronounce the name 'Steven'. Her problem is a common one among learners or nonnative speakers of English who often do not use the schwa (here in the second syllable), which contributes to the giving off of a foreign accent. This problem causes Huang's mispronunciation and might explain Vera's hearing 'wing' as in 'Stewing' as something close to 'veen' as in 'Steveen.'

Vera questions whether she heard Huang correctly by offering as a candidate understanding the name 'Stewing?'. 'Stewing?' may be 'catering' to NNS's talk because 'Stewing' is clearly not a name in the English language, but Vera is willing to go along with it. The prosodic contour in her saying of the name 'Stewing?' does not suggest surprise or incredulity but a mere repetition or confirmation of what she hears. In responding to Vera's OI, Huang indeed treats the problem as one involving her pronunciation. She answers Vera's OI by enunciating more clearly and louder than she had in her first try the initial consonant cluster 'ST' ('STeveen') thereby targeting the consonant cluster as the nettlesome part in her mispronunciation. But in producing the OI, 'Stewing?', Vera was most likely not displaying that she had a problem with the word initial consonant blend.

Not only is Huang's utterance 'STeveen' an answer to the OI, but it constitutes a third try at saying the name that she could not pronounce correctly in her prior two turns. Vera allows Huang two tries at saying the name 'Steven' before she offers an other-initiated repair ('Stewing?'). But even after Huang's third attempt at saying the baby's name, Vera is still unsure of what she heard Huang to have said. Vera offers a second OI ('Steven?') that is stronger than her just prior one ('Stewing?'), despite the fact that Huang reproduced the name 'Steveen' the third time around in a manner similar to how she had produced it upon her first and second tries.

Vera's candidate understanding ('Steven?') is confirmed by Huang at the response token ('mm hmm') after which Vera produces an assessment of the name ('Oh::: that's a very good name'), which can be taken as an indication that the repair sequence, the trouble located but not overtly identified as one involving NNS's pronunciation, has been successfully resolved. Thereafter Huang continues, treating Vera's assessment as a compliment ('thank you'), after initially seeking confirmation that the name is a good one ('You think so?').

The byproduct of these two OI sequences is that it is the *native* speaker who offers a correct rendition of the name 'Steven?' to which an appropriate response from the nonnative speaker is confirmation ('mm hmm'). Vera's OI ('Steven?') not only solicits repair, but becomes a way to indirectly resolve a phonological 'error' produced by NNS. Huang is alleviated, so to speak, from the linguistic or interactional task of pronouncing the name again in what would have been her fourth attempt at saying the baby's English name. Three tries is the interactionally-imposed limit for Huang at pronouncing the name before the problem is addressed in another manner by the native speaker. In fact, asking Huang to make a fourth attempt at correcting her pronunciation when she had displayed three prior 'failed' attempts, moreover, when she apparently did not treat Vera's second OI as 'corrective feedback' (Day *et al.* 1984), possibly runs the risk of upping the ante in terms of interactional salience of her nonnativeness (Kurhila 2001). Recent literature (e.g., Kurhila 2001 and this volume) reveals that NNSs' linguistic errors, which would include ones of pronunciation, are by and large downplayed or ignored in the interaction. This exemplar would lend support to that observation.

The OI seemingly does repair of a *native* speaker's problem in hearing or understanding but not correction of a nonnative speaker's mispronunciation. Correction of Huang's phonological error is sidestepped or, at best, embedded at NS's second OI (Jefferson 1987, 1988). Moreover, had Huang oriented to NS's second OI as 'corrective feedback' (Day *et al.* 1984) or as a 'model of the target language' (Pica 1988) juxtaposed against her own incorrect utterance in the next turn, she might have repeated the name 'Steven' in an attempt to offer more target-like pronunciation. Her uttering of the response token 'mm hmm' exhibits that she treats Vera's OI only as an understanding check and not (simultaneously) as corrective feedback.

In the next example, Sara and Li are engaged in the opening sequences of a telephone conversation.

Extract 3

L: =   Li (NNS)
S: =   Sara (NS)

001	L:	=how <u>are</u> you?
002	S:	pretty good, you?
003		(0.2)
004	L:	uh <u>HUH</u>
005	L:	[fine
006	S:	[how- (0.2) how's school?
007		(0.2)
008	L:	uh huh .h uh:: now:: I choose (0.2) thr- two days at school.
009		(0.2)
010	S:	<u>yeah</u>
011	L:	yeah
012		(0.2)
013 →	S:	oh- jus like Tuesdays Thursdays?
014	L:	uh huh
015 →	S:	an' then ya have Mondays Wednesdays Fridays tuh (0.2) tuh stay it
016		home an' work?
017		(0.2)

```
018   L:   uh huh
019   S:   yeah
```

(Wong 1994, 1:21)

Sara asks Li how school is going to which Li responds in line 008 with the utterance 'uh huh .h uh:: now:: I choose (0.2) thr- two da::ys at school'. This talk later becomes problematic upon which Sara initiates repair at the OI of line 013. Notice that Sara's OI does not occur in the turn immediately after Li's troublesource turn. A number of turns displayed as lines 009–012 separate Sara's OI from the repairable. Sara's OI is delayed past next turn position but not in ways described in talk between native-speaker interactants (Kasper and Ross 2001; Schegloff 2000; Wong 2000a, 2004).

Sara initially responds to Li's talk by producing an acknowledgement token ('yeah'), which displays that she has no problem with Li's response to her question of how school is going. In reply, Li produces an acknowledgment token ('yeah'). The overall sequence does not terminate there, however. There is a pause of two-tenths of a second after which Sara produces an OI (line 13).

It is possible that Sara delays delivery of the OI in order to provide Li with an opportunity to self-repair what later apparently becomes troublesource talk. Li's reply to how school is going is not quite right grammatically or collocationally. It is possible that Li misuses the word 'choose', which does not collocate with the expression 'choose...days at school'. In native-speaker English, we typically do not speak of 'choosing two days at school', but rather 'going *to* school' two days a week or '*being at* school' two days a week. Li's latent troublesource may have been one of finding a proper verb.

Sara's OI appears to be tailored to Li's troublesource talk, targeting the troublesource but not overtly identifying it (Jefferson 1988). For example, instead of producing an OI that focuses on the verb 'choose' as an incorrect lexical item collocationally speaking, Sara locates as the troublesource only the turn final phrase 'two days at school'. Her OI seemingly 'chooses' two days of the week as a means of initiating repair or seeking clarification ('Oh- jus like Tuesday Thursdays?').

By producing an OI formulated in this manner, moreover, after initially responding to NNS's 'troublesource' talk with an acknowledgement token that displays no problem with it, N does other-repair but not other-correction. One interactional outcome is that NS repairs her own understanding and not NNS's misuse of the English lexicon and grammar.

The next relevant business for Li is confirmation of the OI (and the second OI as well), and not a re-doing or re-saying of her 'troublesource' utterance. NS's OI provides a means by which NNS's grammatical 'error' is resolved without overtly attending to the error.

Extract 4, the last example to be discussed, is contrastive with those just treated. Here the context is classroom interaction as opposed to naturally occurring conversation.

Extract 4

T: = Teacher
L1 = Language learner 1
L2 = Language learner 2

```
001  T:   ask erm Sokoop, Sokoop being erm a father. can you ask him?
002       being a father
003  L1:  er yes. do you like being a father?
004  T:   um, hm.
005  L2:  yes, I like. I am er father of four children.
006  T:   yes. listen to her question, though. say again. say it again
007  L1:  do you like er being a father?
008  T:   uhm. do you like being a father? do you like being a father?
009  L2:  yes I like being ... to be
010  T:   um hm yes.
011  L2:  yes I like being. yes I do.
012  T:   yes I do. yes I do. I like being a father
```

(Willis 1992)

In lines 001–002, the teacher asks L1 to ask L2 (Sokoop) how he likes being a father. L1 asks 'Do you like being a father?' to which L2 replies that he does ('Yes, I like.'); moreover, L2 states that he is the father of four children ('I am er father of four children.'). Notice, however, that the teacher treats L2's reply as incorrect. She requests that L2 listen carefully to the question, implying that L2's answer is not what he should have said. The teacher asks L1 to ask the question again, which he does at line 007. Subsequent to that, the teacher repeats L1's question (line 008). Her repetition of the question, as well as her initial request of L1 to ask the question in the first place, contributes to the design of this sequence as classroom discourse, a foreign language learning context, namely, teacher-facilitated talk and interaction which is different from that found in naturally-occurring conversation.

From the teacher's perspective, L2's 'best' attempt at a correct reply may have been his response at line 011 ('Yes I like being. Yes I do.'), but this response gets corrected by the teacher, who rephrases L2's utterance in a way that displays that she was searching for a very specific answer to the question ('Do you like being a father?'). The talk displays that the kind of response for which the teacher was searching was of this nature: 'Yes I do. Yes I do. I like being a father.' It is precisely this kind of utterance that fits the teacher's needs and goals for the lesson.

In this example we see that NS, a teacher in a language classroom, focuses on form and accuracy and not meaning (Seedhouse 1996). The institutional setting of the classroom has an interactional bearing on the shape and form of the talk. L2 may have been attempting to shift into a mode of speaking that is more characteristic of naturally-occurring conversation, stepping out of the 'linguistic' structure or classroom discourse pattern that the teacher was establishing. By moving in and taking control of aspects of the linguistic structure of the talk, the teacher shapes the interaction as one specifically designed for language teaching and learning and, under the circumstances, a focus on meaning is subordinated to that of form and accuracy. The teacher does not sidestep or disattend to NNS's errors. In fact, she *stays within* her bounds and duties as an authority figure and native speaker in initiating correction of NNS's error. This is in keeping with the fact that a language instructor ought to be mindful of a learner's errors in ways that NSs do not necessarily need to be in naturally occurring conversation.

Sidestepping grammar

In Extracts 1–3, the design of the talk is such that NS offers other-repair on her own hearing or understanding of NNS's troublesource talk, and not other-correction of NNS's nontarget-like grammatical or phonological error, which is something that may have precipitated the OI in the first place. NS's OI appears to locate NNS's troublesource utterance but does not identify what was problematic about it. In contrast, in Extract 4 where the 'context' is classroom discourse and a language learning setting, NS, the teacher of the class, *does* overtly locate a problematic utterance of NNS (L2) and shapes the talk or language and action of the sequence to one that is seemingly more in tune with her instructional goals and the needs of the 'interactants' whose identities as language learners appear to take on greater interactional salience, at least, at that particular moment in the unfolding discourse.

In Extracts 1–3, NS's delayed OI might be viewed as providing a repair opportunity space (or spaces) for NNS to do self-repair – *if s/he can*. Yet when the talk displays that NNS does not self-repair, neither does NS offer other-correction. In NS–NNS conversation where linguistic asymmetry between the participants can reasonably be assumed to be, on occasion, more pronounced than it is in native speaker interaction, and quite literally so in Extract 2, NS does not do the talk in a manner that overtly exhibits his or her status as an expert of the language of interaction in contrast with that of NNS. Nonetheless, Extract 4 illustrates that in instructional settings the roles of teacher and student may be more clearly demarcated and oriented to as such in the details of the talk (cf. Koshik 1999).

In naturally occurring conversation, for the not-yet-competent it may be that the issue of overt grammatical correction is sometimes sidestepped in the service of communication and meaning; one way of doing so is for the expert or native speaker to do repair and not correction in response to NNS's troublesource utterance. Correction would highlight NNS's grammatical or phonological error while repair or embedded correction does not necessarily do so, as in Extracts 1–3. By opting for repair as opposed to correction, NS seemingly takes responsibility for NNS's troublesource. But in the language classroom, it may be precisely the highlighting of NNS's error that is the issue – an issue to be pointed out – and under the circumstances NS, the teacher, does correction. And ultimately a language instructor hopes that NNS is able to detect and take responsibility for his/her linguistic or grammatical error and learn from it.

Jefferson (1987) suggests, in relation to NS–NS conversation, that embedded corrections keep issues such as incompetence and/or impropriety away from the conversational surface because they do not make relevant the offering of accountings. Embedded corrections provide a way in which interactants 'correct with discretion' (Jefferson 1988: 100) and that the very need to be discreet with another participant bespeaks lapses of language behaviour or social conduct in the first place. NS's sidestepping of NNS's grammatical problems or incompetences is arguably another form of discretion, one that is potentially different from that in ordinary conversation between native speakers due to the linguistic asymmetry between the participants. Yet in the final analysis, ironically, by downplaying linguistic asymmetry, which may superficially give off the impression that NNS is a competent user of the language, the participants may, on another tacit level, be constituting the talk and their identities precisely as linguistic novice and expert. A different 'standard' of grammaticality appears to be made interactionally relevant.

In terms of the notion of a 'threshold of perceived orderliness', Jefferson (1988) suggests that in ordinary conversation participants orient to the boundaries of phenomena such as responsibility, obligation, propriety and fault. One wonders whether this threshold of perceived orderliness might be somewhat different in NS–NNS conversation in terms of, say, what is allowable or not allowable in terms of grammar and whether social orderliness and linguistic orderliness might be separate or separable phenomena, particularly in NS–NNS conversation. And, if they are separate or separable, one might ask how and when they interact and coalesce in a grammar *in* NS–NNS interaction. Wrestling 'linguistic' or grammatical orderliness out of and throughout conversation so as to generate and regenerate aspects of social orderliness e.g., turn-taking structure, sequence organization, repair mechanisms, may be a daunting, challenging, delicate interactional matter for NS–NNS (or NNS–NNS) participants on a turn-by-turn basis. There are differences not only with conversation between native speakers (Gardner and Wagner 2004; Kasper and Ross 2001; Kurhila 2001; Hosoda 2000; Wong 2000a, 2000b, 2000c, 2004), but also with interaction in the institutional context of the language classroom.

One wonders whether Grice (1975) considered NS–NNS (or NNS–NNS) interaction in his notion of a Cooperative Principle, and whether his maxims of mutual cooperation in social interaction make room for the kind of talk investigated here, that is, NS's sidestepping of NNS's grammatical or phonological error and doing other-repair instead of other-correction. NS focuses on meaning and not language problems. Ways of staying in a NS–NNS conversation or of maintaining the conversational flow may be more difficult and more 'noticeable' than in NS–NS interaction. For example, recent literature reveals that when NNS produce an OI in a delayed position (delayed beyond next turn relative to the troublesource talk), they appear to display understanding of the talk later than they ought to have (Wong 2000a, 2004; Schegloff 2000).

Closing remarks

Given the limited dataset discussed in order to explore in detail what is going on in *particular* moments of naturally occurring NS–NNS interaction, for which research is not abundant but steadily increasing, more exemplars are needed in order to clarify and deepen our understanding and appreciation of grammar *in* NS–NNS conversation. It is precisely along the dimension of syntax and its impact on turn-taking organization, sequential constraints, adjacency pair structure, turn projection, and so on

(Schegloff 1996; Ochs *et al*. 1996; Carroll 2004; Wong 2004), that one might think that a novice speaker's fluency or lack thereof with the language of interaction would lead to some interesting issues to rein in on (Wong and Olsher 2000).

For those in applied linguistics, the notion of a syntax-for-conversation may provide us with a framework by which to revisit and rethink the nature of 'spoken discourse' or what 'conversational English' is about, and offer us a handle by which to grasp issues such as how talk or 'language', social interaction and grammar are inextricably tied and how participants address or skirt issues of language competence or incompetence in 'doing being' native and nonnative speakers for one another (Wong and Olsher 2000). A next step involves seeing how and whether issues in applied linguistics connect to the framework and insights of conversation analysis (e.g., Wong and Olsher 2000; Schegloff *et al*. 2002). Time is ripe for further intellectual pursuit along these lines.

Notes

1 Condensed versions of this chapter were presented as a paper at the convention of the National Communication Association in New Orleans, LA, USA (2002) and at a seminar of the British Association for Applied Linguistics/ Cambridge University Press, 'Conversation Analysis and Applied Linguistics' (2002). I thank the participants at each conference for their comments, in particular, Gene Lerner who served as discussant of the paper presented at the National Communication Association. An excerpt of this chapter was presented as a paper at a panel on Other Repair in Second Language Talk at the International Conference on Conversation Analysis (2002). I thank Catherine Brouwer, Gitte Rasmussen and Johannes Wagner, who organized the panel, and Gail Jefferson, who served as discussant.

2 I thank Debbie Shields and Seth Chorba for these observations.

3 In past literature (Schegloff *et al*. 1977), the notion of OI was referred to as NTRI, which stood for 'next turn repair initiation.' On this changing notion, see Schegloff (2000) and Wong (2000a).

4 Pomerantz (1984b) addresses the notion of preferred and dispreferred actions in talk in interaction. Preferred actions are delivered in the talk early and without delay markers, hedges, and/or hesitations. Dispreferred actions are delivered in the talk late or later and are often accompanied by pauses, hesitations, and/or delay markers.

5 In fact, Schegloff *et al*. (1977) have noted that sometimes interactants joke about errors that speaker make, for example, in cases of other-repair/correction. This does not occur in my NS–NNS corpus of naturally occurring conversation.

11
Discrimination Due to Nonnative Speech Production?

Maria Egbert

Introduction[1]

In 1999 I was a member of a team working on a pedagogical project in which we collected authentic telephone conversations in order to develop teaching materials for migrant workers in Germany designed to foster their interactional skills (*Deutsch am Telefon* 2001). We asked both native and nonnative speakers of German to record their telephone conversations. One call prompted spontaneous claims by several team members that the nonnative speaker was being discriminated against. In this call, a woman with an eastern European accent is inquiring about an apartment advertised for rent. The landlady rejects the caller's request for viewing the apartment. My colleagues felt that the landlady's account – the apartment is too small for a family with two children – is only a cover-up for her concealed racist attitude towards the caller. Our discussions in analysing the data did not yield agreement. The central issue of this chapter is whether the caller is being discriminated against.

This question is not a purely academic one since a researcher's diagnosis of racism is also a serious socio-political matter. We are dealing with a delicate matter, both at the micro and the macro level. Discrimination is related to a characteristic of a person that marks him or her as a member of a particular category of persons. We can think of discrimination as an action of membership categorization (Sacks (1964/ 1965) [1992], 1972a, 1972b) combined with bias, i.e. a person is given special treatment – positive or negative – based on his or her membership. Sexism, racism, classism, anti-Semitism, ageism, and other 'isms' have in common that they are based on a belief that one category of persons is superior or inferior to another category of persons. This belief can be intentional or unintentional, and it can be conscious or subconscious.

In seeking an account for the landlady's rejection of the potential renter in the call to be analysed, the question is raised whether the covert reason is the caller's nonnativeness, or whether the overtly provided account that the apartment, according to the landlady, 'becomes a little cramped for two kids' is credible.

Analytic points supporting claim of discrimination

The analysis will follow the transcript of the call from the opening to the closing. I will first examine how at the beginning of the call, the caller's nonnativeness becomes obvious and that subsequently the landlady disaffiliates more and more, initially by showing reluctance, intermittently by small behaviours inconsistent with a landlady motivated to rent a vacant apartment, and finally by denying the caller an appointment.

Landlady displays reluctance

At the beginning of the call, a male speaker answers the phone and self-identifies by giving his last name. In response, the caller greets him, self-identifies and provides the reason for the call (lines 3–4). The male recipient defers the call to his wife, who also picks up the phone with a self-identification (line 9). Upon this, the caller produces the same turn as before.[2]

Extract 1

01		((*ring*))
02	Called:	berger
03	Caller:	.hh guten tag johnsen wedestett ich rufe wegen anzeige
		.hh hello johnsen wedestett I'm calling about ad
04		in kleinanzeigen von gestern? [.hh
		in yesterday's classifieds? [*.hh*
		[
05	Called:	[ach so ja: meine
		[*oh ye:s my*
06		[frau macht das
		[*wife does that*
		[
07	Caller:	[°e-°

08   ((*6 sec. silence*))

09 Lessor: <u>ber</u>ger?

10 Caller: .hh guten tag johnsen wedestett.
                    .hh hello johnsen wedestett

	Caller shows nonnative speech production

11   ich rufe **wegen** anzeige.
                    I'm calling about ad.

12 Caller: [.hhhh und äh (0.1) zwar möchte.
                    [*.hhhh und uh (0.1) what I would*
                    [

13 Lessor: [°ja:a°

14   ich wissen wie <u>teu</u>er
                    like to know is how <u>mu</u>ch.

	Lessor shows reluctance response to greeting is missing

15   (0.2)

16 Lessor: ja <u>neun</u>hundertzwanzig ma[rk.
                    yes <u>nine</u> hundred twenty   ma[rks.
                                            [

17 Caller: [.hh
                                [*.hh*

18 Caller: neunhundertnzwanzig mark
                    nine hundred n twenty marks

The caller's first turn to the lessor (line 10) contains three features of nonnativeness, one in the area of grammar and two in the area of pragmatics. First, the verb 'anrufen' ('to call') is missing its prefix 'an'. Second, she self-identifies by giving her last name 'johnsen' and the name of the town 'wedestett' from where she is calling. Wedestett is the name of a suburb outside a midsize town about 15 km away from the lessor's residence. In telephone openings among native speakers of German it is uncommon to give the name of the place from where one is calling unless one is calling from very far away. Third, the order of the components – greeting before self-identification – in this call is reversed in comparison to how native speakers open such calls. A small collection of six such calls placed by native speakers to rental ads indicates that the self-identification is positioned before the greeting.

While it is obvious that the caller in Extract 1 is a nonnative speaker of German, the analysis needs to establish whether or not the lessor reacts to this in a negative way. There are two features in her response that may indicate her potential stance of disinclination. First, she does not reciprocate the greeting. In comparison to six other tape-recorded responses to rental ads, the caller's greeting is always reciprocated even in those cases where the apartment is already given away. Second, the landlady receipts the reason of the call with a soft '°ja:a°' (line 13). The next turn by the caller in Extract 1 contains several perturbations, which may be taken as an orientation to the lessor's lack of a greeting. At this earliest point in the interaction, the lessor in Extract 1 shows no inclination to win the caller as a potential tenant. This is all the more surprising since the rental market is advantageous for renters, something the lessor herself mentions towards the end of the call ('there is enough being offered at the moment', line 147).

The caller proceeds with a question about the rental price. This rather conventional question in a call for an advertised apartment is met with more subtle hesitation in that the lessor allows for a gap of 0.2 to emerge (line 15) before imparting the price (line 16). The caller repeats the price and in combination with her succeeding question about more details, she indicates that the price is within her range, thus signalling that there is no impediment on her side to continue with the course of action. While the analysis so far has shown some aspects of the landlady's behaviour, which may be ephemeral displays of a potential reluctant attitude, the conversation continues with a complicated misunderstanding, in which the lessor produces a more tangible negative behaviour.

Landlady shifts the source of a misunderstanding away from herself to the caller

The misunderstanding (cf. data segment below) evolves around two abbreviations in the ad signifying two types of rooms, a storage room and a utility room. In German, storage room is 'Vorratsraum', abbreviated in the ad as 'VR', while utility room is 'Hauswirtschaftsraum', abbreviated as 'HWR'. It should be noted that the abbreviation 'VR' is not known to many Germans, while 'HWR' is more common but is also not known by all. The lessor answers the caller's question about the meaning of 'VR' by explaining it wrongly as 'hauswirtschaftsraum' (line 22). The caller rejects this understanding (line 23), upon which the lessor reacts with a fourth position repair (Schegloff 1992) 'oh V R you mean now?' (line 25). The caller confirms this new understanding and following this, the lessor answers the question from the troublesource turn.

Extract 2

19		.hh und ich möchte noch gerne wissen wo:z- *.hh and I would also like to know fo:r wh-*
1→ 20		wofür steht die *for what stands the*
1→ 21		abkürzung <u>vau</u> <u>er</u>. *abbreviation <u>V</u> <u>R</u>.*

> Confusion evolves around acronyms
> HWR=Haus-Wirtschaft-Raum (utility room)
> VR=Vorrats-Raum (storage room)

2→ 22	Lessor:	haus<u>wirt</u>schaftsraum. *u<u>ti</u>lity room*
3→ 23	Caller:	.h nee das steht <u>e</u>xtra <u>haus</u>wirtschaftsraum *.hh no that stands <u>e</u>xtra u<u>ti</u>lity room*
3→ 24		.hh [komma [v- *.hh [comma [v-* [[
4→ 25	Lessor:	. [ja [ach vau er [*yes* [*oh V R*
26	Lessor:	meinen sie jetzt?= *you mean now?=*
27	Caller:	=ja ja. *=yes yes.*
28	Lessor:	<u>vor</u>ratsraum *<u>sto</u>rage room*
29	Caller:	ach so <u>vor</u>ratsraum. *oh I see <u>sto</u>rage room*
30	Lessor:	ja [vorratsraum *yes* [*storage room* [
31	Caller:	[.hh

> Lessor shifts source of
> misunderstanding to
> caller

(The box "Lessor shifts source of misunderstanding to caller" appears to the right of line 25.)

In the fourth position of this repair, the lessor's use of 'now' in 'oh V R you mean now?', is noteworthy. With this time reference, the lessor implies that the caller is meaning something different 'now' than what she meant before. She thus shifts the source (or blame) of the trouble to the caller and away from herself, where the trouble actually originated.

It is striking that already in the first few turns of this call, the interaction is marred by the same perturbations (hesitations, dysfluencies, errors, and repairs) that van Dijk (1984, 1987) reports in interviews where members of a majority group refer to members of a minority group, thus displaying social distance. So far, the landlady knows very little about the caller. The caller's voice allows for the assumption that she is female, probably in her thirties, and a nonnative speaker of German with an accent typical of persons from eastern European countries, i.e. an accent not considered prestigious by most Germans.[3] Thus, the impression may arise that the landlady's perturbations may be an unfavourable reaction to the caller's nonnativeness.

Diminishing chances of personal contact

After the abbreviations have been clarified, the caller asks a question about whether the apartment is facing south (line 32 below). The lessor first responds in a preferred way by praising the location (lines 33–37) and then, without solicitation, shifts into reverse in that she points to a feature of the apartment which she frames as negative 'though an upper level apartment right? = you saw that right? = U F means upper floor right?' (lines 37–38). She takes a characteristic of the apartment that some renters may find desirable and others may not, and suggests that this could be a reason why the caller may not want the apartment. Although the lessor tries hard to solicit an agreement by extending her turn with 'you saw that right?' (line 38) and by placing a 'nech?' ('right?') (Jefferson 1980, Harren 2001) after each of the two turn-constructional units, the caller withholds agreement.

Extract 3

32 Caller: ja .hh und eh:: ist das süd seit [e?
                yes .hh and uh:: is that south si [de?
                                                  [
33 Lessor: [ja das is alles
                                                  [*yes that is all*

34 Lessor: südseite is das [ja:a und auch ganz <u>ruhig</u> und eh
                south side it is [ye:es and also very <u>quiet</u> and uh
                                 [
35 Caller: [.hh

36 Lessor: hat man auch keinen direkten
                also one has no direct

> Lessor assesses neutral feature of apartment as negative

37	nachbarn .hh is aber *neighbours .hh is though*

38	ne oberwohnung nech? = ham sie gesehn nech?= *an upper level apartment right? = you saw that right?=*

This attempt of discouragement by the landlady additionally contains an unsolicited linguistic explanation about the meaning of the German abbreviation 'OG' ('U F means upper floor', line 39). In this way, the lessor orients to the caller as a person with deficient language knowledge.

Extract 4

39	=[o ge heißt ober [geschoss [*U F means upper* [*floor* [[	Lessor gives unsolicited linguistic help

40	Caller:	=[ja [ja [*yes* [*yes*

41	Caller:	j:a obergeschoss .hhh (0.2) und ähm (0.5) gepfl (0.2) *y:es upper floor .hhh (0.2) and uhm (0.5) ke (0.2)*

42	punkt idyll (0.2) was i [st, *period idyll (0.2) what i[s,* [

43	Lessor:	[ja eine gepflegte idyllische [*yes a kept up idyllic*

44	anlage ☺ also is bisschen schön ru:hig = alles schön *location ☺ so is a little nice and qui:et = all nice and*

45	<u>sau</u>ber .h der garten is schön gepfle:gt das is ganz *<u>clean</u> .h the garden is nice and kept we:ll that is very*

46	ru:hige ecke so .hh wie gesagt man hat da eben kein: *qui:et corner .hh as i said one has there no:*

47	keinen direkten nachbarn der ihnen da so auf'n balkon *no direct neighbours who can look onto your balcony*

48	kucken kann .hhh sie kucken vom balkon so in so n (.) *there .hhh from the balcony you look into like like an (.)*

49	alten <u>baum</u>bestand also nachbarsgarten da er hat noch *old <u>tree</u> area that is neighbour garden there it still has*

50   so alte bäume da stehn
             such old trees standing there

51   Caller: mhm

52   Lessor: al[so ne schöne aussicht so und (0.1) ja einglich ganz
             s [*o a beautiful view like and (0.1) yes really rather*
               [
53   Caller: [.hh

54   Lessor: [ruhig wolln mal so sagen [nich?
             [*quiet shall we say* [*right?*
             [[
55   Caller: [e-   [ich möch- eh ich möchte noch
             [e-   [*i would- uh i would like to also*

This piece of language teaching appears condescending since the lessor
implies that on the basis of one information question, the caller must
have other language deficiencies. This may furnish another slight piece of
evidence that the lessor's reluctance 'though an upper level apartment'
is connected to the caller's nonnativeness.

On the surface, the lessor seems to engage in talk appropriate for
someone interested in finding a renter. She provides factual information
about the price, rooms, view, the surrounding garden and the neighbourhood. Under this surface, her behaviour contains some hardly
detectable negative features, which, when taken individually, may appear
insignificant; however, when viewed together, may indicate an unfriendly
attitude. Among these features are the landlady's lack of reciprocating
the caller's initial greeting, shifting the responsibility of a misunderstanding away from herself to the caller, assessing a neutral aspect of
the apartment (upper floor) as negative, and giving unsolicited linguistic
help. Since the first of these disaffiliate moves occurs after the very first
turn by the caller, it appears plausible that they are an indication of a
covert attitude of unwelcomeness towards the caller's nonnativeness.
As the call unfolds further, the landlady's disaffiliation becomes more overt,
and an account is furnished for her distancing move. After the lessor's
description of the beautiful environment and garden (lines 43–54 above),
the caller mentions that she has two small children, who, she hopes,
will be able to play in the garden. This is taken up by the lessor and
turned into an obstacle. She explains that the previously praised garden
cannot be used by the renters of the advertised apartment (Extract 5
below), and that the apartment is too small for two children (Extract 6).

Extract 5

```
56  Lessor:   [ruhig wolln mal so sagen [nich?
             [quiet shall we say [right?
             [                     [
57  Caller:   [e-                  [ich möch- eh ich möchte noch
             [e-                  [I would- uh I would like to also

58  Caller:   fragen .hh eh wir haben zwei kleine kinder, [und sie
             ask    .hh uh we have two small children, [and you
                                                        [
59  Lessor:                                              [ja:a
                                                        [ye:s

60  Caller:   haben grade erwähnt äh garten dürfen wir dann [garten
             just mentioned uh garden are we allowed then  [garden
                                                           [
61  Lessor:                                                [nee de
                                                           [no the

62  Lessor:   garten is nur für die unterwohnung gedacht.
             garden is only for the bottom floor apartment.

63            (0.2)

64  Caller:   oh das is ja schade=
             oh that is too bad=

65  Lessor:   =ja das is schade dieser- bei der oberwohnung is es
             =yes that is too bad this- with the upper apartment it is

66            immer etwas schwieriger .hh man hat zwar vorne vorm
             always a little more difficult .hh though one has in front

67            haus .hh aber mit zwei kindern wieviel personen wären
             outside the house .hh but with two children how many persons

68            sie denn vier personen?
             would you be then four persons?

69  Caller:   vier personen.
             four persons.
```

Landlady declines to give an appointment

In an extensive tug of turns (Extract 6 below), the caller shows continued interest in the apartment, whereas the lessor keeps insisting that the apartment is too small for two adults and two children. The landlady's reasoning includes a decision about which rooms are to be used for which purpose, a repeated statement of her opinion that the two children should have separate rooms, her reluctance to admit that there is a school and a preschool near by, and attempts to solicit the caller's agreement with this view.

Extract 6

70 Lessor : ja .hh da is nur <u>ein</u> kinderzimmer dabei nech? das is n
          yes .hh there is only <u>one</u> children's room right? that is a

71   bisschen eh (0.2) wird n bisschen
          little uh (0.2) becomes a little.

> Lessor decides for the caller what is appropriate space for caller's kids

72   <u>eng</u> für zwei kinder.
          <u>cramped</u> for two kids

73 Caller: mhm .hh is da auch ein eh kinderspielplatz in der nähe?
          mhm .hh is there also a uh play ground near by?

74 Lessor: n::j:a das is sicherlich is ne
          n::y:es there is surely is a

> Turn-initially, lessor is reluctant to give information that is positive for kids

75   siedlung is das auch und
          development is there too and

76   da is schule kindergarten alles in der nähe.
          there is school play school everything near by.

77 Caller: .hh [mhm
          .hh [mhm
              [
78 Lessor: [das is schon so ja:a .hh aber wie
          [there is like ye:s .hh but as I

> Lessor repeats that space is too small for kids

79   gesagt ich
          said I

80   (be)denk mal m- mit es is nur <u>ein</u> kinderzimmer nich = das
          (con)sider w- with there is only <u>one</u> children's room there = that

81   is n problem glaub ich wie alt sind ihre kinder denn?
          is a problem I believe how old are your children then?

82 Caller: .hhh eine ist eineinhalb,
          .hhh one is one and a half

83   Lessor: ja:a
           ye:s

84   Caller: und die andere ist mm vor kurzem <u>sechs</u> geworden.
           and the other just mm turned <u>six</u>.

85   Lessor: ja
           yes
86   (0.2)

87   Lessor: aber wie ham sie s jetzt <u>auch</u> in einm zimmer noch?
           but how do you have it now <u>also</u> in one room still?

88   Caller: mhm
89   (0.2)

> Lessor implies that she knows better than caller what is appropriate space for caller's kids

90   Lessor: und eh .hh ja es wär ja
           and uh .hh yes it would be a

91   besser wenn die <u>je</u>der n zimmer
           better if they <u>each</u> had

92   hätten nech oder was denken <u>sie</u>.
           room right or what do <u>you</u> think.

> Lessor tries to solicit agreement from caller

93   (0.5)

Overt disaffiliation

While the lessor restates her argument that the apartment would be too small for a family with two children, the caller resists going along with this stance (cf. gaps at lines 78, 93 above) and proceeds to the next relevant step in the course of this call by asking for an appointment in order to be able to see for herself (lines 94–96 below). However, the lessor is quick to step in with a repetition of her perceived impediment that the apartment is too small (lines 97, 99 below). Note that her turn is positioned in midturn at an inbreath, a kind of turn-taking Jefferson (1983) calls progressional or hitch onset. The obstacle is discussed for a long sequence (lines 97–141 below) in which the landlady repeats her argument, produces a condescending move implying that she knows what is best for the caller, and gives an unsolicited recommendation of what is appropriate for the caller's family. She further points to the favourable market situation for renters (line 147).

Extract 7

94   Caller: .hhh also wir können auch einn termin eh abmachen damit
.hhh so we could also make an appointment so that

95   wir uns ankucken wahrscheinlich liegt diese .hh wohnung
we could see for ourselves most likely this .hh apartment will

96   uns so am herz dass wir das .hhh
be so close to our heart that we .hh

97   Lessor: ja ich denke [mal ich sach grade wegen t- m:mit zwei
yes I think [I just said because of t- w:with two
[

98   Caller: [un-

99   Lessor: kindern wird das n bisschen eng in der wohnung .hh
children it gets a little cramped in the apartment .hh

100 Lessor: [weil sie nur ein
[*because you have only one*
[

	Lessor repeats argument that space is too cramped for kids

101 Caller: [mhm

102 Lessor: kinderzimmer haben.
children's room.

103   (0.7)

104 Lessor: ein kinderzimmer .hh und das hat höchstens, also
one children's room .hh and that has at the most, well

105   ungefähr so zwölf quadratmeter .hh und das wird für
at the most like twelve square meters .hh and that gets

106   zwei kinder wird das zu eng.
too cramped for two children.

107 Caller: also auch eh diese zimmer ist nich so gro:ß.
so in addition uh this room is not so bi:g.

108 Lessor: °nein nein ist [nicht so gro:ß° das de- die
°no no   is [not so bi:g° it th- the
[

109 Caller: [mhm

110 Lesser: quadratmeterzahl is vierundachtzig qua<u>dra:t</u>meter .hh
                square meter figure is eighty four squa:are meters. hh

111   aber es geht mehr in den <u>wohn</u>bereich über [.hh das
                but it goes more into the <u>liv</u>ing area   [*.hh the*
                                                                        [
112 Caller: [mhm

113 Lesser: wohnzimmer hat <u>drei</u>ßig quadratmeter alleine schon das
                living room has <u>thir</u>ty square meters alone this is

113   is n ziemlich gro<u>ß</u>es wohnzimmer mit essbereich so
                already a rather big living room with dining area

114   ne[ch? und die küche is noch mal extra,
                ri [ght? and the kitchen is again extra,
                   [
115 Caller: [ja
                  [*yes*

116 Caller: mhm

117 Lesser: und äh wie gesagt dann is eben das <u>elternschlafzimmer</u>
                and uh as I said then is the <u>parents'</u> bedroom

118   .hh da kann man ebm | Lessor decides how
                .hh so there one can | bedrooms are to be
                                                         | used

119   also nur n elternschlafzimmer
                only set up a parents'

120   aufste<u>ll</u>en und das kinderzimmer is ebm wie gesagt <u>nicht</u>
                bedroom and the children's room is as I said <u>not</u>

121   <u>so</u> gro=also für <u>ein</u> kind is es normal aus<u>reich</u>end aber
                <u>so</u> bi=well for <u>one</u> child it is normal sufficient but

122   wenn sie jetzt <u>zwei</u> kinder unterbringen möchten das
                when now you want to accomodate <u>two</u> children it

123   wird n bisschen <u>eng</u>. | Lessor repeats her
                gets a little <u>cramped</u>. | argument

124 Caller: .hhhh okay ic[h h
                hhhh okay i [h
                             [
125 Lesser: [das wird zu <u>eng</u> für zwei kinder ich meine
                           [*that gets too <u>cramped</u> for two children I mean*

| 126 | | das tut mir <u>auch</u> leid aber das is wirklich das kann ich |
| | | *I'm sorry about that <u>too</u> but that is really that I can* |

| 127 | | ihnen schon <u>so</u> sagen und weils eben ne <u>o</u>berwohnung is |
| | | *tell you like <u>this</u> and because it is an <u>upper</u> level apartment* |

| 128 | | in der- die kinder wolln sicherlich auch n bisschen |
| | | *in which- the kids surely want to have a little* |

129		mehr <u>aus</u>lauf haben dan[n nech
		more room to move the [*n right*
		[

| 130 | Caller: | [°m-° |

131 Caller: mja

| 132 | Lessor: | das is ja dann auch nich so <u>toll</u> ich meine .hh sie |
| | | *so then that is then not so <u>great</u> I mean .hh they* |

| 133 | | müssen immer rauf und runter und ha- könn dann nur vorm |
| | | *have to go up and down and then ha- can only play such* |

134		haus da so n bisschen [spielen
		a little in front of the house
		[

| 135 | Caller: | [°°m°° |

136 Caller: °mhm°

| 137 | Lessor: | °so nech?° | Lessor repeats her argument |
| | | °*like this right?*° |

138	Caller:	.hh [ja
		.hh [*yes*
		[

139	Lessor:	[das wäre dann wahrscheinlich zu <u>eng</u> [für zwei
		[*then it would probably be too <u>cramped</u>* [*for two*
		[

| 140 | Caller: | [.hh |

| 141 | Lessor: | kinder |
| | | *children* |

After this extensive reasoning by the lessor, the caller finally gives in
(line 142 below):

Extract 8

142   Caller: da dann- dann werde ich mir was anderes [suchen
              there than- then i will look for something [different

                                                        [
143   Lessor: [ja da kucken
                                                        [*yes look*

144   Lessor: sie mal [noch mal sie müssen
                      [*again you must*

                      [┌─────────────────────────────────┐
145   Caller: [.hh   │ Lessor implies again to know better than │
                                │ caller what is appropriate for caller   │
                                └─────────────────────────────────┘

146   Lessor: einglich <u>vier</u> zimmer haben
              really have <u>four</u> rooms

147   Lessor: denk ich mal [da wird ja auch
              i think   [*there is enough*

                           [
148   Caller: [.hhh   ┌──────────────────────┐
                                    │ Lessor says the rental   │
                                    │ market is good for renters │
149   Lessor: genug angeboten im moment └──────────────────────┘
              being offered at the moment

150   Caller: ich danke ihnen [für gespräch schönen tag [noch tschüss
              i thank you   [*for conversation have a nice day bye*

                              [[
151   Lessor: [ja bitteschön   [jo tschüss.
                              [*yes you're welcome*   [*yeah bye.*

The caller closes the call by thanking the lessor for the conversation, wishing her a good day and bidding her goodbye (line 151). As soon as the preclosing is projectable ('i thank you'), the lessor eagerly produces an agreement and a second pair part and even utters the 'goodbye' before the caller. It is of no small significance that the lessor's quick turn-taking in the closing sequence is just the opposite of her hesitant turn-taking in the opening sequence.

Analysing both the broader course of actions and the small details in this conversation, it appears plausible that the landlady is rejecting this potential renter because of a hardly tangible negative attitude towards the caller's nonnativeness, while giving an overt, socially acceptable, account for her rejection. There are two theoretical frameworks that help explain this finding. Both Critical Discourse Analysis (CDA) and 'modern' or 'aversive' racism theory (Becker 1999; Gaertner and Dovidio 1986; McConahay 1986) report a shift in racism away from open, obvious behaviours of discrimination towards more covert, subtle ways. An example of Old Racism is the belief that so-called aryans or whites are genetically superior to coloured persons. This belief has been the basis of the holocaust, genocide, slavery and segregation. In public opinion polls in the US, such a belief – e.g. blacks are genetically inferior to whites – is nowadays rejected (cf. overview in Kim 2000). Aversive Racism Theory holds that these opinion polls do not show the end of racism. Rather, the situation is more complex and covert. While white Americans now report egalitarian beliefs, many still maintain negative attitudes against blacks. Persons with this conflict suppress their racist belief so that they are no longer aware of it. Aversive Racism Theory describes the resulting behaviour in the following way:

> Aversive racists also typically avoid close contact with minorities or communicate their underlying negative attitudes in subtle, rationalizable ways. Their negativity is likely to be demonstrated in discomfort, uneasiness, fear, or avoidance of minorities rather than in outward hostility. The subtlety of this 'aversive' behaviour (in effect, a non-behaviour) makes it difficult to document aversive racism through the techniques of behavioural research. (Becker 1999)

The analysis so far exemplifies Becker's perspective that a covert negative attitude may not be directly observable. Since a person's disaffiliative inner stance may not surface openly in his or her behaviour, CDA uses interviews as one way in a broader endeavour to detect subtle manifestations of racism. For example, van Dijk and his group (1984, 1987) interviewed members of the majority group in Amsterdam and San Diego in regard to how they talk about 'the Others'. A negative attitude is inferred from how the interviewees talk when referring to members of minorities. The findings show that there is a strong positive presentation of Self in contrast to a negative presentation of members of the minority. In talking about the Others, social distance is observable in the way interviewees talk about the Others. Of particular interest to this chapter is that the interviewees' speech is marked by perturbations, such as hesitations, dysfluencies, errors and repairs, which typically occur in the speech of members of the majority group when referring to the Others. In the case of the landlady rejecting the nonnative caller, hesitations, dysfluencies and repair occur right at the beginning of the call; in contrast, once the caller gives up her efforts to view the apartment, the landlady's conduct is smooth. The difficulty of the analysis lies in the nature of the object being studied; a negative interactant's attitude towards her co-participant may be subconscious or concealed, and to the co-participant as well as to the researcher only the actual behaviour is observable. Unless there is leakage in the cover-up of a negative attitude it cannot be detected, so we do not know for sure whether it is there. In this part of the analysis I have pulled together those aspects of the landlady's conduct that are potential indications of such leakage. Will this line of argument hold against an opposing analysis?

Analytic points disclaiming discrimination

The analysis above has shown clearly that the landlady is discouraging the caller's interest in different ways, and that she is unwilling to show the rental property to the caller. The point of contention is why she behaves this way. So far I have assembled observations and interpretations in an attempt to find grounding in the data for the impression by many Germans who, when listening to the call, feel that the landlady displays a negative attitude to the caller's nonnativeness. I will now develop an alternative second line of analysis scrutinizing the analysis to set against this.

Landlady displays reluctance in telephone opening

The analysis above sets out to establish that the initial behaviour by the landlady – in particular the absence of a reciprocatory greeting and her hesitant turn-taking – may include slight displays of a negative reaction to the caller's nonnative speech production. Clearly, there are pragmatic, grammatical and articulatory features of nonnativeness in the caller's first turn, and the landlady's reaction may be connected to this, yet the source of this conduct may not lie in her negative attitude towards non-Germanness but rather in the ordering of components in the nonnative speaker's first turn. In comparative calls by native speakers, the recipient of the call picks up the phone with a self-identification. In response, the caller first provides the second pair part to the identification sequence and then starts the greeting sequence with a first pair part, thus completing the identification sequence before opening the greeting sequence. In reversing this order, the nonnative caller's turn design pre-empts the proper place for a reciprocatory greeting, hence the landlady's absence of a greeting. The soft volume of the landlady's '°ja:a°' (line 13) may also be accounted for by the unusual turn-design by the nonnative speaker. The landlady may simply be unclear about what will follow next by the native speaker. By signalling receipt she behaves sequentially appropriately, and by doing this in a soft voice, she only weakly claims turn space, thus leaving room for the nonnative speaker to say more, which she indeed does. We may thus support the impression that the landlady is orienting to the caller's nonnativeness, yet this is done in an accommodating way due to the nonnative speaker's irregular positioning of turn components rather than to a potential negative attitude by the landlady.

Occurrence of dysfluencies and repair

Repair is the mechanism for signalling and resolving trouble in speaking, hearing and understanding (cf. seminal work by Schegloff *et al.* 1977; for German, cf. Egbert 2002) and it often co-occurs with or precedes other kinds of interactional friction. This has been observed in naturally occurring conversation (e.g. Schegloff 1995; Egbert 2002). In CDA dysfluencies and repairs have been interpreted in interviews (van Dijk 1984, 1987) as indications of a covert racial attitude by the interviewee when they co-occur in references to members of minority groups. While the parallels between CA and CDA are interesting here, it should be noted that these features may be present in talk about minorities but not in talk to minorities, which is the case here.[4] Most importantly, it has not been established that the reverse is true, i.e. not every instance of repair is an indication of discomfort or unease. As Schegloff points out (personal communication), sometimes a repair is just a repair.

Misunderstanding around abbreviations

The misunderstanding occurs in a sequence where the caller asks about the meaning of the abbreviation 'VR'. In answering the caller's inquiry, the landlady confuses 'VR' and 'HWR', i.e. two rooms with similar functions, one being the storage room ('VR') and one the utility room ('HWR'). The analysis above suggests that the landlady shifts the responsibility of this misunderstanding away from herself to the caller by saying 'oh VR you mean now?' (line 25). Such an interpretation rests on the assumption that the landlady remembers who said what around these abbreviations; however, given the accumulation of abbreviations in the ad, she may not remember exactly and may actually erroneously assume the caller asked about 'HWR'. Here again the analysis enters the grey area of making psychological or cognitive inferences from an observable verbal behaviour where the evidence is inconclusive.

Giving unsolicited linguistic advice

When is a native speaker's linguistic advice to a nonnative speaker appropriate? Are there preferred and dispreferred ways of offering this?

This question pertains to the part in the analysis above where the land-lady gives unsolicited advice to the caller by explaining the German abbreviation 'OG' in her ad in the following way: 'U F means upper floor' (line 39). She thus orients to the nonnative speaker as a person with deficient language knowledge. It is doubtful that this can be taken as a covert sign of the landlady's negative attitude towards the caller, since earlier in the call the nonnative speaker herself displayed deficiency by asking about the abbreviation 'VR'. Whether this is being condescending or being eagerly helpful remains open to interpretation. Granted, the landlady gives this linguistic assistance in connection with the description of a negatively evaluated element, thus making sure that the caller understands this. However, it does seem significant that the nonnative speaker herself reacts to this unsolicited linguistic help in a receptive way by soliciting more assistance about other abbreviations in the ad (see Extract 4).

Here again, the analysis would have to rest on inference in order to explicate the motivation or attitude underlying the landlady's behaviour. Once we rely on inferencing, the interpretation is vulnerable to political or personal bias, i.e. the action of giving unsolicited linguistic help can equally be supported as indicating an interactant's positive or a negative attitude.

Landlady's overt account for her disinclination

When the landlady learns that the caller has two children (line 58 in Extract 5 above), she inquires about how many persons in total would move in. She then voices the opinion that one small room is too cramped for two children (line 70–72). While a scaffolding of small pieces has been assembled – and possibly disassembled – to show the plausibility of a concealed negative attitude, only very faint signs of inconsistency in the landlady's open account have been furnished. Let us consider these.

If we assume that the landlady honestly considers the apartment too small for this family, it seems reasonable that she would be reluctant to expand the discussion further. So when the caller asks about a play-ground (cf. line 73), the landlady starts her turn with a lengthened 'n::' projecting a negative 'nein', which she turns into an affirmative 'ja:a' (line 74). It appears reasonable that for her, once she has deemed the apartment too small for the caller's family, she is slightly reluctant to follow positive aspects related to children, yet nonetheless she does confirm that there is a playground near by and even volunteers the additional information that there is also a school and play school in the vicinity.

In the first course of the analysis, much is made of the fact that the landlady pre-empts any opportunity for the caller to view the place for herself in order to decide whether it is appropriate after all. Such a behaviour may not be very forthcoming, and it may even be condescending; however, this may arise from her not wanting to have children in the neighbourhood rather than being the product of a covert racial attitude. It is just as likely, perhaps even more likely, that the landlady wishes to keep the neighbourhood quiet. Even before she learns that the caller has two small children, she emphasizes in a positive way that the neighbourhood is quiet (line 34). This would contrast with the idea of two children in a small upper-level apartment without access to a garden.

Discussion

The goal of this analysis was to examine the transcript for potential pieces of evidence that would provide grounding in the data for the initial impression by several native Germans that the German landlady rejects the nonnative caller because of a veiled racist attitude. The analysis shows without doubt that the landlady is disaffiliating with the caller and denies her an appointment to view the apartment. As an account for this rejection, she explains that the place advertised is too small for a couple with two children. The analysis cannot substantiate the hypothesis that the landlady shows a racist attitude. Neither a single aspect of her conduct nor her overall behaviour warrants the indisputable conclusion that she has a negative attitude due to the caller's non-nativeness. How can we explain the fact that several Germans report to detect a racist attitude in the landlady's interaction? Possibly, elements in the voice quality or intonation might lead native speakers of German to assume that the lessor is discriminating based on the caller's non-nativeness, but we know too little about these elements of interactional behaviour to make analytic claims.

There are many ways in which discrimination can surface in interactional behaviour, but when a person conceals a discriminating attitude, it may be difficult to address this – both for the co-participant and for the conversation analyst. While it is of political and social importance to detect the ways in which discrimination is constructed in interaction, in particular when this is done in subtle and concealed manners, the issue of concluding that a given person's behaviour is racist is such a sensitive one that we should position any analysis on safe grounds in order not to accuse anybody unjustly. At the same time, much more research is called for to broaden our insights into this matter.

Application to anti-bias training

One central goal of most anti-bias and intercultural training is to make participants more aware of interactional conduct of discrimination. Human rights movements across the globe strive to implement equal rights in the legislature so that discrimination can be identified and offenders can be sued in court. For participants in anti-bias training and for legal experts, an analysis of video- and audio-recorded naturally occurring interaction like the phone conversation investigated in this paper would be useful in the pursuit of shedding light on any grey areas of what exactly constitutes discriminatory conduct. In existing anti-bias training, a module could be included in which a set of data segments could be played and analysed together in order to define the line between discrimination, borderline discrimination and the absence of discrimination. These interactions could then be used as a point of departure for role-plays and the reflection of instances the participants have observed or experienced themselves. For law-makers, an analysis of authentic conduct could help to develop clearer descriptions of which behaviours are regarded as discriminating.

Notes

1   I would like to thank Jörg Bergmann, Paul Drew, Sandra Harrison, Franz Januschek, Claudia Lohrenscheidt, Keith Richards, Manny Schegloff, Paul Seedhouse, Anette Wenderoth and my students for their ideas on earlier versions of the analysis.
2   The caller gave her permission for tape-recording before she placed the call, the lessor was telephoned directly after this phone call and also granted permission. The names have been changed to ensure anonymity.
3   Here the issue of the label 'nonnative' becomes very political since this speaker's accent suggests that she is a 'Spätaussiedlerin', i.e. a person from an area that belonged to pre-WWII Germany, and who is seeking residence in Germany based on the claim that she has German heritage.
4   For a methodological debate between members of CA and CDA, cf. Schegloff 1997, Billig 1999; Schegloff 1999, Wetherell 1998, Schegloff 1998.

Part IV
Language Learning

12
The Organization of Off-task Talk in Second Language Classrooms

Numa Markee

Introduction

How do we know when second/foreign language (S/FL) learners are 'off-task' during small group work? Teachers and learners probably know intuitively when this kind of event occurs. However, there is no empirical work on how such talk is constructed. This chapter uses conversation analysis (CA) to explicate the achievement of off-task talk in terms of its sequential placement, and examines the difficulty of maintaining such talk in the face of co-occurring on-task talk in the wider classroom. Finally, the chapter discusses the value of CA insights for second language acquisition (SLA) studies, classroom research (CR) and S/FL teacher education and training.

What is off-task talk?

A vernacular definition of off-task talk characterizes such talk as interaction that diverges from whatever topic(s) teachers designate as the current class agenda. But this definition is circular: it claims that off-task talk is any interaction that is not on-task, begging the question of what on-task talk is in the first place. Let us instead formulate the issues in terms of the different organizational practices to which participants orient in more or less distinct speech exchange systems. Classroom talk – or, more accurately, classroom talks[1] – is an instance of institutional talk and in the most familiar form is teacher-led. That is, teachers 'do' being teachers by exercising privileged rights to nominate conversational topics, and by deciding which learners may talk when. Conversely, learners do being learners by participating in this unequal power speech exchange system. When teachers (Ts) ask learners (LL) questions, LL are in the sequential position of providing answers. Finally, Ts also 'own' the third commenting or evaluating slot in this three-part conversational object, yielding the prototypical Question–Answer–Comment (QAC) preference organization of teacher-led classroom talk (McHoul 1978; Mehan 1979; Sinclair and Coulthard 1975; van Lier 1988).

However, when teachers use collaborative learning techniques (particularly those that involve no direct teacher participation), they not only increase the number and range of speech exchange systems to which participants have to orient but also relax the pre-allocated turn-taking practices of teacher-led talk (Markee 2000). Thus, the range of classroom talks to which members may orient in a given class is potentially large.

One problem with the vernacular definition of off-task talk is that the notion of topic is notoriously difficult to pin down (Brown and Yule 1983; Givon 1983; Jefferson 1984; Keenan and Schieffelin 1975; Maynard 1980; Schegloff 1979; van Lier 1988). For present purposes, I treat ordinary conversation (and, more generally, talk-in-interaction) as a series of topics that occur during a single extended speech event (Maynard 1980). Topics are thus analysed in terms of their sequential structure and ordering vis-à-vis other topics rather than their semantic content. This is consistent with Schegloff's (1979) theoretically agnostic formulation of topic as whatever-members-understand-the-current-conversation-to-be-about.

Although this formulation of topic allows us to deploy CA techniques to explicate how members 'do' topics, topics-as-conversational-objects are still difficult to identify. They frequently do not have clear-cut boundaries because they often imperceptibly shade into each other (Jefferson 1984; Schegloff *et al.* 2002). In addition, topics are often done as multiple attempts to talk about something (Markee 2000). Each reprise of a given topic is separated by other topics, and, during the course of each reprise, members' formulations of what is currently being talked about may change. Finally, there are some forms of 'talk-that-occurs-in-the-classroom' that are nonetheless *not* institutional because participants observably orient to the topic nomination and turn-taking conventions of ordinary conversation.[2] With these caveats in mind, let us now proceed to the empirical analysis of the data.

Background information

The talk analysed here consists of an invitation to a party issued by L11 to L9, which was issued during a class whose official topic was the reunification of East and West Germany. The site of this audio/ video-recorded interaction was a 50-minute intermediate undergraduate ESL class of 12 learners at an American university, taught by T, who had also written the relevant content-based unit. The methodology was task-based, and utilized small group work, during which T circulated from group to group. The lesson consisted of two phases. During phase 1, five groups of varying sizes each read and discussed a different article on the topic of German reunification. During phase 2, three newly configured groups exchanged and synthesized information from these articles prior to writing a term paper on the pros and cons of German reunification. L9 and L11 constitute Group 3. The off-task invitation talk analysed in this chapter occurred at the end of phase 1.

The data

The database for this chapter consists of 447 lines of audio/video-recorded talk (Invitation to a party) lasting for three minutes 32 seconds. Transcribed using standard CA transcription conventions (Atkinson and Heritage 1984), it includes information about eye gaze (Goodwin, 1981). Talk is written in bold type in this chapter only to distinguish it from the many non-verbal actions. Additional symbols unique to this chapter are:

⊃ ⊃   foot steps
{   talk from another conversation to the one that is being analysed
≈   fortuitous overlap between another conversation and the one that is being analysed

Finally, the layout of the classroom and the positions of the teacher as she moved around the classroom during this off-task talk are shown in Figure 12.1. The data are from camera 1.

The sequential placement and achievement of off-task talk

The talk (not reproduced here) immediately prior to Extract 1 instantiates the QAC structure of teacher-led classroom talk and focuses on the topic of whether Günter Grass is an East or West German writer. At line 002 of Extract 1, T asks the whole class whether class members have almost finished. This question is a closure-relevant device that T uses to encourage students to move on to the next class activity (see also lines 375, 383 and 393 of Extracts 8 and 9). Although another activity occurs by default in this extract – T responds to a request for help by L14 at line

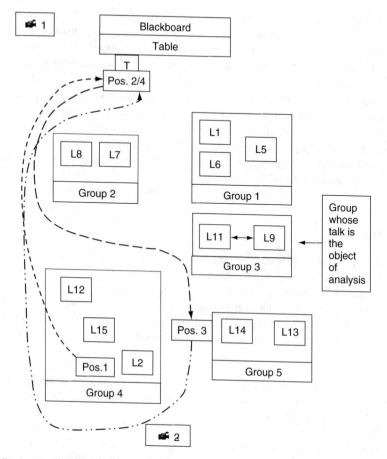

Figure 12.1 Classroom layout

025 and then engages in small group interaction with L14 and L13 – T does not specify what learners should do next.

Extract 1

((T walks from Position 1 at the back of the classroom to Position 2 in front of the table. Three steps before reaching Position 2, she starts to speak, addressing the whole class. Two steps before stopping, she ends her first turn at line 002. When she comes to a stop at Position 2, she remains standing, with her arms crossed, facing the class. L11 watches T as she makes her way to the front of the class. L11 keeps looking at T through T's turn at line 002 and 1.3 seconds into the silence at line 004, L11 looks down at his handout. Two seconds into the silence at line 004, L11 raises his gaze and looks toward L9. Throughout this time, L9 is looking down at his handout.))

```
001 T:      [⊃1 ⊃2        [------------------ ⊃ 3 ----------------------- ] ⊃4 ⊃5]
002 T:                      [OK ARE YOU ALMOST FINISHED.]
003 L11:    [X_____ ]
004         (2.3)
005 L11:    --- [X _____
006 L11:       [are we finished, you are finished,
007         (1.0)
008 L11:    _____
009 L9:     ((L9 looks up slightly but is still looking down at his handout))
010 L11:    _____        [, , ,]
011 L9:     ☺ <I think. so.>☺  [hhh]
012         (0.3)
013 L11:    huh=
014 L9:     =h=
015 L9:     [((L9 leans toward L11)) ..  [X _____ . , .   [X , , , , , , , , , , ,
016 L11:    ┌ [= [☺ huh huh huh      <[I [↓ thin:k so↓> ☺  [
017 L11:    │                                    [ , , , , , , , , , , , ,  [((L11 tilts head back))
018 L9:     │      X ____ . . . , , , , [X _
019 L9:     └ huh huh huh huh [ ˙hhh
020 L9:     _____        [, , , , , , , , , , , , , , , , , , , , , ,
021 L11:    ☺˙ hhh oh no:. ↓☺ [((L11 turns a page of his handout))
022         (2.0)
023         [((T clasps her hands and starts walking to her right))]
024 T:      ⊃1 ⊃2]
025 L14     [((L14 raises his hand))
026 T:      [⊃3]
027         [((T moves from Position 2 to Position 3 in the back of the class))]
028         [⊃4 ⊃5 ⊃6 ⊃7 ⊃8 ⊃9] ((T remains at Position 3 until line 299))
```

(All extracts from Numa Markee: Invitation to a party)

The learners in groups 1, 2, 4 and 5 all return to the official topic of German reunification during the three and a half minutes of small group work that ensue. In contrast, group 3 (L11 and L9) engage in off-task talk. Thus, the switch from on-task to off-task work by L9 and L11 is sequentially located immediately after the QAC-mediated topic of Günter Grass's nationality has been closed down at line 002 and in the gap that has been created by T's lack of precise pedagogical instructions at this moment.

How is the sequential opportunity for off-task talk converted into action by L9 and L11? At line 006 of Extract 1, L9 and L11 begin to orient to the locally managed conventions of ordinary conversation. Following a 2.3 second silence at line 004, L11 asks L9 at line 006 to confirm that they have finished. After a 1.0 second silence at line 007, during which L9 considers L11's question, L9 confirms in a smiley voice at line 011 that they have indeed finished. After another pause of 0.3 second at line 012, L11 and L9 laugh in close alignment at lines 013–021.

These verbal behaviors are observable traces of the conversational work that L9 and L11 do to accomplish a switch from one speech exchange system to another. By 'work,' I mean how L9 and L11 resolve the sequential ambiguity that is involved in transitioning from a licit to an illicit form of talk. This sequential ambiguity is also possibly manifested in the striking lack of mutual eye gaze between L9 and L11 during Extract 1. L11 first shifts his gaze from T to L9 at line 005 as T is walking to the front of the class. L11's gaze remains fixed on L9 through line 010, when he averts his gaze. L11's gaze does not return to L9 during the rest of this extract. Similarly, L9 first makes eye contact with L11 and then immediately averts his gaze again at line 015, just as L11 tilts his head back at line 017. L9 then laughs. Meanwhile, L9's gaze returns to L11, momentarily falls away and then briefly returns to L11 at the end of line 018. L9's gaze remains focused on L11 at the beginning of line 020 and then falls away again as L11 turns a page of his handout at line 021.

The fact that L9 and L11 are in the process of switching from teacher-directed classroom talk to ordinary conversation in Extract 1 does not by itself prove that the following talk is going to be off-task. The whole point of teacher-sanctioned small group work is to relax the norms of institutional talk so that learners may explore a teacher-licensed topic more freely than they could during lock step work. Furthermore, up to this moment, a new topic has yet to be suggested by either L9 or L11. Extracts 2 and 3 show how they negotiate the introduction of an off-task topic.

Extract 2

```
029 L9:                              [X _____ , , , , , , , , , , , , ,
030 L9:     this writer has a ra[ther- [com- pli-] this is ┌ co- ┐ writer has a
031 L11:                         [X _____     ┌┘      └┐
032 L11:                         [I slept five ho-]      └ huh ┘
033 L9:     [X _____
034 L9:     [complicated uh,
035 L11:     _____   [ ... ....................................................
036 L11:    yea:h ┌ (h) ┐  [((L11 looks left, lifts his left hand to his mouth
037 L11:          │     │   , , , , , , , , , , ,
038            │     │   and looks down))
039 L9:          └ h ┘    heh heh ˙hhh
040 L11:    (what'd I say.)
041        (1.0) ((L9 scratches his forehead with his right hand.
042        Simultaneously, L11 drops his hand back to his lap.
```

```
043          As L11's hand reaches his lap, he begins his turn at line 045))
044 L11:     [ . . . . . X _____ [ , , , , , , , , , , , , , , , , , , ,
045 L11:     [I'm so tired I slept ┌ five hours [((L11 looks at his watch))
046 L11:     , , , , , , , , , , , , , , , , |, , , , , , , , , , , , , , , , , , , , , , , , , , , , ,
047 L11:     that night         │    ((L11 drops his hand back to his lap))
048 L9:              . . . . . . . . └ X_____
049          (0.6 )
050 L9:      _____
051 L9:      a:::h. ((L9 uses a tone of mock sympathy))
```

At lines 030 and 034 of Extract 2, L9 tries to shift the talk back to the official topic of discussion, but L11 overlaps at line 032 by saying that he slept five hours. L9 continues with his turn-in-progress, but several trouble-relevant perturbations occur in L9's and L11's turns at talk. There are three cut offs in L9's turn at line 030, and he never finishes his turn (034). Similarly, both the first overlap in L11's turn at line 032 that causes him to cut off his own announcement and the second (the cut-off laughter) also provide evidence of trouble.

At lines 036 and 039, L11 and L9 both acknowledge a misalignment in topic orientation (notice too how at this moment L11 looks away from L9 at lines 035, 036, 037 and 038, and also lifts his hand to his mouth at line 036). At line 040, L11 attempts to regroup, but the silence at line 041, the head scratching gesture by L9, and L11's hand movements all suggest that the problem of what to talk about next has not yet been resolved. A possible resolution is offered by L11 at line 045, who reinstates his previous off-task topic nomination that he only slept five hours that night, this time, without overlap by L9. After a short pause at line 049, L9 aligns at line 051 with L11's off-task topic nomination by expressing mock sympathy.

Following another 25 lines of transcript in which L9 and L11 continue to align topically with each other by talking about how tired they *both* are, L11 nominates the second, main topic that he has probably been trying to introduce into the talk all along: at line 81 he invites L9 to a party in his dormitory.

Extract 3

```
076          (1.0)
077 L11:     >there are so many things,- <
078          ┌ ((L11 touches L9 lightly with his left hand
079          │   and leans toward L9))
080 L11:     │ [X_____
081 L11:     └ [ hh d'you want to join a party-? tonight?
082 L9:        [X_____
```

```
083 L11:        we have a party in sherman hall.
084 L11:        _____
085         ┌ (0.3)   ((L11 raises his left hand in a motion
086         │  indicating direction))
087 L11:    │   _____
088 L11:    └ in our do:rm. ((L11 drops his hand back to his lap))
089 L9:         _____
090 L11:        ____
091             (0.3)
092 L11:        _____
093 L9:         uh huh,
                ...
```

By initiating this invitation topic, L11 casts himself as an inviter and L9
as an invitee, identities topically and sequentially incompatible with
the predetermined role of learner. It is in this *technical* sense that this
interaction is constituted as off-task talk.

Some observable problems in maintaining off-task topic talk in the face of co-occurring on-task talk in the wider classroom

Teachers may interrupt or close down small group work (be this on- or
off-task) whenever they choose. But, as I now show, a special problem
that L9 and L11 face is that their invitation talk does not go smoothly.
Consequently, they have to repair potential damage to their social
relationship as T makes simultaneous claims on the attention of class
members, including L9 and L11.

While L9 and L11 pay close attention to each other's talk in Extract 3
(their eye gazes are firmly on each other at lines 080, 082, 084, 087,
089, 090 and 092), L9 does not accept the invitation immediately after
L11's cut off at line 081.[3] Furthermore, L9 does not respond at all at line
085. This slot becomes a 0.3 second intra-turn pause that is ended by
L11's continuation at line 088. At line 091, there is another 0.3 second
pause. Although this time L9 self-selects as next speaker at line 093, he
does so via a minimal passing turn, which puts L11 in the sequential
position of having to provide more information about the party in next
turn.

The interaction proceeds for another 106 lines of transcript (not
reproduced here), but by line 209 in Extract 4, L11's attempt to invite
L9 to a party has run into serious trouble (see also Extract 5). L9 bluntly
turns down L11's invitation by saying that the party venue is a bad

place for a party (notice also that L9 concurrently averts his gaze at line 208, as does L11 at line 211).

Extract 4

```
199 L9:      [where is it held, (0.3) what pa- what part of (0.2) the hall.
200          (0.3)
201 L11:     _____
202 L11:     [it's in the lobby.]
203          [((L11 rotates with left hand and simultaneously nods his head))]
204 L9:      _____
205 L9:      in the lobby.
206 L11:     _____
207 L11:     yeah=
208 L9:          [ , , , ,
209 L9:      = >°yeah.=it's bad.° <
210 L11:     _____
211 L11:     ≈ , , , , , , , , , , , , , ≈
212 T:      ≈{OK. (0.3) WHERE-≈ ≈THERE IS A:: UH...
213 L11:                           ≈ ((L11 turns back to looks at T in Position 3,
214                                 touches his microphone and brings his gaze back
215                                 down to his chest))
216 L9:      [X_____
217 L9:    ┌ [I might (0.2) go there but uh (1.0) ((During the silence, L9 glances
218       │                              toward T briefly and then looks
219       │                              back at L11. In the meantime, L11
220       │                              brings his hand back down
221       │                              to his lap.))
222 L11:   └ X_____
223 L9:      _____
224 L9:      [I have a busy]
225 L11:     _____
226 L11:     [° (yeah there is)°]
227 L9:      _____
228 L9:      week ...
```

L11 would normally deal with this dispreferred response in next turn. However, T fortuitously happens to raise her voice as she talks with Group 5 at line 212, which causes L11 to briefly look at T at lines 213–15.

At line 217 of Extract 5, L9 realizes that his declination of L11's invitation is problematic, so he tries to retrieve the situation by saying that he is busy (lines 217–34 and 239). L11 responds to this excuse with an invitation to a second party at lines 226 and 237–51. This provokes mutual laughter tokens at lines 243, 249, 253 and 255, the use of smiley voice by L9 at lines 257 and 263 and by L11 at lines 260, and the fanning motion by L9 at lines 244–56. This embodied action visually says: 'come on, give-me-a-break'. Furthermore, both participants look intently at each other for most of the interaction between lines 236–75. Indeed, when L11 elaborates on the circumstances of this second invitation at lines 269–75, L9 responds with a sympathetic nod at line 273. Thus, the social relationship between L9 and L11 seems well on the way to being repaired. Furthermore, because of the fortuitous interruption by T at line 212, this process has been initiated by L9 rather than by L11.

Extract 5

```
212 T:      ≈[OK. (0.3) WHERE-≈ ≈THERE IS A:: UH...
213 L11:              ≈ ((L11 turns back to looks at T in Position 3,
214                       touches his microphone and brings his gaze back
215                       down to his chest))
216 L9:      [X_____
217 L9:    ┌ [I might (0.2) go there but uh (1.0) ((During the silence, L9 glance
218        │                                      toward T briefly and then looks
219        │                                      back at L11.  In the meantime, L11
220        │                                      brings his hand back down
221        │                                      to his lap.))
222 L11:   └ X_____
223 L9:      _____
224 L9:      [I have a busy]
225 L11:     _____
226 L11:     [°(yeah there is)°]
227 L9:      _____
228 L9:      week (0.3) big project for next week=
229 L11:     ,,,,,
230 L11:     =a:oh. [ (0.3) ]
231                [((L11 leans forward))]
232 L11:   ˙hhh=
233 L9:      _____
234 L9:      =monday 'ti:l.
235            (0.3)
236 L11:     ...   [X_____
237 L11:     yeah > [I have a pa┌rty to  mo̲:rrow ┐ <
238 L9:      _____   │               │
239 L9:                         └ °(wednesday)° ┘
240 L11:     _____
241 L11:     ((L11 quickly rotates his left hand.))=
242 L9:
243 L9:                          =hhhhh
244          ((L9 leans back. He is holding a hand out in his right hand,
245          which he waves four times at L11 in a fanning motion throughout lines 239–56.
246          L11 turns head away to his left after L9's first fanning motion
247          and then returns his gaze to L9 at the end of the second fanning motion))
248 L9:      _____
249 L9:      [HUHHH]
250 L11:     _____
251 L11:     [if↓you want↑]
252 L9:      _____
253 L9       HUHhh °huhh.°=
```

```
254 L11:      _____  ... ͵ ͵ ͵
255 L11:      =↑GHU::GH huh huh ↓(0.6) ↑ghu::h
256 L9:       _____
257 L9:       hhh. (0.3) ((L9 stops his fanning motion.)) ☺ to↑morrow ↓ ☺
258           (0.3)
259 L11:      [X_____ ]
260 L11:      [☺ yeah.☺]
261           (0.3) ((L9 nods twice))
262 L9:       _____
263 L9:       ☺danie┌lle is right. ┐☺
264 L11:      _____┤           ├ ͵ ͵ ͵ ͵ ͵
265 L11:          ☺└ the reason-┘ >no no< the reason an u::h (↑/prastic/↓)
266           party.☺
267           (0.6)
268 L11:      [X_____  ͵ ͵ ͵
269 L11:      [a girl invited me and-(0.6) ((L11 raises his left hand briefly.))
270 L11:                    [X_____
271           and- (0.2) said- [bring your↑friends with you:: ↓ so ˙h
272 L9:       _____
273 L9:       ((L9 nods))
274 L11:      _____
275 L11:      ≈if you [vant].≈
```

However, L9 has not yet explicitly accepted this second invitation. Before L9 and L11 can close this invitation topic, T fortuitously raises her voice as she assesses the adequacy of an answer provided by L14 within the ongoing T/Group 5 discussion (see line 276 of Extract 6), overlapping the last part of L11's turn at line 275. After a 0.3 second pause at line 277, T again fortuitously overlaps L11's turn with another interruption at line 280 as she looks up and her gaze falls on Group 1. Meanwhile, as a result of this interruption, L11 seems to have difficulty remembering where the second party is to be held (see the cut-off after the word 'I' and the lengthening of the word 'in:' at line 279, and L11's thinking gesture at lines 282–3). L11 (and probably L9 also) then visually orient to T's question at lines 285–7. For the next 58 lines, L11 and L9 visually focus on, and listen to, the class-oriented talk between L1 and T, temporarily abandoning their off-task invitation talk.

Extract 6

```
275 L11:      ≈if you [vant].≈
276 T:        {≈OK YOU'RE≈CLOSE
277           (0.3)
278 L11:      _____
279 L11:      ≈I- it's in:≈
280 T:        ≈u::H     ≈ LET'S SEE. ((T raises her head and looks toward Group 1))
281           (.- - [- - - -)]
```

```
282 L11:      [((L11 leans forward and puts his head in his left hand in a thinking
283             gesture]))
284 T:        [X_____
285 T:        U::HM (0.6) SANTIAGO ((L11, L6 and L1 turn to look at T. L9 probably
286                              looks forward but is hidden by L6. L11 begins to
287                              look toward L6 in front of him))
288 L6        [X
289 L6:       [yes
290 T         [... X____
291 T:        [OR FELIPE ((L11 briefly returns his gaze toward T as she
292           re-allocates next turn to L1. L1 turns his gaze away from T
293           and turns back to face front))
294 T         _____
295 T:        ˙H WHY: D'YOU THINK GERMAN.
                            .

349 L11:      THAT'S HISTO::RICAL FA:::CTOR.
350           (- - -)   ((L9 turns his gaze toward T as L11 makes a forward motion
351                       with his hand))
352 L11:      _____
353 L11:      THAT'S- THAT'S- ˙HHH THE BO::RDERS BETWEEN FF FRANCE
354 L11:      _____
355 L11:      AND /T/GE::RMANY? (0.3) WERE ALWAYS SHIFTING YEA::H, (0.3)
356 L11:      _____
357 L11:      ONE TIME TO THE- TO THE LE::FT? ONE TIME TO THE RIGHT?
358 T:        _____
359 T:        ((T nods))
360 L11:      _____
361 L11:      ˙HHHH ((L11 brings his left hand up to his chin in a thinking gesture.))
362           (- -[- - - - - - - -)]
363 L11:          [, , , , , , , ,]
364 L11:          [((L11 makes a punctuating gesture with his left hand and then
365               brings it down to his lap.))]
366 T:        _____
367 T:        YEAH.
368 L11:      °THE SAME WITH POLAND.°
```

At lines 349–68, L11 contributes his own information to the whole-class discussion. However, the invitation topic remains unfinished business between L9 and L11. As we will see shortly, this is an issue to which both L9 and L11 attend. However, before they can do this, T asks the whole class at line 375 of Extract 7 whether it has finished, and directs the same question of L9 and L11 at line 383. L11 responds that he has finished.

Extract 7

```
375 T:        °GOOD° (0.3) OK! (0.3) [ARE WE ↑FINISHED,]
376                                 [((T raises palm slightly off her thigh))]
377           (1.6 )
378 L5:       °huh no way ˙hh ok (0.3) that°
379           (- - - - - -)[
```

```
380 L11:              [X ((T looks up momentarily, catches T's eye and
381                        immediately looks down again, touching his nose
382                        with the back of his left hand as he does so))
383 T:      ((to Group 3)) are you almost finished,
384 L9:     [X_____ ,,,,,,,,,,,,,,,,,,,,,,,,,,,,,,,,,,,, ]
385 L11:    [X_____ ,,,,,,,,,,,,,,,,,,,,,,,,,,,,,,,,,,, ]
386         [(- - - - -) ((L11 brings his left hand down to his lap))]
387 L11:    °yeah.°[hhh ((sigh))
```

As I suggested earlier, this type of teacher question potentially functions
as a transition to another activity. This is observable in lines 399 and
405 of Extract 8 and lines 417–18 of Extract 9, where T's class
announcement frames the next pedagogical activity. Perhaps anticipating
this eventuality, L9 tells L11 in a low voice at line 390 of Extract 8 that
he still has 'my telephone number'. The use of the pronoun 'my' at this
point in the talk seems to be an error that is induced under the communicative stress of trying to finish the invitation talk. At line 404, L9
repairs this turn, saying 'I still have your number'.

Extract 8

```
389 L9:     _____
390 L9:     [°first make clear⌈ ≈I still have- my number so.°≈ ⌉((L9 cocks his
391                           |                                |  head left))
392 L11:    [X_____|_____|  ]
393 T:               ⌊ {≈°are you (   ) finished,°    ≈⌋((T addresses
394                                                         Group 5))
395 L13:                      {yeah
396         (0.6) ((timed from L9's turn at line 379))
397 L11:    _____
398 L11:    ≈°yeah°≈
399 T:      {≈YEAH OK≈ ˙H ⌈ ≈WHAT I WANT TO DO (0.3) ≈
400                       |  ≈((L11 moves his left arm to his left side ≈))
401         (- - -)       |  ((pause is timed from L11's turn at line 394))
402 L11:    _____|
403 L9:                   | _____ [((L9 nods slightly))] _____
404 L9:               ⌊ ≈ ° I [still have your number ] so- uh°≈
405 T:      [IS FORM GROUPS=
```

At lines 412 and 416 of Extract 9, L11 also orients to the fact that he
and L9 are running out of time to bring their covert invitation talk
to a more or less satisfactory close (see the rush through and the low
volume of L11's response). Furthermore, even though L9 nods at line
413 in response to L11's request for L9 to call, L9 is simultaneously

gazing at T. Thus, the matter of whether L9 has accepted L11's invitation is unresolved and it is left to L9 to resolve this after class is over.

Extract 9

404 L9:	≈ ° I [still have your number] so- uh°≈
405 T:	⌐ [IS FORM GROUPS ≈ ((L11 makes a downward chopping ≈ ⌐
406 L9:	[X___._____ movement with his left hand as he begins his turn.
407	at line 411. He moves his hand slightly closer to L9
408	to coincide with 'you' as he says 'I can
409	say you' and then withdraws it back to his lap.))
410 L11:	[X_____ , , .
411 L11:	[X ___((L11's eye gaze is now directed at L9)) _____
412 L11:	≈[° you can **call** me and then [I can say you] the the address
413	[((L9 nods 4 times] but continues to look
414	at T throughout the rest of the extract))
415 L11:	_____
416 L11:	**of the party tomorrow.°**
417 T:	≈(0.3) **I'D LIKE TO SEPARATE YOU NO:W** (0.3) ≈ ⌐
	INTO GROUPS I DON'T-
418	└ (0.9) <u>CA:RE</u> ... ≈ ⌐

Implications for CA-for SLA

This chapter has shown that off-task talk occurred when T closed a previous topic and tried to encourage students to move on to another topic. However, because she did not frame the next topic, an interactional gap opened up, which L11 exploited to initiate off-task talk. It has also shown that L9 and L11 had to *achieve* this shift to another topic and to another speech exchange system. Finally, this analysis has shown that off-task talk is particularly vulnerable to interruptions from T in the wider classroom.

This analysis also suggests that the construction of member-relevant identities is more complicated than Firth and Wagner (1997) and their critics (see Long 1997, 1998, and Gass 1998) allow. The identities that L11 and L9 construct during the off-task invitation talk are those of inviter and invitee respectively. These identities are what constitute this interaction as off-task. But L9 and L11 also monitor T's talk in the larger classroom and construct their roles as inviter/invitee on the one hand and as learners on the other with considerable skill. The most interesting example of how the learners achieve a 'skilful schizophrenia' occurs in

Extract 9. As L9 listens to T's final announcement and simultaneously nods in acknowledgement of L11's invitation talk, he displays a concurrent orientation to the norms of ordinary conversation and institutional talk.

Why is this empirical demonstration of skilful schizophrenia important in SLA terms? Researchers in 'mainstream' SLA studies have long assumed that SLA is a psycholinguistic discipline. So, for example, the point of doing research on the structure of repair in non-native/ non-native conversation (see Varonis and Gass 1985) is to show that repair is a *psycholinguistically* important catalyst for SLA. *Sociolinguistic* approaches to SLA (which includes CA-for-SLA) have come under increasing pressure to demonstrate how and why an understanding of social structure *per se* illuminates SLA processes (see Eckman 1994; Gass 1998; Kasper 1997; Long 1997, 1998).

CA-for-SLA takes psycholinguistically interesting extracts of S/FL learners' talk – such as repair[4] – and re-interprets these actions as micro moments of socially distributed cognition (Markee 2000; Schegloff 1991). Since ordinary conversation and institutional talk offer different structural opportunities for repair, different contexts of talk should also provide different opportunities for language learning (Markee 2000; Tarone and Liu 1995). However, the data analysed in this chapter complicate this hypothesis by showing that learner/inviters and learner/invitees (or whatever combinations of identities are relevant to a particular piece of talk) are capable of orienting to multiple speech exchange systems and agendas at the same time. Thus, while we need to have empirical research that investigates how SLA works in ordinary conversation (Liddicoat 1997; Kasper 2002) and in institutional contexts (Markee 2000), we also ultimately need to disentangle how SLA works in hybrid contexts of talk, whose behavioural and psycholinguistic complexities are only just beginning to emerge.

Implications for teacher education and training

Curriculum specialists, teacher educators, teacher trainers, materials writers and teachers (whether experienced or neophyte) are all natural consumers (and, indeed, potential producers) of CA-for-SLA research (see Packett this volume). Whereas experimental research usually hides interactional data behind statistical data, CA preserves the participants' voices and actions as the principal object of enquiry. CA should therefore have an inherent appeal for second language teaching practitioners, who all too often have little use for SLA classroom research (Markee 1997).

The present chapter has illustrated 'what really happened' in one instance of small group work. An obvious lesson to be drawn from these off-task data is that teachers who use small group work should have reserve tasks up their sleeve in order to keep those students who finish earlier than others gainfully employed with on-task work. On the other hand, if the goal of task-based instruction is to engage learners in meaning-focused talk, does it matter whether what they actually talk about is on- or off-task?

From an SLA perspective, it probably does not. Indeed, off-task interaction may be just as valuable as on-task interaction, because off-task interaction may be closer to learners' 'real-life' interactional needs than on-task interaction. In addition, off-task data, because they are so naturalistic, may also provide language testers with valuable insights into learners' levels of interactional competence that would be difficult to obtain from more formal assessment instruments (Jacoby and McNamara 1999).

But from the perspective of university level, content-based instruction, it is surely important to stretch learners with challenging topics that go beyond the intellectually vacuous language games that are the habitual fare of task-based instruction. More specifically, the Auschwitz data analysed in Markee (2000) demonstrate that the learner in that collection was unable to understand why the phenomenon of Auschwitz and other concentration camps in recent German history might be used as an argument against German reunification because she knew nothing about the Holocaust. Quite apart from the fact that topic familiarity is thought to be a factor that affects learners' ability to get comprehensible input in a S/FL (Gass and Varonis 1984), it is surely crucial for university students to have a reasonable understanding of issues of such immense human importance. Being on-task matters, and the use of CA-for-SLA techniques is a resource that can help language teaching professionals understand what happens in their classes, how it happens, and why.

Notes

1 I use the plural 'classroom talks' because classroom talk is not a monolithic phenomenon, but consists of a nexus of interrelated speech exchange systems, some of whose turn-taking practices are relatively pre-allocated, while others are relatively more locally managed.

2 More specifically, irrespective of whether talk is mediated through an L1 or an L2, turn size, content and type are all free to vary in ordinary conversation, as is turn-taking: thus, who speaks to whom, when, and about what is not pre-determined, and there is a preference for a minimization of turn

length (Sacks *et al.* 1974). Furthermore, ordinary conversation is characterized by a preference for self-initiated, self-completed repair (Schegloff *et al.* 1977).

3 This would be the preferred response to an invitation (Davidson 1984).
4 For recent work on the function of repair in SLA, see Doughty and Varela (1998); Gass (1997); Gass *et al.* (1998); Long (1996); Long, Inagaki and Ortega (1998); Lyster (1998); Lyster and Ranta (1997); Mackey and Philp (1998); Nicholas *et al.* (2001); Oliver (1995, 1998, 2000).

13
Vowel-marking as an Interactional Resource in Japanese Novice ESL Conversation

Donald Carroll

Introduction

Novice Japanese speakers of English as a foreign language are often stereotyped, fairly or unfairly, as speaking in what might be described as *kana-speak*, that is, English spoken as if written in the Japanese hiragana/katakana syllabary.[1] In fact, many EFL texts designed for the Japanese market provide katakana transliterations for English words and phrases. For example, 'What is that thing?' might be rendered as 'What-o iz-u zat-o shing-u?' One specific feature of this style of speech, that of adding vowels to word-final consonants, will be referred to in this paper as *vowel-marking*. Extract 1 below contains eight instances of vowel-marking.

Extract 1

```
01 →  A:  um mm but-o but-o mm (0.59) good-o good-o
02 →      (0.45) good-o[:::
03    S:              [experien[ce?
04    A:                       [yes [experience
05    K:                            [huh huh huh
06 →  S:  good-u chance?
07 →  A:  ye:s [good-u] good-o
08    S:       [yea::h ]
```

For the most part, EFL teachers have treated this as a 'pronunciation problem,' resulting from 'negative transfer' from Japanese. In their efforts to deal with this problem, teachers have devised drills, mocked their students' speech, and generally bemoaned the unwilling tongue and ear of Japanese students. It has also been suggested that some students consciously adopt this style of speech in order to avoid a perceived social stigma attached to speaking English 'too well'. Anecdotally, EFL teachers have complained that the same student who speaks 'perfectly' outside of class will lard his or her speech with vowel-markings when speaking in front of peers in English class. Joan Smith (personal communication) of the University of Canterbury comments:

> I teach English part-time to visiting Japanese students, and am sometimes frustrated by the fact that students prove repeatedly that they can pronounce words without the vowels, they just don't. I wondered if it might be a dual identity marker (given that all the students in my classes are Japanese), something like Myers-Scotton's unmarked Code-switching where the two languages index dual identities. Something along the lines of 'even though I am speaking English, I am still Japanese'.

My conversational data, however, paint a more intriguing picture. I will argue that vowel-marking, while it may have its roots in L1 phonological patterns, is not oriented to by these novice L2 speakers as a pronunciation problem but employed as a situated resource for organizing aspects of their interaction. The most frequent use of vowel-marking occurs within the conversational phenomenon of *forward-oriented repair* (Schegloff 1979) also known as *word search* (Goodwin and Goodwin 1986; Lerner 1996; Brouwer 1998; Hayashi 2000). Vowel-marking also appears to be implicated in the construction of multi-TCU 'projects' and the management of overlap resolution.

The data

The database for this chapter consists of a set of seven face-to-face English conversations video-recorded in the fall of 1999, of approximately 30 minutes, with most examples being drawn from the group 6 conversation. Participants were, at the time of the recording, second-year English Department students at Shikoku Gakuin University in Japan, working at the approximate level of advanced beginners (TOEIC scores in the low to mid 200s). In order to minimize the 'doing being a guinea pig' effect commented on by Wagner (1998) participants selected their own groupings of three and most elected to be with friends or at least long-time classmates. Each group was allowed several opportunities over several weeks to 'just talk' before the recordings were made in a quiet area close to the classroom which is commonly used by students.[2]

Initial observations

One immediate observation is that a rough phonological patterning exists in terms of which vowel is attached to which final sound (see Table 13.1). For example, final /m/ is exclusively followed by /-u/ and never /-o/ or /-i/ despite the fact that 'mo' and 'mi' both exist in the katakana syllabary. Similarly, final velar consonants /k/ and /g/ are always paired with /-u/ rather than /-o/. It is also apparent that /t/ and /d/ may be marked with either /-o/ or /-u/.

A more relevant observation to the concerns of this chapter is that if vowel-marking were exclusively a matter of L1 phonological interference,

Table 13.1 Sample of vowel-marked words in the data

Vowel-marking with /-o/	Vowel-marking with /-u/	Vowel-marking with /-i/
but-o	but-u	stage-i
eat(0.39)-o	eat-u	
what-o	what-u	
wet-o	last-u	
absent-o	ate-u	
hot-o	and-u	
best-o	cold-u	
and-o	food-u	
cold-o	boyfriend-u	
food-o	like-u	
second-o	dark-u	
stand-o	speak-u	
made-o	morning-u	
	raining-u	
	climbing-u	
	same-u	
	time-u	
	school-u	
	have-u	
	staff-u	
	cheap-u	
	soup-u	
	is-u	
	Japanese-u	

one would expect it to occur regularly throughout the data – at least for the same speaker. But this is not the case. Instances can be found in the data where the same speaker uses a given word with vowel-marking on one occasion and without vowel-marking on an immediately subsequent usage as in Extract 2 below.

Extract 2

```
01      S: .hh I::[y
02  →   A:        [an' (0.73) other staff-u
03      K: mm
04         (1.00)
05         a-huh
06         (0.95)
07      A: cor-u   (("call"))
08         (1.17)
09      S: [un:  ]
10  →   A: [other] staff call-u[:
11      S:                      [you?
```

In line 2, speaker A vowel-marks her production of 'staff' and this is followed by K's minimal continuer 'mm' (Schegloff 1982; Gardner 1997). After this minimal continuer, a longish silence emerges before K offers an additional, more substantial, continuer ('a-huh'). Then, in line 10, speaker A recycles her prior TCU beginning (Schegloff 1987), this time uttering the word 'staff' without vowel-marking. Such variation within the talk of a single speaker should strike observers as suspicious to say the least. It certainly contradicts the L1 interference argument; this is clearly not just a pronunciation problem.

A third initial observation is that a large number of the instances of vowel-marking in the data were found to occur prior to an intra-turn pause. Below are a few isolated turns illustrating this:

and ah don't like-u (0.16) rain
I: I(h): huh (h)rike-u (0.14) brue sky
uh-i I:-e-, (0.40) I ate-u (0.34) doria,
oldest child-u is-u (0.21) um:: twenty,

Together these initial observations, particularly the occurrence of intra-speaker variation and the fact that vowel-marking regularly prefaces

silence, suggest that something more than just L1 phonological interference underlies the phenomenon of conversational vowel-marking.

Vowel-marking as a micro-practice in forward repair

The examples above involving vowel-marking look suspiciously like the
phenomenon Schegloff (1979) termed *forward-oriented repair* (also widely
known as *word search*). In contrast to backwards-oriented repair which is
initiated, often via cut-offs, in order to carry out repair on some already
produced element of the turn-so-far, forward-oriented repair targets
repairables that 'loom on the horizon' in the not-yet-produced portion of
the turn. As might be imagined, forward repair is an extremely common
phenomenon in novice-to-novice L2 talk-in-interaction.

In native speaker talk forward repair is quite commonly heralded by
'production hitches'. Sound stretches, in particular, are strongly associated with *possible* incipient word search and can act as repair initiators
(Schegloff *et al.* 1977; Schegloff 1979). Schegloff (1984: 270) asserts that:

> As some item enters the 'projection space,' as it 'comes into play,' as
> it first becomes a specifically planned-for item, if it is sensed or rec-
> ognized by speaker as a possible trouble-source (e.g., *the exact word is
> not available* [this author's emphasis], a difficult sound pattern is
> involved, how to say it is unclear, etc.), then a hitch appears in what-
> ever is being produced – whatever is in the process of being said – *at
> the moment*. (By momentarily delaying the point at which the pos-
> sible trouble-source is to be said, the possibility is enhanced that the
> trouble will be solved before that point arrives. Also notice is given
> interactionally of possible trouble ahead.)

The first sign of possible trouble in each of the examples below (from
a collection of native speaker word searches) is, in fact, a sound stretch.
Notice the stretches on *i:n, Bradley:*, and *ha:d*.

turned in my term paper i:n h-uh:: (0.4) .tch Psychology

thet he thought Mister Bradley: (.) was uhm (1.2) .tch uh::m (0.5)
condoning hhhhh .hhhh (0.3) uh thin:gs

He ha:d u:m (1.0) Whuh wuz iht. (0.3) Oh. He had some paint: (.)
da:mage.on iz car.

In my data, sound stretches alone are sometimes used to both initiate as well as manage repair once initiated. In the first example below (Extract 3), taken from the group 6 data, speaker S employs an *opportunistic stretch* on an existent word-final vowel (the /u/ in 'to:::') to both initiate and sustain the search until she is able to produce the *sought-for-item*. In the second example (Extract 4), speaker A also employs a stretch on a word-final vowel and then maintains the vowel for more than a full second, but is still unable to produce a repair resolution and the elongated vowel ends up fading into silence.

Extract 3

```
01    S:  I wen' to::: Bedorow's university?
02         (0.13)
03    K:  ohn yeah good
```

Extract 4

```
01  →  A:  ye::::s:: oh yes Iy::: (0.16) I wen' to:::::::::
02         (0.59)
03    A:  kenya:= ((breathy))
04    K:  =oh.
05    A:  d:is summa:(hh) ((release of /d/ is held))
```

Word-final vowels, more common in Japanese than English, ideally provide for the opportunistic use of a stretch in initiating and managing the activity of forward repair. In cases where no word-final vowel is available for an opportunistic stretch, these speakers simply provide their own vowel as a means of initiating forward repair. Below are just a few of the many instances in my data where vowel-marking initiates forward repair, i.e., where it is the first indication of delayed turn progressivity (Lerner 1996). Note that the vowel-marking in these examples is not preceded by any other sound stretch.

Extract 5

```
01  →  S:  yeah they- (0.14) do they like-u (0.46) eating?
02         (0.37)
03    A:  ye[: : : : : : : : : : ][s ye:s ye:s    ][oh you ][too huh =
04    K:     [uh huh huh][.hhh me too][heh heh]
05    S:                              [heh heh][you too =
```

Extract 6

```
01 → S:  does your (0.52) do your father have-u (0.44) your shop?
02        (0.36)
03    K:  [oh >yeah][yeah yeah yeah<]
04    S:  [eh       ][ own shop      ]
05        (0.08)
```

Extract 7

```
01 → A:  small smalle[r ch]ild is-u (0.46) °°u::nto ne°°(0.50) ah-=
02    S:             [un ]
03        =BABY BABY
04    K:  [BABY!]
05    S:  [BABY [o::::h::]
```

Extract 8

```
01 → K:  =un (0.38) I ate-u: (0.30) eto japanese food-u
02        (1.04)
03    A:  hohn
04    S:  °°what°°,
```

In each of these instances, the vowel-marking is followed by an intra-turn pause. In Extracts 5 and 6 the silence, and with it the search, is brought to conclusion when the initiating speaker provides a resolution. More commonly, however, a pause leads to further micro-practices also associated with forward repair such as the use of *pre-pausal tokens*, i.e. so-called 'thinking noises', like *um, uh, ah* or the Japanese *eto* and *eto ne*.[3] Vowel-marking, however, does not invariably lead to pauses. In the examples below, the vowel-marking is followed immediately by either the *sought-for-item*, as in 'its-u: raining', 'what-o interesting-u,' and 'schoo:l-u festival,' or by some intermediary item, as in 'is-u very...'

K: its-u: raining tod[ay:::]

A: what-o what-o interesting-u (0.43) e:to schoo:l-u festival

A: = [u:h] u:h toda:y is-u very COLD-o

Vowel-marking, in delaying the production of some *next-item-due*, serves to buy the speaker initiating the repair a bit more time to achieve self-repair, which according to Schegloff *et al.* (1977) is the preferred outcome and, in the case of forward repair/word search, amounts to self-resolution. Furthermore, vowel-marking alerts co-participants to the fact that a search is underway and to their possible role in resolving it as in Extracts 9 and 10 below where S provides collaborative completions to A's incomplete and vowel-marked turns.

Extract 9

```
01    A: other staff call-u[:
02  → S:              [you?
```

Extract 10

```
01    A: =u:h u:h toda:y is-u very COLD-o
02       (0.16)
03    S: yeah[::]
04    A:    [so]:: I absent-o[::            [ah huh
05    S:               [huh huh huh .hhh [HUH hum
06    A: e:to:: °°e:to:: °° morning-u:[::    ]
07  → S:                     [second] class?
```

Note that vowel-marking itself can be stretched. In Extract 11 below, speaker A tacks on the vowel-marking/–u/ to buy herself added time but, when a resolution still does not present itself, she extends the production of the vowel-marking for a full 1.26 seconds before finally falling silent.

Extract 11

```
01  → A: un:to (0.38) other staff-u:::::::::((-u lasts 1.26 sec.))
02       (0.50) a::nto(h) ca(h)al-u ..hhh call-u s- >eto< other =
03       = staff-u stand-o stage-i
```

From the examples provided thus far, it should be apparent that these (Japanese) novice speakers of English employ and orient to vowel-marking as a situated resource which, depending on the exigencies of the interaction, may be employed *or not*, stretched *or not*, and followed by a pause *or not*. This phenomenon *does not* appear to be a mere pronunciation problem.

One further clue to the interactional origins of vowel-marking comes from the observation that Japanese speakers employ *u::* as a 'stand-alone' object similar to *uh* in word search environments as seen in the follow-ing example:

Extract 12

01 → Kooji: ..hh maa sonna::: are   ga:::: (1.5) u:::::
              well such   that one SB   uh
02   meedo san ga iru yoona: ie ya nai kara
         maid TL   SB exist like family CP not because

[Hayashi, 2000:309]

Vowel-marking and gaze aversion

So far, this discussion of vowel-marking has relied entirely on the verbal/vocal dimension of the interaction. The next section will examine in fine-detail several specific instances of vowel-marking and how they are placed relative to any attendant physical actions. In Extract 13, the participants are discussing the weather and their reactions to it. The following discussion is centred on S's pronunciation of 'like' at three points in this extract, in lines 9, 14, and 18 (the instance in line 20 will be discussed later). In line 9, speaker S utters 'like' without an attendant vowel (although there is marginal breathiness) demonstrating that she is capable of uttering the word without tagging on a terminal vowel; this is also demonstrated at other points in the talk where S does not vowel-mark 'like,' for example:

S: I like to live in (.) Spain.

Yet in the exemplars in lines 14 and 18 speaker S *does* vowel-mark her production ('like-u'). Once again we see an example of 'suspicious' intra-speaker variation. This section of the analysis will focus on what speaker S is doing visually as the talk unfolds.

Extract 13

01   ˈS: are you:: fi:ne today?
02   (0.21)
03   K: yes::
04   S: yea(h)huh [oh go-]
05   A: [oh do] do you: fine?
06   (0.49)

```
07   A: today?
08      (0.42)
09 → S: yeah↑ (0.22) but (0.49) but I don't like(h) raining(-u),
10      (0.14)
11   K: [um::::]
12   A: [a::h:: ] very dark-u
13      (0.14)
14 → S: da- yeah [I::a I      ] I like-u
15   A:          [un un un]
16   K:          [a::h::    ]
17      (1.19)
18 → S: I:  I(h): huh (h)rike-u (0.14) brue sky
19   A: o::h:: [yes yes [yes yes ]me too [me too
20 → S:        [u::n::  [I like-u]       [fine day
21      (0.18)
22   A: hm-hm-[hm-hm
23   S:       [yeah
24      (0.50)
```

The sequence in which these instances of 'like' are produced starts
with S's type-conforming response (Sacks 1987; Raymond 2000) to
A's question about S's health in lines 5 and 7. However, the pitch rise
on S's initial response ('yeah↑') indicates some discomfort with this
response and, thereby, adumbrates further talk (Raymond 2000).
That S's co-participants hear and orient to this is displayed in the
fact that neither self-select following S's 'yeah'. Following a brief
silence, speaker S produces the further TCU: 'but (0.49) but I don't
like(h) raining-u'.[4] There is a very momentary delay in the production of the next-item following 'like' and, in fact, speaker S begins to
turn her head away from A (her addressed recipient) as she starts to
say 'like(h)', keeping her gaze averted until just after beginning to
utter 'raining', at which point she begins to bring her head and gaze
back around to A, so that by the end of the word she is gazing fully
at A. We might think of this as an 'incipient word search' that is
resolved almost immediately – even before vowel-marking becomes
necessary.

In the second instance of 'like' in line 14, vowel-marking is very evident
and the entry into a search is more overt. As speaker S begins to say
'like-u' she moves her head away from A (see Figure 13.1 below) as she
had done in the previous instance. However, this time she is not able to
move so quickly into a resolution and instead vowel-marks the word
while at the same time quickly shifting her gaze even further to the left

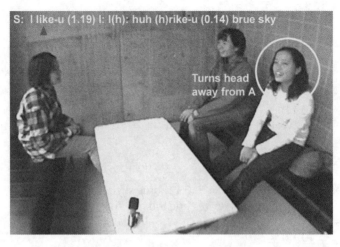

Figure 13.1   S's head begins to turn away

(as in Figure 13.2 below), i.e., she does what can be called a *step-wise visual disengagement* on the vowel-marking.

Both S's body behaviours and her vowel-marking signal to her co-participants that she is involved in a search – in this case a *solitary search* (Goodwin and Goodwin 1986) for a way forward in her turn construction. The co-ordination of S's step-wise visual disengagement with her use of vowel-marking provides supporting evidence that vowel-marking is, indeed, an interactional resource and that it is can be used to initiate forward repair.

As S's search continues, specifically as she reaches the end of her vowel-marking (see Figure 13.3 below), her eyes shift back towards the middle but she does not yet re-establish gaze with either A or K. In other words, she displays to her co-participants that she is still involved in a solitary search and they make no attempt to intrude into the nearly 1.2 second pause that emerges at this point, although it must be clear to both that speaker S's intended turn will involve a contrast with her just previously stated dislike of 'raining', something along the lines that she likes 'good weather', 'clear skies', etc.

During the 1.19 second pause speaker S begins what might be called the 'setup for the onset' of a gesture which has 'blue sky' as its lexical affiliate (Schegloff 1984) such that at the point where she reinitiates her TCU the movement towards this gesture's onset position is approxi-

Figure 13.2 At vowel-marking S visually disengages further

Figure 13.3 Upon termination of vowel-marking S begins to return gaze

mately halfway complete. Speaker S is still not making eye contact with either A or K.

This brings us to S's third instance of 'like' in this extract. Once again S does not move immediately from the end of 'like' into the next-item-due ('blue sky'). Again she vowel-marks the word and there is a brief

Figure 13.4   Vowel-marking in pre-pausal position

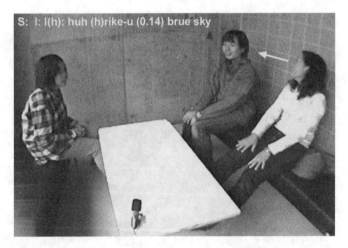

Figure 13.5   S visually re-engages with A at turn completion

hesitation (see Figure 13.4) before S launches the gesture (pointing with both hands towards the sky) and begins to say its lexical affiliate.

Speaker S's repair, as well as her turn construction, are brought to completion by her production of one possible object for the verb 'like', namely 'blue sky', and as S utters the final word 'sky' her head and gaze returns to A (as in Figure 13.5).

My argument *is not* that vowel-marking is always accompanied by gaze aversion. This would clearly be false – just as it would be observably false to claim that all instances of forward repair/word search are accompanied by gaze aversion. My argument is simply that, given that gaze aversion is highly indicative of *repair-in-progress* (Goodwin and Goodwin 1986), the regular co-occurrence of vowel-marking with gaze aversion in this novice-to-novice L2 talk argues strongly in favour of vowel-marking being an interactional resource and not just a pronunciation problem.

Additional interactional uses of vowel-marking

Even a quick glance through the transcripts from the group 6 data reveals instances of vowel-marking not involved in forward repair. But do these instances really represent counter-evidence to the claim advanced in this paper? As it turns out, an examination of these *deviant cases* only strengthens the argument supporting vowel-marking as an interaction resource.

One class of deviant cases might be called *TCU-final vowel-markings*. All of the instances of vowel-marking provided in prior examples occur at points where the TCU-in-progress is not possibly complete, that is to say, they occur *TCU-medially*. Extract 14 is one example of several to be found in the group 6 data of TCU-terminal vowel-marking.

Extract 14

```
01      A: me too me [too      ][uh: ] uhm (0.24) eh =
02      S:              [°me too°][yeah]
03   →  A: = u:h u:h toda:y is-u very COLD-o
04   →      (0.16)
05      S: yeah[:: ]
06   →  A:       [so]:: I absent-o[::                [ah huh
07      S:                    [huh huh huh .hhh [HUH hum
08      A: e:to:: °°e:to:: °° morning-u:[::        ]
09      S:                            [second] class?
```

In this extract, speaker A produces an assessment of the weather that might be *possibly complete*, i.e. possibly hearable by co-participants as complete, at the conclusion of 'cold'. This TCU is syntactically complete, presented as an intonational whole with final-falling intonation, and carries out a pragmatically complete action ('making an assessment'), thus fulfilling the criterion for completeness proposed by Ford and Thompson (1996). Notice, however, the absence of immediate uptake by both S and K. After a brief silence, S does provide an agreement token ('yeah') but, possibly due to A's overlapping start-up at line 6, does not add a further TCU to her turn.[5] It is significant that speaker A constructs her new talk, in line 6, as a continuation of the prior talk by means of the conjunctional 'so'. In this instance, then, the TCU-final vowel-marking served not to initiate repair but to foreshadow further talk belonging to the same 'project'.

Another example of this can be seen in Extract 15 below. Here too S's (somewhat reduced) vowel-marking on 'raining-u' vaguely adumbrates further talk. Once again it is followed by a lack of immediate uptake by either A or K despite the fact that both A and K regularly provide immediate response tokens such as *yeah, yes-yes-yes, un* throughout this talk (see Carroll 2000 for a demonstration that nonnative speakers are both capable of precision timing and orient to *no-gap* transitions).

Extract 15

```
01  →  S:   yeah↑ (0.22) but (0.49) but I don't like(h) raining-u,
02          (0.14)
03     K:   [mm::::]
04     A:   [a::h::  ] very dark-u
05          (0.14)
06  →  S:   da- yeah [I::a I      ] I like-u
07     A:            [un un un]
08     K:            [a::h::   ]
09          (1.19)
10  →  S:   I: I(h): huh (h)rike-u (0.14) brue sky
```

While K does speak (after a gap), it is only to provide a minimal continuer, produced in overlap with a receipt token ('a::h::') by speaker A, who goes on to provide a short evaluative comment on 'raining'. Speaker S's partial repetition (and then abandonment) of A's 'dark' dismisses A's intervening talk. Then, in lines 6 and 10, speaker S adds the second part of a common rhetorical device: a two-part contrast (see Atkinson 1984). Once again we see vowel-marking prefiguring further talk.

Co-participant orientation to TCU-final vowel-marking is revealed in the following two examples. In Extract 16 line 1, K has told A and S what she had for lunch, namely, Japanese food. On its own, 'I ate Japanese food' would be a perfectly satisfactory sort of statement. However, K vowel-marks 'food-u' and neither A or S intrude either vocally or physically in any way into the full one-second silence that emerges. When they do speak it is only to provide a minimal sort of receipt token (A's nasal *oh*) and a quiet prompt for more information by S. In other words, even if K did consider her own talk as fully rhetorically complete at line 1, her co-participants apparently did not.

Extract 16

```
01  →  K: = un (0.38) I ate-u: (0.30) eto japanese food-u
02         (1.04)
03     A: hohn
04     S: °°what°°,
05         (0.32)
06     K: u-hm (0.26) rice: a:::[:::n:::]
07     S:                  [(fried)]
08         (0.67)
09  →  K: rice a:::n::::-nu (1.86) fish,
10         (0.20)
```

In the next example, K's turn is syntactically and pragmatically (in the context in which it occurs) projectably complete at the conclusion of 'eat' in line 2, but speaker S does not respond. Instead, K holds the release of the final /t/ for almost four tenths of a second and then tags on the vowel-marking /-o/ which she then stretches. This leads into a silence which lasts approximately seven tenths of a second before S indicates that she 'gets the drift' of K's question with 'yeah' and then provides a word ('lunch') which would complete what, *at least to S if not also to K*, was K's incomplete TCU. Speaker K then ratifies S's contribution in line 6 by repeating it. In both of these examples, recipients of TCU-final vowel-marking treat the talk as somehow lacking or insufficient or incomplete.

Extract 17

```
01     A: o::h nn [eto huh huh huh huh huh huh]
02     K:        [whe:re huh huh di(h) dch(h)u ] did =
03     = you eat (0.39)-o::
04     (0.74)
05     S: ieah (0.12) lunch,
06     K: lunch =
```

In conclusion, TCU-final vowel-marking shares with TCU-medial vowel-marking a displayed sense of incompleteness; the difference appears to lie in the scope of this incompleteness. *Vowel-marking, when it occurs TCU-medially, is employed by these participants to retard the progressivity of the turn towards possible completion and, thereby, allow time for a possible resolution of the search to emerge.* In contrast, TCU-final vowel-marking appears to project that the just-completed TCU is part of some larger rhetorical project (Selting 1996), that *while this TCU is finished, there is more to come.*

A second class of deviant cases in my data can regularly be found to occur in what Schegloff (2000) refers to as the *pre-resolution phase* and the *post-resolution phase* of overlap. In the following example, Schegloff illustrates the way that speakers can stretch the production of a word in hopes of being able to finish in the clear.

Extract 18

```
01    Deb:    How [come you get thiz:: thi:s v::::::]ersion of          ]...
02    Anne:         [W'd you please concentrate on drivi]ng the ca:r,]
```

[Schegloff 2000:13]

The novice speakers in my data appear to be using vowel-marking in a comparable manner, i.e., as a practice designed to allow them to 'survive' overlap. In the first two examples below (19 and 20), vowel-marking is found in the post-resolution stage, that is, the vowel-marking is the first bit of talk uttered 'in the clear' after the resolution of the overlapping talk:

Extract 19

```
01    S:  I went to:: Bedlow's university?
02        (0.16)
03    A:  [O:::H
04    K:  [o::h ye[ah good]
05  → S:          [a::n::d  ]-u mm uh (1.11) °a(kh)nd(h)a°=
06        = (0.45) a:hm::::: criffs criffs
```

Extract 20

```
01    A:  da- eto every day [dancing   ] ((gestures 'dance' at 'da-'))
02    K:                    [DANCING]
03    S:                    [dancing   ] oh
04        (0.26)
```

```
05    ?:  [um ]
06  → A:  [and]-o (0.75) [wa:lk]-u
07    K:              [sss-s ]
08    K:  un
09        (0.46)
```

Examples of *in-the-clear* vowel-marking following overlap resolution abound in my data and represent one practice for re-establishing speaker rights. Extract 21 below (taken from another set of novice L2 data) provides a particularly strong demonstration of this.

Extract 21

```
01    K:  no (1.21) mm (2.61) people (0.35) people in (0.21) Kochi
02        (0.89) is-u (0.39) are (0.49) people (0.70) drink =
03  →     = a lot[-- ]-o
04    M:         [un]
05        (0.88)
06    K:  but but my family my:: (0.62) my mother . . .
```

Here speaker K (a different speaker K) states, *sans* repairs and linguistic inaccuracies, that 'People in Kochi are people who drink a lot'. On the face of it, this TCU seems complete and co-participant M responds precisely at this point with Japanese 'un' which, like English 'yeah,' can function as either a continuer or a receipt token. But K has not released the [t] in 'lot' and immediately upon the cessation of 'overlap' between M's 'un' and her own *holding silence* (Local and Kelly 1986) she re-establishes speakership by releasing the stop into a vowel such that this delayed instance of vowel-marking gets done perfectly in the clear. This is also a fine example of TCU-final vowel-marking projecting further talk as K goes on to state that, in contrast to 'Kochi people' in general, her own mother (also from Japan's Kochi prefecture) doesn't drink at all.

The following instance illustrates vowel-marking in the pre-resolution stage, i.e., just prior to the resolution of the overlap. Notice that in this case, the vowel-marking would have emerged in the clear, had the other speaker not lengthened production of competing talk.

Extract 22

```
01  → S:  I joined school festival,[wi::ss-u ]
02    A:                           [a:h um::]
```

03   (0.92)
04   S: mizu [Kayo]:ko =

Below is one further instance of vowel-marking in the pre-resolution stage which readers will recognize as the fourth instance of 'like' from the discussion of gaze aversion above. In this instance, however, S's vowel-marking on 'like-u' appears to be responsive to an overlapping series of yes-tokens by A. Notice the fine timing between the conclusion of A's 'me too' and S's utterance of the next part of her TCU. Speaker S is clearly attending to A's talk and attempting to fit her own talk around it.

Extract 23

19   A: o::h:: [yes yes [yes yes]me too [me too
20   → S: [u::n::   [I like-u]   [fine day

These instances, and many more like them in the data, argue that these novice L2 speakers also utilize vowel-marking in order to survive overlap in a manner comparable to sound stretches in native speaker inter-action. The three uses outlined thus far (*vowel-marking in forward repair, TCU-final vowel-marking, and vowel-marking as a resource for overlap resolution*) account for the vast majority of instances of vowel-marking in my data.

Conclusions

This chapter has presented evidence that strongly suggests that the vowel-marking common in talk by Japanese novice speakers of English cannot simply be attributed to L1 phonological interference, but rather that the novice speakers in these data utilize and orient to vowel-marking as a situated resource in the management of their conversational inter-action. Most frequently vowel-marking is employed as a micro-practice within the extremely common conversational activity of forward repair/ word search where it can serve both to initiate repair as well as manage aspects of the search prior to resolution. Additionally, vowel-marking, when it occurs TCU-finally, signals that while the current speaker may have finished with *this* TCU, he or she is working on some larger multi-TCU rhetorical project. And co-participants display their orientation to this hearing by withholding talk at points that might otherwise be considered suitable points for speaker transition. The novice L2 speakers in my data also employ vowel-marking as a means of 'surviving' overlap and, thereby, reasserting their speaker rights.

But just how germane is this phenomenon of vowel-marking to the broader study of so-called nonnative speaker interaction? After all, this phenomenon is, almost certainly, limited to *Japanese* speakers of English as a second language, and probably to *novice Japanese* speakers of English as a second language, and quite possibly only to *novice Japanese speakers of English as a second language engaged in talk with other (novice?) Japanese speakers of English as a second language.* There are, nevertheless, practical as well as methodological points that can be drawn from this investigation of vowel-marking.

First, on a practical note, teachers of English as a second language intent on ridding their Japanese students' speech of vowel-marking are advised to forget pronunciation drills and ridicule, and instead concentrate on training students to use interactionally equivalent conversational micro-practices, such as the use of *uh* and *um.* Explicit instruction not just in the 'grammar' (in the traditional sense of that term) but also in the micro-practices of the target language/culture, including those of self-repair, may resolve a number of difficulties and may even significantly improve subjective impressions of students' spoken abilities.[6]

Second, this study of vowel-marking highlights the problems facing analysts of nonnative discourse. The application of conversation analysis to nonnative speaker data has inevitably led to new methodological challenges (see Firth 1996; Wagner 1996; Seedhouse 1998, as well as an interview with Schegloff in Wong and Olsher 2000; Schegloff *et al.* 2002). As just one example, how does one capture on a transcript the sound of 'anomalous' language without slipping into linguistic stereotyping (Jefferson 1996)? What level of transcription is suitable? If it were not for a decision taken by the present author to transcribe one of several characteristic 'pronunciation problems' for Japanese speakers of English, namely, word-final vowel extensions, the previously unreported conversational practice of vowel-marking might never have been observed. Researchers working with nonnative speaker data should heed Heritage's warning (1984: 241) that '...no order of detail can be dismissed, *a priori*, as disorderly, accidental or irrelevant'.

A third point raised by vowel-marking is the possibly transient nature of some of the interactional practices in talk among 'not-yet-competent' speakers of a second language. Researchers can expect to find greater individual speaker variation in terms of which specific practices are employed. For example, in the data examined in this chapter, vowel-marking is far more prevalent in talk by speaker A as compared to speaker S, who more frequently employed additional practices to initiate and manage forward repair, as when she initiates forward repair with multiple progressive cut-offs, e.g. 'o- ong- onny: (0.36) onny that s-s-s'tuation?', which is almost never seen in A's speech.

As a final point, the delicate ways that these speakers deploy and orient to vowel-marking hint at the hitherto little explored range of inter-actional competencies adult speakers bring to talk in another language. Even supposedly 'low-level' novices, such as those in this study, display a degree of interactional sophistication previously unimagined. In the end, perhaps one of the most valuable contributions conversation analysis can make to the field of applied linguistics is to demolish once and for all the crude stereotype of language learners as deficient, unsophisticated communicators.

Notes

1 Hiragana and katakana are alternate versions of the same syllabary with katakana frequently used to transliterate foreign words and names and on product packaging.
2 The Hi8 tapes were transferred to miniDV cassettes and imported to iMovie 2 on the Mac. In producing the transcripts I watched the video clips in Quick-time Pro and listened to the audio (and measured the silences to the nearest one-hundredth) using CoolEdit 2000 for Windows. The frame grabs were also produced with Quicktime Pro and then the text and graphics added in Photoshop. One very convenient feature of Quicktime Pro is that it allows the user to create movie sub-clips which occupy only 2-3k and this then allows the researcher to make 'video collections' without clogging up the hard disk.
3 The term *pre-pausal* is preferable to more frequently heard labels, such as 'fillers' or 'filled pauses,' as it provides a better description of the interactional goals of these conversational objects. What pre-pausals are designed to do is warn of a possible upcoming silence which may or may not materialize. That pre-pausals can also be found to occur in post-pausal positions does not alter the interactional goal.
4 Speaker S looks away during the 0.49 second pause and then reestablishes gaze with A as she begins to say 'But I . . .'.
5 There is some debate as to whether 'yeah' projects a greater degree of possible incipient next-speakership (see Drummond and Hopper 1993a, 1993b, 1993c).
6 Streeck (1996:208) suggests that '. . . the very question as to whether some-thing is "a grammatical feature" or a "cultural performance characteristic" may become obsolete'.

14

Teaching Patterns of Interaction in English for Specific Purposes

Andrew Packett

Introduction

Journalistic broadcast interviewing is talk produced for absent viewers or listeners, and should thus be seen as a form of institutional interaction whose primary, though unaddressed, recipient is the overhearing audience (Heritage 1985). A basic institutional demand of broadcast journalists, therefore, is that they manage interview interaction as talk for overhearers, an orientation that requires the deployment of an institutionalized 'footing' (Goffman 1981; Clayman 1992) attentive to the needs of this absent audience. The special interactional work the deployment of such a footing entails is the focus of this chapter, which considers the pedagogic applications of CA within my own work as a teacher of English to Portuguese students of Journalism. In taking a comparative perspective, interview data from both professional and learner contexts will be analysed in order to show how a routine sequential practice commonly found in professional broadcast interviewing might be seen as a means of raising learners' awareness over a particular interactional problem evident in the learner data.[1] To approach data in such terms is, in itself, a reflection of CA's distinctive methodological perspective:

> CA is a structural methodology for the analysis of talk. The sequential regularities and patterns that it discovers, however, reveal how specific features of talk are used by participants to accomplish tasks that are central to the organization of talk, i.e. *how they function to create solutions for recurrent problems of talk*. (Schiffrin 1994: 341, emphasis added)

The recurrent problem of talk that this chapter focuses upon can be seen as an oriented-to product of the institutional context of broadcast interviewing, since, in having to manage face-to-face interaction for the benefit of an absent public audience, interviewers must constantly monitor the talk-in-interaction from the epistemological perspective of an idealized third-party. The interactional footing produced as a result of this institutional demand can be seen particularly clearly in a routine, yet previously unexamined, sequential practice of broadcast interviewing in which the interviewer departs from the question–answer turn-taking format in order to briefly add a point of detail to a description given in the prior turn. Such 'insertion sequences', as collaborative interactional achievements, are constitutive of 'doing interview', and are thus worthy of pedagogic attention, especially given that they are either absent or problematically deployed in the learner data. The classroom use of professional data argued for in this chapter is informed by what is a basic analytic strategy of CA – 'taking what people are doing and finding out the kind of problem for which this doing might be a solution' (ten Have 1999: 17) – suggesting that pedagogic application can be derived not only from the cumulative findings of the research tradition, but also, and perhaps more importantly, from CA's distinctive method of inquiry[2] (Schegloff *et al.* 2002).

We begin with a brief consideration of pedagogic context, underlining the particular relevance of CA to the teaching of the specialized speech exchange systems found within the field of English for Specific Purposes (ESP), before moving on to comparative analyses of the data. Here the approach taken mirrors the pedagogic cycle learners themselves experience in class, since we begin by identifying, through deviant case analysis, the pre-allocated nature of the turn-taking organization found in broadcast interviewing. The focus then shifts to sequence organization, in which the differential distribution of turn-types is revealed in the recursive question–answer patterns of which interview talk is comprised. The candidate phenomenon is then identified in the professional data as a tightly organized sequential practice which is briefly inserted within these question–answer sequences. Finally, a pedagogic warrant for highlighting such insertion sequences is revealed by the way in which learner interviewers can be seen to be either failing to deploy this practice, or, when attempting to do so, delaying its inception such that its familiar shape is disrupted.

Pedagogic context: teaching English for Specific Purposes

While key descriptive categories of CA, such as turn-taking, repair or adjacency relations, have long formed part of the terminological mainstream in TESOL (Teaching English to Speakers of Other Languages), the research tradition from which such terms are drawn remains a source of suspicion for many teachers, who see its fine-grained approach to the details of naturally occurring interaction as somehow implying the study of 'defective' language use (McCarthy 1998). Applications of CA within the field must therefore be carefully argued for, and ESP (a sub-field of TESOL) presents itself as an area of particular relevance, as its content and objectives are determined by the specific needs of particular groups of learners, in the case of the present study those planning to work in the field of journalism. Broadcast interviewing is naturally a key target need for such learners, and students who opt to study English as part of their journalism degree course at the University of Coimbra, Portugal, are required to record a face-to-face interview for potential radio broadcast as part of their assessed course work. Although this is inevitably only a simulation, task guidelines are designed to encourage an orientation to the particular roles, tasks and relevancies which together comprise the constituent features of institutional talk (Drew and Heritage 1992b). In particular, they are required to specify an appropriate audience, focus and goal for the interview based on research carried out into their interviewee, thus underlining from the outset the position of the overhearing audience as a key institutional determinant of broadcast talk. Furthermore, learners are required to transcribe the interview in full as well as producing a critical commentary on selected sequences, thus encouraging close attention to the details of talk-in-interaction. The application of CA argued for in this chapter should therefore be seen as intrinsic to a pedagogic cycle that aims to combine experiential learning with informed reflection in order to develop the interviewer as reflective practitioner.

Turn-taking organization in broadcast interviewing

In raising students' awareness of broadcast interviewing as a specialized form of institutional interaction, it is first of all necessary to identify the overall turn-taking system. This pedagogic objective is facilitated by CA methodology, which views this higher level of interactional organization as a useful starting point for any analysis (Heritage 1997; ten Have 1999), and which, through 'deviant case' analysis, offers an effective means by which participants' normative orientation to the constraints of such turn-taking systems can be revealed. This approach, a key methodological tool of CA, involves analysing cases in which there is some form of departure from a normal pattern of interaction, paying particular attention to the way in which participants orient to such departures through their actions. Extract 1 below is one such instance and is all the more valuable pedagogically for having occurred in a learner interview, thus indicating how an orientation to the constraints of doing interview form part of participants' tacit interactional competencies even as neophytes. The interviewee, as is often the case, is the interviewer's ex-English teacher who in line 2 refers to a secondary school translation course (*'técnicas de tradução'*), which it is assumed the recipient of the turn had taken. A further statement-formatted utterance at the beginning of line 3 is then abruptly cut off by a polar question. What happens now is highly significant since, even before the interviewee has a chance to respond, the action of asking a question is topicalized and thus seen as morally accountable, thereby underlining the questioner's incumbent identity of interviewee and revealing an attendant orientation to the specialized constraints of roles and turn-types that are constitutive of 'doing interview'. The sanctioned nature of this departure is further underlined by the explanatory work the interviewee undertakes in order to mitigate her role departure in lines 6 and 7 prior to the interviewer's projected reassertion of control in line 8.

Extract 1

IE: = interviewee
IR: = interviewer

```
001   IE:   →   ... what I wanted to say is (1.0) you ↑ also had English (1.0)
002                 when you lear::nt (.) er > tecnicas de tradução em Inglês <
003                 so i- (0.5) do you think it was helpful? (0.5) or:: (.) or ↓ not.
004         →    now I'm asking you(h) a que(h)stion hhhh ha =
005   IR:        = yes I(h) think it was very helpful h[h ha
006   IE:                                              [.hhhh ok ok so (.) it was-
007                 >it was a game.< so (.) uh huh I(h) jus'
008   IR:        ok and now to end the interview ....
```

(June 2000. Student interview project)[3]

It is through highlighting speakers' orientations, then, that deviant case analysis enables attention to be drawn to the normativity of speakers' shared practices. Furthermore, it underlines the fact that within CA's distinctive mode of inquiry the social-structural context is not to be invoked as 'an external interpretative resource' (Heritage 1984b: 283) but rather endogenously grounded in the fine-grained details of participants' actions (Schegloff 1997). This methodological canon has obvious pedagogic application in terms of the selection of material for classroom use.

[A] major requirement is that the matters selected for study are those that persons in the setting are themselves demonstrably aware of and/or oriented to in the course of their actions. (Psathas 1995:46)

In this way a CA-informed pedagogy requires learners to inductively discover in the empirical details of talk-in-interaction what it actually means to 'do interview'.[4] This pedagogic challenge draws upon two key analytic issues in CA, 'relevance' and 'procedural consequentiality' (Schegloff 1991, 1992b; see also Gafaranga and Britten this volume). The former can be invoked straightforwardly in the excerpt above in terms of the co-participants' demonstrable orientation to the institutional roles of interviewer and interviewee. The latter, however, presents a particular analytical difficulty since it requires going a step further to 'give an account of how the interaction proceeded in the way in which it did, how it came to have the trajectory, the direction, the shape that it ended up having' (Schegloff 1992b: 111) as a consequence of the local social structure. To examine this further, and, in so doing, address the interactional issue this chapter focuses upon, we must turn to sequence organization, another core idea of CA's analytic strategy (ten Have 1999) and a further key site for probing the 'institutionality' of interaction (Heritage 1997: 168).

Sequence organization: insertion sequences in broadcast interviews

Although the distribution of roles and turn-types oriented to in Extract 1 underlines how broadcast interviewing should be seen, in CA terms, as a pre-allocated turn-taking system (Atkinson and Drew 1979), this system is nevertheless still *locally* managed on a turn-by-turn basis. In this way, the central methodological resource in CA, for participants and analyst alike, is the understanding shown of prior talk in a next turn (Sacks *et al.* 1974). This is seen particularly clearly in the question–answer sequences that structure interview talk across a range of institutional domains. Such sequences establish recursive patterns in which third-position actions in answer-subsequent turns assume particular strategic importance as the site for displaying orientation to, and hence control of, the ongoing talk (Button 1992; Drew and Sorjonen 1997). This imparts a distinctive shape to broadcast interviewing that is seen to operate even at the very opening of an interview, as illustrated, albeit somewhat minimally, in Extract 2 below. Here the interviewer's third-position turn (arrowed) neatly embeds an exhibited understanding of the prior turn in the form of an anaphoric indexical ('that'), thereby using prior talk as a resource in the construction of a current turn. While this is recognized in CA as a generic property of 'third actions' (Heritage 1984b: 258), the discursive power hereby granted to interviewers is also a consequence of an asymmetric institutional turn-taking system that gives interviewers 'the structurally provided ability to constrain the actions of others' (Hutchby and Wooffitt 1998: 170).[5]

Extract 2

```
001   IR:    Sumner Redstone a very warm welcome to the programme.
002   IE:    thank you (.) [ glad to be here
003   IR:                   [ how much-
004          how much do you care about journalistic integrity.
005   IE:    I care a lot about journalistic integrity =
006   IR: →  = is that at the top of your pr- list of priorities, =
007   IE:    = I wouldn't say that, but it's certainly important . . .
```

(11.7.01 BBC World 'HARDtalk')

While second-position slots are, of course, usually far more extended in journalistic interviewing, the key pedagogic insight this minimal exchange underlines is that the three-part pattern of question–answer sequences constitutes a powerful interactional framework through which neophytes can begin to gain a sense of the orderliness of interview talk. Adjacency relations – of which question–answer pairs are a particularly clear example – are, of course, one of the earliest and most well known of CA's discoveries, yet their analytic value is overlooked if considered merely as CA jargon (Schegloff 2001). In turning now to an analysis of insertion sequences, it is worth underlining that only through a basic understanding of adjacency can learners come to recognize the pattern of the sequential practice shown in Extracts 3 to 7 below, and, in so doing, come to an understanding of the interactional work achieved.

As an initial exercise in awareness-raising, learners can be presented with a number of examples illustrating the distinctive shape of this common sequential practice. This is clearly seen in Extracts 3 to 5, where the arrowed interviewer turns indicate the initiation of the insertion sequence. In departing from the question–answer format, the interviewer, in each excerpt, effectively interrupts the interviewee's answer turn prior to any projection of closure.

Extract 3

```
001   IR:      what about er- Gillespie the- the red-neck police chief in
002            er- in the heat [ of the night]
003   IE:                      [ .hhhh well ] that's a ↓ different thing .
004            that was- (.) Sidney poitier was a friend of mine for many years
005            before we did that . =
006   IR:  →   = he was the homicide detective in it
007            who (.) [ helps you out (.) helps you solve the murder ]
008   IE:              [ yeah he was the (.) black guy (.) a- a- a-      ]
009            he was the detective, (0.4) an' we were friends long before
010            we did the picture, . . .
```

(BBC Radio 'Desert Island Discs')

Extract 4

```
001   IR:      How (0.7) hard has it been for you (.) all these years
002            to fight (0.6) piece by piece (0.4) document by document (0.5)
003            .hh[hh =
004   IE:         [ °Hmm°
005   IR:      = to be lied to:, = to be blocked, (0.6) to have (.) so many disappointments
006            pile up over the years = what's that been like for you.
007   IE:      .hhh well honestly Ed Horman (.) er:m was leading the charge,
008   IR:  →   Charles's father
009   IE:      Yes (.) uh initially, (0.5) uh when we went to congress, . . .
```

(16.3.01. BBC World 'HARDtalk')

Extract 5

```
001   IR:      .hh you say if you'd had (.) Jo::hn's some of John's (.)
002            >abilities or talents and he'd had some of yours <
003            which were those. Which would he've [ liked to (  ) between you
004   IE:                                          [ .hhh well I think John-
005            John er (0.2) John no::w (0.2) having obviously been married to Chris
006            an-an- an- =
007   IR:  →   = >Chris Evert yah.< =
008   IE:      = yeah, and basically living a lot in- in the states . . .
```

(15.8.00. BBC Radio 'On the Ropes')

The CA notion of adjacency relations is helpful in understanding how these sequences are organized so as to interrupt only minimally the question–answer format of the interview. In particular, the powerful normative mechanism of conditional relevance explains how, in each case above, the interviewee, having briefly receipted and thus completed the insertion sequence, returns immediately to the precise point of the prior answer turn which the insertion sequence had interrupted. The first pair part represented by an initial question is therefore seen as conditionally relevant insofar as expectation of a second pair part of answer is maintained across the embedded utterances represented by the insertion sequence.

To approach an analytic object in terms of the interactional contingencies it deals with is a common method of CA, and the main pedagogic relevance of these sequences lies in a closer consideration of what actually occasions these interviewer-initiated departures. In each of the arrowed turns above there is a perceived need on the part of the interviewer to expand upon a description given in the prior turn. What the interviewer provides, however, is merely a further detail to the category term given in the prior turn, the understanding of which, intersubjectively, had been warrantably presupposed by the interviewee. Interactionally, then, this amounts to a curious footing in which the co-participants are, in one sense, merely confirming knowledge they both know to be true. However, these insertion sequences are designed to redress the indexicality of the prior description, which, as a pervasive phenomenon of natural language, can be considered as a seen but unnoticed feature of interaction. Such sequences are, therefore, useful pedagogically in raising awareness of how an institutionalized footing mandates a distinctive inferential framework (Drew and Heritage 1992b) which learners, as will be shown below, find difficult to grasp. The crucial point is that these sequences, while addressed to the interviewee, are performed primarily for the benefit of the overhearing audience, and it is the particular analytic method of CA that provides this pedagogic insight since the basic analytic question implicit in CA's concern with the sequential organization of talk is precisely the relevant pedagogic question to be asked of each of the arrowed turns above:

> For those trying to understand a bit of talk, the key question about any of its aspects is – *why that now* (Schegloff & Sacks 1973)? What is getting done by virtue of that bit of conduct, done that way, in just that place? This is, in the first instance, the central issue *for the parties to the talk* – both for its construction and for its understanding. And

for that reason, it is the central issue for academic/professional students of the talk. (Schegloff *et al*. 2002: 5–6, original italics)

The activity focus of CA – its concern with action in *inter*action (Schegloff 2001) – is a decisive distinguishing feature of its approach (Drew & Heritage 1992b), and it is certainly appropriate pedagogically to talk of interactional practices as 'work', a 'doing' by which the participants themselves actively produce the context of the talk-in-interaction. In this sense, insertion sequences constitute special interactional work, the action import of which can be brought home to learners through careful selection of exchanges in which the CA methodological requisite of demonstrable orientation can be identified.

Extract 6, for instance, is notable for the manner in which the insertion sequence is receipted in line 7, standing as a clear indication of how such practices are interactional achievements contingent upon the collaboration of the interviewee. CA's next-turn proof procedure is particularly illuminating here since the interviewee's 'thank you' reveals an understanding of the work achieved by the insertion sequence, thus accounting for the relevance of the interviewer's fuller description of Guzman to the overhearing audience's understanding of her answer turn.

Extract 6

```
001  IR:      Last year you filed suit (0.4) in the Chilean courts (0.3) against General
002           Pinochet = you also asked the supreme court for an investigation (.) into
003           your husband's death, = how far has that got.
004  IE:      .hhh well er:: (1.4) there were two petitions = one went to Guzman's docket,
005           (0.3) er:: with the case itself,
006  IR:  →   Guzman is the magistrate who's been leading (0.3)
007  IE:  →   Thank you =
008  IR:  →   = The charge
009  IE:      Ye[s
010  IR:         [ against Pinochet =
011  IE:      = that's absolutely right. a::h a-all of the cases against Pinochet get filed
012           with Judge Guzman, .hhhh and we also petitioned the supreme court ...
```

(16.3.01. BBC World 'HARDtalk')

Extract 7 further highlights how the audience-directed nature of these insertion sequences should be regarded as a seen but unnoticed feature.

Unlike the previous examples, this insertion sequence is initiated in overlap (line 11) and is tied to prior talk through means of a reason clause, thus constituting a more abrupt departure from the turn-taking system which, furthermore, is projected as being relatively expansive. In mitigation the interviewer orients to this in line 12 as a morally accountable action, and in so doing explicitly reveals the institutionalized footing that underpins this sequential practice.

Extract 7

```
001  IR:   .....hh um (.) now I understand it- Mr- Mr- Powler- er Mr Tyler
002        > tell me if I'm wrong < I understand that (.) what (.) Robin Cook wanted to
003        do .hh was give (0.3) MPs more power to decide who became the chairmen
004        of select committees .hhh why would MPs vote against that.
005  IE:   well there was a nasty little conspiracy putting it bluntly
006        between the labour and con ↑ servative whips.
007        it was a re ↑ venge attack (0.2) on Robin Cook.
008        .hh the: government whips felt that he hadn't been sufficiently robust
009        in defending their position (.) la:st summer er – sa- on the occasion that you
010        referred t[o          (                    )
011  IR:            [ because it's the whips who have a lot-
012  →     > just so that people understand < it's the whips who have .hhh
013  →     th- ba- basically >sort of< hand out the black spots. = decide who gets to be
014        chairmen and who:: doesn't get to be chairmen of these committees.
015  IE:   that's the position at the moment, and we were trying to reform it . . .
```

(15.5.02. BBC Radio 'Today')

This section has identified a sequential practice common to broadcast interviewing, and, following a basic analytic strategy of CA, argued that this particular 'doing' of professional journalists should be seen as a solution to an interactional problem inherent in managing talk produced for an absent audience. In this way, the key pedagogic application of CA is that of encouraging a particular analytic mentality that seeks to account for the orderliness of sequential practices in terms of the interactional contingencies they are addressing. This emic perspective extends to the comparative analysis of learner data, to which we now turn.

Insertion sequences in the learner data

This section, in aiming to provide a pedagogic warrant for the focus upon insertion sequences, addresses two issues arising from the preceding discussion. First, we briefly identify a common problem in learner interviews in which the absence of an insertion sequence indicates the failure to achieve the requisite institutionalized footing. Secondly, we examine how the delayed initiation of insertion sequences disrupts the familiar shape of such sequences as identified in the professional data. This feature of learner interview talk is significant in that it illustrates how the identity of the interviewer as non-native speaker can be seen to have procedural consequentiality.

Though common in professional interviewing, insertion sequences are relatively rare in learner interviews, and it is therefore important to highlight exchanges in which the absence of such an action might be seen as potentially problematic for the overhearing audience. As an analytic procedure, the noticing of such an absence requires that learners, as analysts, adopt a particular perspective with regard to the data. This perspective corresponds to the institutionalized footing identified in the professional data, since the absent action can only be noted if interviewee turns are retrospectively monitored from the epistemological perspective of the absent listener. So, in Extract 8, the interviewee's references in line 3 to local student festivals require further contextualization for the overhearing audience rather than merely being repeated in the question turn of line 6.

Extract 8

```
001  IE:      ... But I still like the um- (1.0) the ↑atmosphere
002           in the student ↑town an' everything =
003      →    = I think its- (0.3) like with the ↑queima and the cor↑tejo [ yesterday
004  IR:                                                                   [ (yes)
005           (0.8)
006      →    d-do you like (.) queima,
```
(Interview project, June 1999)

This stands as a representative example of the kind of intersubjective understanding commonly achieved in learner interviews, in which the interviewer's response merely ratifies the indexicality of the prior turn. However, given that the task instructions stipulate that such interviews should be designed for an English-speaking audience, there is clearly a failure to adopt the kind of institutionalized footing observed in professional insertion sequences that would function precisely to orient the talk to this putative audience as prime recipient. Simply highlighting this professional practice in class therefore serves to raise awareness of one way in which the institutional context of broadcast interviewing is 'talked into being' (Heritage 1984b: 290).

While a warrant for highlighting insertion sequences might be seen in the relative absence of such sequences in previous learner interviews, the outcome can only be measured by the extent to which learners, having noticed the action import of insertion sequences, are now able to deploy the more proactive role such practices require. In this respect, evidence from more recent projects would suggest that, although insertion sequences are certainly being attempted, the delayed nature of their initiation is an issue that requires further pedagogic attention. Recall that in the professional data presented above a constitutive feature of insertion sequences was the way in which they were designed for minimal disruption to the answer turn in progress. To achieve this, the insertion sequence is initiated at a point proximate to the trouble source, that is to say, at the next available transition relevance place, as seen in line 8 of Extract 4 (reprinted below for ease of reference).

```
007  IE:        .hhh well honestly Ed Horman (.) er:m was leading the charge
008  IR:   →    Charles's father
009  IE:        Yes (.) uh initially, (0.5) uh when we went to congress . . .
```

What seems to occur in the learner data, however, is that initiation is typically delayed beyond the initial transition relevance place, which results in the markedly different trajectories seen in Extracts 9 and 10 below. In the former, it should be noted, first of all, that the interviewer's orientation in line 5 to an institutional role is exemplary, showing awareness of the indexical properties of abbreviations and, in so doing, also displaying the research carried out into the subject matter of the interview.[6] By initiating the sequence in overlap with the interviewee's turn, however, the intelligibility of the talk is seriously affected.

Extract 9

```
001  IR:      . . . what does the Oromo students' movement do.
002           (0.7)
```

```
003   IE:      the Oromo (0.5) m-m-movement, (0.2) not only Oromo movement = the
004            (.) OLF. Oromo movements are under th[e (OLF)
005   IR:  →                                        [ OLF is the Oromo Liberation
006            Front =
007   IE:      = yes. (.) front. And then er::: well we- we just appealed to the
008            international er community, . . .
```

(Interview project, June 2002)

It should also be noted that overlap is, in any case, obviated by an institutional turn-taking system that grants the interviewer licence to re-examine any chosen aspect of prior talk in any future turn. Such discursive rights notwithstanding, the consequence of delaying the insertion sequence still further can be observed in Extract 10 below. In choosing to highlight the significance of Caxito's close proximity to Luanda, the Angolan capital, the interviewer, as in the previous excerpt, displays an exemplary orientation to the overhearing audience. However, its relative removal from the referent in line 14 necessitates delivering the insertion sequence as an accountable action in line 17. The fluent deployment of what are designed in the professional data as minimally shaped sequences is thereby disrupted with the sequence only being terminated in line 23 where the interviewer has to retrieve the conditional relevance of the original question through a restatement of the turn-taking rules. In this way, the identity of the interviewer as non-native speaker is shown to be procedurally relevant to the talk.[7]

Extract 10

```
001   IR:     . . . er:: lets talk er now about erm:: (0.2) er: the: the:: (0.8) Angolan
002           (0.6) peace process (0.5) er you- you said er- erm::
003           Mr S- Savimbi > Jonah Savimbi < death .hh er was important,
004           er hhhh make change in- in this process, (0.6)
005           .hhh what do you think erm (0.6)
006           (he'll) f- first quest- my first question is .hhh erm
007           (1.5) you- you:: (1.2) was surprised with erm:: (0.5) this er
008           fast running (0.5) of process.
009   IE:     .hhhh (1.0) yes I was. = erm (.) b'coz last year (0.8) it was really
              difficult
010           what would happen with the future of Angola = erm (1.0)
011           it seemed that (0.4) the FAA was er:: having some victories
```

```
012              against UNITA but at the same time UNITA was still able
013              to::: (.) carry out some serious attacks.
014        →     > I mean < they attacked Caxito:: they attacked Uige twice.
015              they attacked many smaller villages.
016              .hhh really last year I didn't think the war was about to end =
017   IR:  →     = I think is better we- we explain that Caxito is:: near Luanda
018        →     [[ it's a- a =
019   IE:        [[ that's right
020   IR:  →     = a fifteen fifty .hh er ki↑lometres (1.0) um near Luanda
021   IE:        yeah that's right
022              (0.7)
023   IR:        yeah (.) so (.) go on.
```

(Interview project, June 2002)

Conclusion

This chapter has focused on one particular sequential practice found in journalistic broadcast interviews, identifying how the deployment of insertion sequences can be seen as an interactional resource through which journalists fulfil the institutional task of managing talk for over-hearers. The data analysed are intended as classroom material, selected so as to raise learners' awareness of the kinds of special interactional work required in order to achieve an institutionalized footing for the overhearing audience. Such selection was informed by CA notions of demonstrable relevance and the procedural consequentiality of this as revealed in a particular sequential practice. This has significant pedagogic implications in that claims regarding the social-structural category of 'broadcast interviewing' (or any other of the specialized speech exchange systems taught in ESP) can only be warranted through empirical analysis which is able to reveal the demonstrable relevance of this category to the participants.

Furthermore, in its very organization this chapter has revealed how CA can inform a pedagogic procedure whose aim is to develop future journalists as reflective practitioners. That is to say, we focused first on how the CA methodological tool of deviant case analysis can be used to show how learners can be initially sensitized to the specialized turn-taking system of broadcast interviewing, before moving on to the more detailed considerations of sequential organization. Comparative use of professional data could here be seen to illuminate interactional problems in learner interviews through the application of CA's action-oriented heuristic procedures. An immediate outcome was revealed in learners' subsequent attempts to deploy the kinds of sequential practices identified in professional data, albeit with markedly delayed initiation, recognition of which underlines the value of CA as a tool in the elaboration of further pedagogic intervention.

Notes

1 The learner data are taken from a corpus of interviews produced as assessed project work for the English component of the Journalism degree course at the University of Coimbra, Portugal over the period of 1997 to 2002. A parallel professional corpus comprises material recorded off-air from a range of British media sources.

2 CA has paid particular attention to the news interview as a key social institution, producing a wealth of findings concerning its basic rules and practices. Although the learner interviews in the present study are of a less adversarial nature, institutional constraints such as neutrality and orientation to the overhearing audience must still be invoked. (See, *inter alia*, Clayman 1991, 1992, Clayman and Heritage 2002, Greatbatch 1988, 1992, Heritage 1985, Heritage and Greatbatch 1991, Heritage and Roth 1995)

3 The transcribed excerpts in this chapter have all been used as teaching material, and, for this reason, use standard orthography rather than the so-called 'eye' dialect of much CA work.

4 While journalism textbooks refer to a range of interview types (such as, 'hard news', 'personal', 'adversarial', etc. Herbert 2000: 255) such labels are of little pedagogic value if simply invoked *a priori* when analysing interview material in class. In this respect, CA's insistence on the demonstrable relevance of context as well as the inductive methodology through which it achieves its findings should be seen as key determinants of the pedagogic approach argued for in this chapter.

5 Although the concern here is with third position actions that display understanding of prior talk, an orientation to prior talk must still be shown even when shifting topic, insofar as such actions must be signalled as representing a break with prior talk. The pedagogic relevance of CA's focus on third position actions has been to reveal the disjunctive nature of question turns as a key interactional problem evidenced in the learner data.

6 The following extract from the interviewer's commentary is illustrative of the kind of reflective practice the CA-informed pedagogy outlined in this chapter can encourage:

> Being aware that there would be a third listener, the audience, I tried to produce the interview for those absent listeners. I believe that I was well-briefed and I wanted to pass along the information. Acting on behalf of the listener I tried to intervene so as to give him the information I had,

allowing the listener a better understanding of the facts, for example, when I add 'OLF is the Oromo Liberation Front'. (Cristina Bastos, Interview Project, June 2002)

7   Delayed actions as a feature of non-native speaker talk have also been identified in relation to repair sequences (Wong 2000a).

15
Conversation Analysis as Research Methodology
Paul Seedhouse

The aims of this concluding chapter are to tie together a number of themes that have emerged from the chapters in the collection and to reflect on the processes of research manifested in the chapters, positioning these in relation to linguistic and social science research paradigms. A frequent complaint by researchers outside CA is that CA practitioners tend not to make their methodology and procedures comprehensible and accessible to researchers from other disciplines. It has sometimes been acknowledged by CA practitioners (Peräkylä 1997) that more could be done in this respect. A full explication of CA methodology and procedures would start with a discussion of the ethnomethodological principles underpinning CA. Considerations of space prohibit such a discussion here; however, see Bergmann (1981), Heritage (1984b) and Seedhouse (2004). Similarly, this chapter cannot provide an introduction to CA methodology; however, see Hutchby and Wooffitt 1998; Psathas 1995; Seedhouse 2004; ten Have 1999. In this first section I will focus on two areas relevant to this collection, namely the CA view of language and the emic perspective.

CA's origins in sociology and specifically ethnomethodology entail a different perspective on the status and interest of language itself from that typical of linguistics. CA's primary interest is in the social act and only marginally in language, whereas a linguist's primary interest is normally in language. In descriptivist linguistics, the interest is in examining how aspects of language are organized in relation to each other. CA, by contrast, studies how social acts are organized in interaction. As part of this, CA is interested in how social acts are packaged and delivered in linguistic terms. The fundamental CA question 'Why this, in this way, right now?' captures the interest in talk as social action, which is delivered in particular linguistic formatting, as part of an unfolding sequence. The CA perspective on the primacy of the social act is illustrated by chapters in this collection. For example, Gafaranga and Britten found that general practitioners systematically use different 'social' opening sequences to talk different professional relationships into being and hence to establish different professional contexts. This is an example of CA analysts' interest in linguistic forms; not so much for their own sake, but rather in the way they are used to embody and express subtle differences in social actions with social consequences.

The distinction between emic and etic perspectives is vital to the argument in this chapter. The distinction originated in linguistics and specifically in phonology, namely in the difference between phonetics and phonemics. Pike's definition of etic and emic perspectives broadened interest in the distinction in the social sciences:

> The etic viewpoint studies behaviour as from outside of a particular system, and as an essential initial approach to an alien system. The emic viewpoint results from studying behaviour as from inside the system. (Pike 1967: 37)

There is no sense that either perspective is inherently superior to the other, and CA does not claim that social actions and emic perspectives are inherently more important than language or etic perspectives *per se*; it is simply the case that CA's unrelenting aim is to portray social action in interaction from an emic perspective. What CA means by an emic perspective, however, is not merely the participants' perspective, but the perspective from within the sequential environment in which the social actions were performed. Here the interactants talk their social world into being by employing the context-free interactional architecture in context-sensitive ways. The participants display in the interaction those terms of reference which they employ and these provide us with access to the emic perspective.

This point can be illustrated using an example from Bloch (this volume) which reveals how a dysarthric individual is able to co-construct words and multi-word utterances with the help of another person. The norms of turn-taking in conversation (Sacks *et al.* 1974) specify that one speaker usually speaks at a time and that turns may be exchanged when a turn-constructional unit is complete; this constitutes the context-free machinery. Although the mother (M) does not follow these norms, we understand the significance of her social acts by reference to them. The degree of M's help in co-construction is indexed and documented by the intervention of repetition before TCUs are complete and by the candidate expansions. In other words, the interactants perform their social actions *precisely by normative reference to the model of turn-taking.* The interactional organizations (turn-taking, sequence, repair and preference) themselves are stated in context-free terms, but the vital point is that participants employ these context-free organizations in a context-sensitive way to display their social actions. It is because the participants (and we as analysts) are able to identify the gap between the context-free model and its context-sensitive implementation that they (and we as analysts) are able to understand the social significance of the context-sensitive implementation. So the CA conception of an emic perspective cannot be disembedded from the sequential context, which provides the interface between context-free architecture and context-sensitive implementation. This is why CA considers that interviewing participants post-hoc cannot provide an emic perspective as understood here.

Research methods and concepts

It follows from the discussion above that CA's aim to develop an emic perspective on talk means that many of its assumptions and practices will necessarily be radically different from research methodologies with different goals. At this point I will attempt to position CA in relation to typical social science research methods and concepts such as validity, reliability, generalizability, epistemology, quantification and triangulation, as well as explicating the CA position on 'context'. The aim of this section is to facilitate mutual understanding between the different paradigms in which CA, linguistics and social sciences operate. A number of points need to be made beforehand. First, qualitative researchers often object that the concepts of validity and reliability derive from quantitative approaches and sometimes propose alternative criteria to be applied to qualitative research; these issues are discussed by Bryman (2001: 31–2). Secondly, as Peräkylä (1997: 216) notes, 'The specific techniques of securing reliability and validity in different types of qualitative research are not the same.' Thirdly, the goal of developing an emic perspective on naturally occurring interaction means that CA has had to develop many procedures and practices that are rather different to mainstream research methodologies. Fourthly, Peräkylä (1997: 202) notes that, until his own publication, there had been 'no accessible discussions available on issues of validity and reliability in conversation analytic studies'. This does not mean that CA practitioners have not been interested in these issues. On the contrary, it may be argued that all CA work has been (on one level) an attempt at a process exposition of what exactly is involved in and meant by ensuring validity and reliability in the analysis of talk. However, CA practitioners have often phrased the discussion in terms only accessible to other practitioners, with the unintended result that the CA perspective has often been misunderstood by social science and linguistic researchers.[1]

Reliability

Peräkylä (1997: 206) identifies the key factors in relation to reliability as the selection of what is recorded, the technical quality of recordings and the adequacy of transcripts; ten Have (1999) provides a very detailed account of this area. Another aspect of reliability is the question of whether the results of a study are repeatable or replicable (Bryman 2001: 29), and the way CA studies present their data is of crucial significance here. Many research methodologies do not present their primary data in their publications and hence the reliability of major sections of the researchers' analyses is not available for scrutiny. By contrast, it is standard practice for CA studies to include the transcripts of the data, and increasingly to make audio and video files available electronically via the Web. Furthermore, because CA studies (as exemplified in this collection) display their analyses, they make transparent the process of analysis for the reader. This enables the reader to analyse the data themselves, to test the analytical procedures which the author has followed and the validity of his/her analysis and claims. In this way, all of the analyses of data in this collection are rendered repeatable and replicable to the reader in so far as this is possible. For example, Packett (this volume) describes how he recorded expert interviewers using insertion sequences and also noticed that his student interviewers failed to produce these sequences in the practice interview situation. His chapter provides sufficient information to permit others to replicate his procedure with other groups of journalism students. Is Packett's analysis reliable? The analysis was originally presented at a seminar for comment and was then peer-reviewed by a number of editors and reviewers. Indeed, it is standard practice for CA practitioners to take their data and analyses to data workshops and to send their work to other practitioners for comment before sending them for publication. Most importantly, however, the data and the analysis are publicly available for challenge by any reader; in many other research methodologies readers do not have access to these.

Internal validity

We will now consider four kinds of validity in relation to qualitative research: internal, external, ecological and construct validity (Bryman 2001: 30). Internal validity is concerned with the soundness, integrity and credibility of findings. Do the data prove what the researcher says they prove or are there alternative explanations? Many CA procedures which seem strange to non-practitioners are based on a concern for ensuring internal validity whilst developing an emic perspective, which reflects the participants' perspective rather than the analyst's. How do CA analysts know what the participants' perspective is? Because the participants document their social actions to each other in the details of the inter-action by normative reference to the interactional organizations, as explained above. We as analysts can access the emic perspective in the details of the interaction and by reference to those same organizations. Clearly, the details of the interaction themselves provide the only justi-fication for claiming to be able to develop an emic perspective. There-fore, CA practitioners make no claims beyond what is demonstrated by the interactional detail without destroying the emic perspective and hence the whole internal validity of the enterprise.

Ten Have (1999: 27) details a number of aspects of CA practice which often astound non-practitioners. These can be explained (from one angle) as being absolutely necessary in order to maintain validity in an emic perspective. The first aspect ten Have mentions is obsession with 'trivial' detail. However, since the emic perspective can only be portrayed by reference to the minute interactional detail, this is vital. Secondly, CA does not tend to use existing theories of language, society, psychology etc. to explain the interaction. This would replace the emic perspective with an analyst's perspective, unless it can be shown in the details of the interaction that the participants themselves are orienting to such theories. Thirdly, CA allegedly refuses to take context into account as it declines to invoke 'obviously relevant' contextual features such as participants' social status, gender, race etc. Since there are an indefinite number of 'external' aspects of cultural, social or personal identity or context that could be potentially relevant to any given instance of talk-in-interaction, an emic analysis must show which of these innumerable, potentially relevant characteristics are actually procedurally relevant to those participants at that moment; this can only be accomplished by analysing the details of the interaction. Benwell and Stokoe (this volume), for example, avoid the *a priori* assumption that resistance to academic identity is linked to gender in UK university tutorials. They find that both male and female students use the same interactional strategies to resist academic identity and conclude that the participants themselves do not display an orientation to gender in this regard. Similarly, Egbert (this volume) considers the extent to which the category 'non-native' is procedurally relevant to the interaction.

External validity

External validity is concerned with generalizability or the extent to which the findings can be generalized beyond the specific research context. A typical criticism of qualitative studies is that they are context-bound and therefore weak in terms of external validity. Peräkylä (1997: 214) points out that generalizability 'is closely dependent on the type of conversation analytic research' and indeed there is variation in the generalizability of the studies in this collection. It is sometimes not appreciated that CA studies may analyse on the micro and macro level simultaneously. So, by explicating the organization of the micro-interaction in a particular social setting, CA studies may at the same time be providing some aspects of a generalizable description of the interactional organization of the setting. This is the case because interaction is seen as rationally organized in relation to social goals (Levinson 1992: 71). CA studies in effect work on the particular and the general simultaneously; by analysing individual instances, the machinery that produced these individual instances is revealed: 'The point of working with actual occurrences, single instances, single events, is to see them as the products of a "machinery" ... The ethnomethodological objective is to generate formal descriptions of social actions which preserve and display the features of the machinery which produced them' (Benson and Hughes 1991: 130–131).

For example, Bloch's chapter (this volume) makes the generalizable point that different research methodological approaches provide different pictures of the same individual's communicative competence. A focus on the individual in dysarthric speech production using a speech signal intelligibility model tends to provides a 'deficit' picture, with the degree of severity being based upon a perceptual or instrumental analysis. Seen from this perspective, dysarthria is a medical label that describes a form of speech production but does not indicate the consequences of that production upon conversation or social action. Bloch, by contrast, reveals how the dysarthric individual is able to co-construct words and multi-word utterances with the help of another person, so the picture presented is one of competencies.[2]

Ecological validity

Ecological validity is concerned with whether findings are applicable to people's everyday life; laboratory experiments in the social sciences can often be weak in terms of ecological validity. CA practitioners typically record naturally occurring talk in its authentic social setting, attempting to develop an emic, holistic perspective and to portray how the interactants perform their social actions through talk by reference to the same interactional organizations which the interactants are using. Therefore CA studies tend to be exceptionally strong by comparison to other research methodologies in terms of ecological validity. Vinkhuyzen and Szymanski's study (this volume) of requests for service in one very specific ecological system (a reprographics shop in California) reveals that requests linguistically formatted as other-oriented interrogatives tend to cause problems for the service providers, whereas those packaged as self-oriented declaratives do not. Because the analysis is so firmly grounded in the specific ecological system, the reflexive relationship between linguistic formatting and institutional context is abundantly clear. Contrast this with the disappointing results of decontextualised studies of requests reviewed by Levinson (1983). Since, as mentioned in the previous section, CA portrays individual instances as products of a machinery, the analysis is not limited to one particular reprographics shop, so some generalizable findings emerge. For example, different linguistic packaging of requests can expose the inherent conflict in service industries of satisfying the customer and maximizing profits.

Construct validity, epistemology and ontology

In this section I will consider construct validity, epistemology and ontology together. Construct validity[3] is a vital concept in a positivistic, quantitative paradigm (Bryman 2001). However, in an emic paradigm the question is: whose construct is it? Typically, descriptivist linguists look for etically specifiable methods of description, so that an analyst can match surface linguistic features of the interaction to constructs and categories. In an emic perspective, however, we are looking for constructs to which participants orient during interaction, which is not necessarily the same thing. Epistemologically, CA is based on ethnomethodology (for a discussion, see Heritage (1984b) and Seedhouse (2004)) located (Lynch 2000) in a phenomenological paradigm, which considers that 'it is the job of the social scientist to gain access to people's "common-sense thinking" and hence to interpret their actions and their social world from their point of view'. (Bryman 2001: 14). Ethno-methodology's ontological position can be associated with construc-tionism or the belief that 'social phenomena and their meanings are constantly being accomplished by social actors'. (Bryman 2001: 18). Hence, CA sees social constructs as being talked in and out of being by interactants.

I will illustrate how this position with respect to construct validity, ontology and epistemology functions in practice by reference to Markee's chapter (this volume). Task-based Learning (TBL) has assumed a central role in applied linguistics research, particularly in Second Language Acquisition (SLA). TBL/SLA operates predominantly in a quantitative paradigm[4] (Lazaraton 2000) which in turn assumes the importance of construct validity (Long 1997) and a fundamentally object-ivist ontological position. This means that the construct 'task' has to have a tangible objective reality of its own and be concretely specifiable. In TBL/SLA, task is conceived of as a workplan (Ellis 2003: 9) made prior to classroom implementation of what the teachers and learners will do. This is therefore specified etically, reflecting the objectivist position (Bryman 2001: 17) that social phenomena and their meanings have an existence independent of social actors. Though the task-as-workplan may materially exist in the physical shape of a lesson plan or course-book unit, it does not exist as an interactive event since it is defined as a plan.

Markee's chapter demonstrates how learners recorded working on a pairwork task can switch instantly from on-task institutional talk to off-task social talk. Markee demonstrates how the learners in the extract carefully disguise their social talk (relating to a party invitation) from the teacher and are able instantly to switch back on-task when required. In other words, the interactants can talk the relevance of the construct 'task' in and out of being from one moment to the next. A number of research studies (Coughlan and Duff 1994; Donato 2000; Foster 1998; Mori 2002; Ohta 2000; Seedhouse, 2004) confirm that there is often a very significant difference between what is supposed to happen (inten-ded pedagogy) and what actually happens (actual pedagogy) in task-based pedagogy. From the ontological perspective, this causes fundamental problems for an objectivist position. The task-as-workplan, which is taken to be the basis of construct validity with an objective reality, may be re-interpreted, ignored or marginalized by the interactants and hence have a very weak ontology in interaction. By contrast, the constructivist position is ontologically strong; the object of study is simply whatever the interactants actually orient to during the interaction.

The constructs which are revealed by CA are those to which the participants themselves orient during interaction, rather than those that may be pre-specified in *a priori* fashion by analysts. The knowledge created is that of the social world, social phenomena and categories that are talked into being in a sequential environment by the participants themselves. From a broader perspective, CA creates knowledge of how social acts are performed in interaction and of how interaction itself is organized. Ontologically, CA studies that which the interactants themselves make relevant or talk into being. The constructs studied are therefore those that have reality for the interactants.

Quantification

The short and simple way to present the CA attitude to quantification would be to state that CA is a qualitative methodology that tries to develop an emic perspective, so quantification is generally of peripheral interest to CA practitioners. It has often been mistakenly reported that quantification is prohibited in CA. However, informal or methodological quantification has been widely used from the beginnings of CA. Schegloff *et al.* (1977), for example, report self-correction as 'vastly more common than other-correction'. The classic statement of the CA position on quantification is Schegloff (1993), who warns specifically against premature quantification in relation to superficially identifiable interactional phenomena, which will tend to divert our attention from detailed analysis of individual instances. As Schegloff (1993: 114) puts it, 'Quantification is no substitute for analysis.' Nevertheless, Heritage (1999: 70) considers the likelihood that CA will become more quantitative during the next period of its development and identifies (1995: 404) a number of possible uses for statistics in CA:

- As a means of isolating interesting phenomena.
- As a means of consolidating intuitions which are well defined, but where the existence of a practice is difficult to secure without a large number of cases.
- In cases in which independent findings about a conversational practice can have indirect statistical support.
- In almost all cases where a claim is made that the use or outcome of a particular interactional practice is tied to particular social or psychological categories, such as gender, status etc. statistical support will be necessary.

Gardner's chapter (this volume) provides an excellent example of quantification built on and complementary to CA qualitative analysis. Gardner's CA analysis of a mother and a therapist working on speech with the same child identifies two phenomena (length of bout and the focus of repair-initiation) as constituting significant differences in approach by the two adults, the CA analysis uncovering an emic logic connecting the two phenomena. Schegloff (1993: 114) notes that 'We need to know what the phenomena are, how they are organized, and how they are related to each other as a precondition for cogently bringing methods of quantitative analysis to bear on them' and in Gardner's chapter this stage has been reached. Quantification then confirms that there is an overall significant difference in length of bout in relation to the two adults. Furthermore, Gardner quantifies different turn types which had previously been identified during the CA stage, relating these findings to the therapeutic outcomes achieved by the therapist and the mother. When considering applications of CA in professional and institutional contexts, we should take into account that many professions and institutions use numerical data as a prime source of evidence for their decision-making. Therefore, Gardner's combination of qualitative and quantitative approaches is likely to strengthen the professional credibility of her claims.

Triangulation and ethnographic data sources

Given the emic goal of CA, there is no substitute for detailed and in-depth analysis of individual sequences; interviews, questionnaires and observations are not able to provide this, which is why *triangulation* and other data-gathering techniques typical of ethnography are not generally undertaken. However, there is currently a movement to integrate CA and ethnography. Recent papers (Auer 1995; Silverman 1999) have attempted a rapprochement between these two methodological approaches. Silverman's basic argument is that the two approaches are compatible and may be applied to the same instances of talk. An initial CA analysis of *how* participants locally produce context for their interaction can be followed by an ethnographic analysis of *why* questions about institutional and cultural constraints, thus moving from the micro to the macro levels. Auer (1995: 427) points out that data collection procedures in ethnography are eclectic by principle and therefore incorporate CA methods. Another issue of recent interest (e.g. Arminen 2000) has been the extent to which CA analyses of institutional discourse make use of ethnographic or expert knowledge of the institutional setting. Arminen's argument is that CA analysts inevitably do make use of such knowledge and should make as transparent as possible the extent to which their analyses derive from the details of the interaction or from use of ethnographic or expert knowledge.

This collection contains two studies which demonstrate the possibility of combining CA and ethnography in a mutually reinforcing way. Vinkhuyzen and Szymanski's recorded data derive from one stage of a three-year ethnographic study, the other two stages being ethnographic observation, shadowing and interviewing as well as participant observation. The expert knowledge they obtained of the economics of the business helps the authors explain the institutional significance of the different ways customers package their requests. Gafaranga and Britten carried out pre- and post-consultation interviews with patients and doctors were interviewed post-consultation. In a deviant case, where a doctor used *What can I do for you?* with a patient he knew very well, a post-consultation interview revealed that this patient had abused the health system and the doctor was deliberately and strategically distancing himself from the patient by choice of topic initial elicitor. In this case, then, ethnographic information was able to shed light on a deviant case and this served to reinforce the argument which the authors had already built on sequential analysis.

Attitude to context

CA has a dynamic, complex and highly empirical perspective on context. The basic aim is to establish an emic perspective, i.e. to determine which elements of context are relevant to the interactants at any point in the interaction. The perspective is also an active one in which participants are seen to talk a context into being or out of being. The perspective is dynamic in that, as Heritage (1984b: 242) puts it, 'The context of a next action is repeatedly renewed with every current action' and is transformable at any moment. A basic assumption of CA is that contributions to interaction are *context-shaped* and *context-renewing*. Contributions are context-shaped in that they cannot be adequately understood except by reference to the sequential environment in which they occur and in which the participants design them to occur. Contributions are context-renewing in that they create a sequential environment or template in which a next contribution will occur. So Markee's chapter (this volume), for example, shows how interactants instantly talk out of being the official pedagogical context and talk into being an alternative 'social' context. We cannot assume that one single contextual feature or membership category will remain relevant throughout a whole inter-actional sequence. Different contextual elements may be talked in and out of being and relevance as the sequence progresses and the partici-pants themselves may negotiate or dispute their relevance. Kurhila's chapter (this volume) demonstrates a dynamic perspective on context and shows how the participants themselves may orient differently to contextual features or membership categories. In Kurhila's Extract 4, one participant tries to foreground his identity as non-native speaker and have his conversational partner help with his problems with linguistic form. The other participant, however, resists this by foregrounding their respective institutional identities as secretary and student and prioritizes the institutional business of completing a form.

CA sees the underlying machinery that generates interaction as being both context-free and operating in context-sensitive ways. The structural organizations can be seen as the context-free resources in that their organization can be specified as a series of norms in isolation from any specific instance of interaction, but the application of these organiza-tions is context-sensitive in that interactants use the organization of (for example) turn-taking to display their understanding of context. So professionals and lay clients may talk an institutional context into being through the professional taking control of the turn-taking system; we understand this by reference to the context-free norms. By tracing how the context-free resources are employed and manifested locally in a context-sensitive manner, we are able to uncover the underlying machinery. As Hutchby and Wooffitt (1998: 36) put it, 'The aim of con-versation analysis . . . is to explicate the structural organization of talk in interaction at this interface between context-free resources and their context-sensitive applications.'

The final aspect to the rather complex CA perspective on context is that sequential location is as a major part of what we mean by context. Two examples are provided, one from non-verbal communication and one from verbal communication. Dickerson *et al.*'s chapter (this volume) demonstrates the significance of sequential placement as context. Traditionally, gaze abnormalities (particularly gaze aversion) are cited as a 'symptom' of autism by many professional groups. However, Dickerson *et al.* carefully relate gaze activity in a sequential location to the activities of referring and addressing and demonstrate that children diagnosed as autistic can deploy 'competent and sophisticated eye gaze practice'. Sequential location, then, provides a 'context' for the significance of gaze. Vowel-marking by Japanese novice ESL learners has been generally treated as an L1 interference phenomenon. However, Carroll's chapter (this volume) shows that learners systematically and strategically employ vowel-marking as part of forward-oriented repair, so that sequential location determines where vowel-marking is most likely to occur. In Carroll's data, vowel-marking tends to precede intra-turn pauses (oh dees dees is-u (0.22)) and to precede a sought-for-item (it's-u: raining).

Themes for development

In this final section I tie together themes which have emerged in the collection and look to possible future research developments.

CA has proved able to provide a 'holistic' portrayal of language use that reveals the reflexive relationships between form, function, sequence and social identity and social/institutional context. In all chapters we see that the organization of the talk relates directly and reflexively to the social goals of the participants, whether institutional or otherwise. In Bloch's chapter we see how the participants develop an extraordinary speech-exchange system in orientation to their goal of having as 'ordinary' a relationship and a conversation as possible under the circumstances. Gafaranga and Britten's chapter demonstrates how doctors systematically use different 'social' opening sequences to talk different professional relationships into being. Packett's chapter identifies an insertion sequence that is directly related to the institutional goal of informing an unseen but overhearing audience. Gardner's chapter shows how a therapist and a mother organize their talk with a child differently owing to their different belief systems. In Markee's chapter we see how the students cunningly organize their verbal and non-verbal communication in order to conceal from the teacher their project of off-task social talk.

A recurrent theme in this collection is that interactants do not always share the same social goals or the same understanding of context and their respective roles. Egbert demonstrates the very different orientations a landlady and potential tenant have towards the prospective goal of letting a flat. Vinkhuyzen and Szymanski show how staff and customers in service encounters may have very different views of how the service should proceed. Benwell and Stokoe's and Markee's studies demonstrate how students may resist tasks teachers ask them to carry out. Both Kurhila's and Wong's chapters reveal different orientations to grammatical correctness on the part of native speakers and non-native speakers. In all cases, however, CA is able to portray the progress of the participants' intersubjectivity. Taken as a whole, the collection demonstrates that in naturally-occurring interaction, social actors negotiate an extremely diverse range of social and institutional goals by deploying an equally diverse verbal and non-verbal repertoire in a dynamic and mutable environment. The collection shows that CA is able to handle this level of heterogeneity and mutability and also make itself relevant on a practical level in terms of applications. This is the case because, whatever the specific type of human activity, CA is able to provide the emic perspective and to portray the reflexive relationship between the social and interactional levels.

CA is able to grow organically to accommodate new dimensions. Its current stage of growth is marked by linguistic and cultural diversity. There are now CA studies of interaction in a number of different languages (reviewed in Schegloff *et al.* 2002; Seedhouse 2004) and early criticisms that CA was biased as it was based almost exclusively on English native-speaker interaction are no longer founded. This collection contains chapters on NS–NNS interaction in Finnish (Kurhila) and German (Egbert) as well as English (Wong), multilingual code-switching (Torras) and all the indications are that the trend towards multilingual and multicultural applied CA studies will continue; see in particular Gardner and Wagner (2004). Torras's chapter shows that CA is particularly well suited to the portrayal of the social dimensions of language choice. Torras uncovers the subtle, complex and reflexive relationship between multiple social identities in relation to language choice, roles in service transactions and degrees of acquaintanceship. The chapter challenges static and monolithic conceptions of social identity and presents language preference as a platform for the display of identity sets relevant to the interaction. Interactants are shown to negotiate and switch between multiple identities, multiple types of relationship with each other and multiple languages; these are shown to be interdependent.

The finding in several chapters that oral production problems are sometimes related to interactional issues rather than internal mechanisms has many implications for future research. Chapters by Dickerson *et al.*, Markee and Carroll demonstrate the importance of delicate transcription and analysis of gaze and non-verbal communication as interactive resources. A particularly strong theme to emerge from the collection was the similarities between native speaker–non-native speaker talk and talk in communication disorder settings. The similarities emerged in interactional patterns but also in the way in which a CA approach challenged static linguistic deficit models and highlighted interactive competencies. This approach may be used to investigate a wider range of settings in which speakers are assumed to be less than competent. An important epistemological point is that the knowledge we build of the communicative abilities of individuals depends crucially on the methodology used to study them. If individuals are asked to produce speech in isolation, which is then segmented, quantified and compared to a norm, the result will inevitably be presented in terms of deficit. By contrast, a holistic view of the same individuals in interaction may reveal the inventive ways they are able to co-construct meaning with their interactional partners: see also Gardner and Wagner (2004).

Individual chapters suggest areas for future research and the individual chapters provide models of applied CA research. The three chapters on communication disorders suggest fruitful areas for research in therapeutic contexts, while the range of the four chapters on professional interaction indicates what an enormous scope there is for CA studies in diverse professional areas; see also Asmuss and Steensig (2003). A theme common to all of the studies is how professionals are best able to orient their clients to the institutional goal, and this is likely to be applicable to all professional contexts. The study of discrimination introduced by Egbert (this volume) is one with considerable potential for development, as is the theme common to the three chapters of how native speakers invoke and negotiate identities through talk. There are many areas for CA to explore in the area of native speaker–nonnative speaker interaction and language learning. For example, Carroll (this volume) reveals the potential of studying learner talk, while Packett (this volume) demonstrates that analysis of professional talk may be very relevant to the teaching of Languages for Specific Purposes. The issues and possibilities are discussed in Jacoby (1998a, b), Koshik (2000), Markee (2000) and Seedhouse (2004). Language proficiency assessment design may be informed by CA, as previous work in this area by Young and He (1998), Lazaraton (1997) and Kasper and Ross (2001) demonstrates. The finding of this collection that communicative competence is not a static construct invites future research. The collection demonstrates that CA is able to tackle many areas of interest to applied linguistics. Richards' and Drew's chapters (this volume) outline the relationship between CA and AL, and all indications are that this will continue to be fruitful and that applications of CA are likely to increase in volume and scope.

Notes

1 For an example of a 'linguistic' misunderstanding of CA, see Seedhouse (2004, chapter 1).
2 Bloch (personal communication) points out that we cannot generalize that all dysarthric conversations are like those analysed here. However, because

they appear so unusual, they require a method that allows us to describe the mechanism beneath the surface individuality.

3   Construct validity has to do with the question of 'whether a measure that is devised of a concept really does reflect the concept that it is supposed to be denoting' (Bryman 2001: 30).

4   The assumption of a predominantly quantitative paradigm does not of course imply that qualitative work is not undertaken in TBL/SLA; see, for example, Hall and Verplaetse 2000; Ohta 2000. However, Lazaraton (2000) found in a study of empirical articles in four prominent language teaching/SLA journals over a seven-year period that 88% were quantitative. There is considerable debate as to the legitimacy of the term 'quantitative paradigm'. This study adopts Bryman's (2001) position with respect to quantitative and qualitative research. This is that it is possible to distinguish differences between quantitative and qualitative research strategies in terms of the role of theory in research, epistemology and ontology. However, these should be seen as tendencies and there are complex interconnections between the two strategies. Furthermore, in some circumstances and if carefully planned, the two strategies may be combined in multi-strategy research.

Bibliography

Allwright, R.L. 1984. The importance of interaction in classroom language learning. *Applied Linguistics*, 5(2): 157–71.

American Psychiatric Association (4th edn) 1995. *Diagnostic & Statistical Manual of Mental Disorders-DSM IV.*

Antaki, C. and S. Widdicombe 1998. Identity as an achievement and as a tool. In C. Antaki and S. Widdicombe (eds) *Identities in Talk*. London: Sage, pp. 1–14.

Antaki, C. and S. Widdicombe (eds) 1998. *Identities in Talk*. London: Sage.

Arnold, A., R.J. Semple, I. Beale and C.M. Fletcher-Flynn 2000. Eye contact in children's social interactions: what is normal behaviour? *Journal of Intellectual and Developmental Disability*, 25(3): 207–16.

Asmuss, B. and J. Steensig (eds) 2003. Samtalen på arbejde – konversationsanalysen og kompetenceudvikling. Copenhagen: Samfundslitteratur.

Aston, G. (ed.) 1988. *Negotiating Service: Studies in the Discourse of Bookshop Encounters*. Bologna: The PIXI Project.

Atkinson, J.M. 1984. *Our Master's Voices: The Language and Body Language of Politics*. London: Methuen.

Atkinson J.M. and P. Drew. 1979. *Order in Court: the Organisation of Verbal Interaction in Judicial Settings*. London: Macmillan.

Atkinson, J.M. and J. Heritage. 1984. Transcript notation. In J.M. Atkinson and J. Heritage (eds) *Structures of Social Action*. Cambridge: Cambridge University Press, pp. ix–xvi.

Atkinson, J.M. and J. Heritage (eds) 1984. *Structures of Social Action. Studies in Conversation Analysis*. Cambridge: Cambridge University Press.

Auer, P. 1984. *Bilingual Conversation*. Amsterdam: Benjamins Publishing Company.

Auer, P. 1995. Ethnographic methods in the analysis of oral communication. In U. Quasthoff (ed.), *Aspects of Oral Communication*. Berlin: Walter de Gruyter, pp. 419–40.

Baltaxe, C.A.M. 1977. Pragmatics deficits in the language of autistic adolescents. *Journal of Paediatric Psychology*, 2(4): 176–80.

Baron-Cohen, S., A.M. Leslie and U. Frith 1985. Does the autistic child have a theory of mind? *Cognition*, 21: 37–46.

Batts, Valerie 1989. Modern Racism: New melody for the same old tunes. In A. Koopman (ed.) 1997. *Shifting Paradigms*. Early Learning Resource Unit. Lansdowne, South Africa (in consultation with Helen Robb), pp. 18–29.

Beach, W. 1993. Transactional regularities for 'casual' "okay" usages. *Journal of Pragmatics*, 19: 325–52.

Becker, J. 1999. *The Cyberspace Regionalization Project: Simultaneously Bridging the Digital and Racial Divide*. The Secretary's Conference on Educational Technology. http://www.ed.gov/Technology/TechConf/1999/whitepapers/paper7.html#V (downloaded in June 2002).

Benson, D. and J. Hughes 1991. Method: evidence and inference – evidence and inference for ethnomethodology. In G. Button (ed.), *Ethnomethodology and the Human Sciences* Cambridge: Cambridge University Press, pp. 109–36.

Benwell, B. 1996. The Discourse of University Tutorials. Unpublished PhD dissertation, University of Nottingham, UK.

Benwell, B. 1999. The organisation of knowledge in British university tutorial discourse: issues, pedagogic discourse strategies and disciplinary identity. *Pragmatics*, 9(4): 535–65.

Benwell, B. and E.H. Stokoe 2002. Constructing discussion tasks in university tutorials: shifting dynamics and identities. *Discourse Studies*, 4(4): 429–53.

Benwell, B. and E.H. Stokoe (forthcoming). The organisation of knowledge displays in tutorial talk. Manuscript in preparation.

Beretta, A. (ed.) 1993. Theory construction in second language acquisition. *Applied Linguistics* (Special Issue), 14(3).

Bergmann, J.R. 1981. Ethnomethodologische Konversationsanalyse. In P. Schröder and H. Steger (eds) *Dialogforschung. Jahrbuch 1980 des Institus für deutsche Sprache*. Düsseldorf, pp. 9–51.

Bettelheim, B. 1967. *The Empty Fortress: Infantile Autism and The Birth of the Self*. New York: Free Press.

Billig, M. 1999. Whose terms? Whose ordinariness? Rhetoric and ideology in Conversation Analysis. *Discourse and Society*, 10(4): 543–58.

Blum-Kulka, S., J. House and G. Kasper (eds)1989. *Cross-cultural Pragmatics: Requests and Apologies*. Norwood NJ: Ablex.

Boddy, F.A. 1975. General Practice medicine. In J.H. Barber and F.A. Boddy (eds) *General Practice Medicine*. London: Churchill Livingstone, pp. 1–25.

Boden, D. 1994. *The Business of Talk: Organizations in Action*. Cambridge: Polity Press.

Boden, D. and D.H. Zimmerman (eds) 1991. *Talk and Social Structure. Studies in Ethnomethodology and Conversation Analysis*. Oxford: Polity Press.

Bower, P., L. Gask, C. May and N. Mead 2000. Domains of consultation research in primary care. *Patient Education and Counselling*, 45: 3–11.

Boyle, R. 2000. 'You've Worked with Elizabeth Taylor!': Phatic Functions and Implicit Compliments. *Applied Linguistics*, 21(1): 26–46.

Britten, N., F.A. Stevenson, C.A. Barry, N. Barber and C.P. Bradley 2000. Misunderstandings in prescribing decisions in general practice: qualitative study. *British Medical Journal*, 320: 484–8.

Brouwer, C. 1998. On doing being a language learner: Word searches in NNS–NS interaction. A paper presented at IPrA conference, 1998, Reims, France.

Brouwer, C. 2000. L2 listening in interaction. Unpublished doctoral thesis, Institute of Language and Communication, University of Southern Denmark, Odense University.

Brown, G. and G. Yule 1983. *Discourse Analysis*. Cambridge: Cambridge University Press.

Brown, P. and S. Levinson 1978. Universals in language use: politeness phenomena. In E. Goody (ed.) *Questions and Politeness*. Cambridge: Cambridge University Press.

Brown, P. and S. Levinson 1987. *Politeness: Some Universals in Language Usage*. Cambridge: Cambridge University Press.

Bryman, A. 2001. *Social Research Methods*. Oxford: Oxford University Press.

Button, G. 1991. Conversation-in-a-series. In D. Boden and D. Zimmerman (eds), *Talk and Social Structure. Studies in Ethnomethodology and Conversation Analysis*. Oxford: Polity Press, pp. 251–77.

Button, G. 1992. Answers as interactional products: two sequential practices used in job interviews. In P. Drew and J. Heritage (eds) *Talk at Work: Interaction in Institutional Settings*. Cambridge: Cambridge University Press, pp. 212–31.

Button, G. and N.J. Casey 1984. Generating a topic: The use of topic initial elicitors. In J.M. Atkinson and J. Heritage (eds) *Structures of Social Action: Studies in Conversation Analysis*. Cambridge: Cambridge University Press, pp. 167–90.

Butts, E. 2000. Overcoming Student Resistance to Group Work. *TETYC* September: 80–3.

Candlin, C.N., Y. Maley and H. Sutch 1999. Industrial instability and the discourse of enterprise bargaining. In S. Sarangi and C. Roberts (eds) *Talk, Work and Institutional Order. Discourse in Medical, Mediation and Management Settings*. Berlin: Mouton de Gruyter, pp. 323–49.

Carroll, D. 2000. Precision timing in novice-to-novice L2 conversations. *Issues in Applied Linguistics*, 11(1): 67–110.

Carroll, D. 2004. Finding a way forward: Word searches in novice-to-novice L2 talk. In R. Gardner and J. Wagner (eds) *Second Language Conversations*. London: Continuum.

Carter, K. and J. McNeill 1998. Coping with the darkness of transition: students as the leading lights of guidance at induction to higher education. *British Journal of Guidance and Counselling*, 26(3): 399–415.

Celce-Murcia, M. and E. Olshtain 2000. *Discourse and Context in Language Teaching: A Guide for Language Teachers*. Cambridge: Cambridge University Press.

Chenery, H. 1998. Perceptual analysis of dysarthric speech. In B. Murdoch (ed.) *Dysarthria — A Physiological Approach to Assessment and Treament*. Cheltenham: Stanley Thornes Ltd, pp. 37–67.

Clarke, M.A. 1994. The dysfunctions of the theory/practice discourse. *TESOL Quarterly*. 28(1): 9–26.

Clayman, S. 1991. News interview openings: aspects of sequential organization. In P. Scannell (ed.) *Broadcast Talk: A Reader*. Newbury Park: Sage, pp. 48–75.

Clayman, S. 1992. Footing in the achievement of neutrality: the case of news interview discourse. In P. Drew and J. Heritage (eds) *Talk at Work: Interaction in Institutional Settings*. Cambridge: Cambridge University Press, pp. 163–98.

Clayman, S. and J. Heritage. 2002. *The News Interview: Journalists and Public Figures on the Air*. Cambridge: Cambridge University Press.

Clayman, S.E. and J. Whalen 1988. When the medium becomes the message: The case of the Rather-Bush encounter. *Research on Language and Social Interaction*, 22: 241–72.

Clift, R. 2001. Meaning in interaction: the case of 'actually'. *Language*, 77(2): 245–91.

Collins, S., I. Markova and J. Murphy 1997. Bringing conversations to a close: the management of closings in interactions between AAC users and 'natural' speakers. *Clinical Linguistics and Phonetics*, 11(6): 467–93.

Comrie, P., C. Mackenzie and J. McCall 2001. The influence of acquired dysarthria on conversational turn taking. *Clinical Linguistics and Phonetics*, 15(5): 383–98.

Coughlan, P. and P. Duff 1994. Same task, different activities: Analysis of a second language acquisition task from an activity theory perspective. In J.P. Lantolf and G. Appel (eds) *Vygotskian Approaches to Second Language Research*. Norwood, NJ: Ablex Press, pp. 173–94.

Couper-Kuhlen, E. 1992. Contextualizing discourse: The prosody of interactive repair. In A.D. Luzio (ed.) *The Contextualization of Language.* Amsterdam: John Benjamins Publishing Company, pp. 337–64.

Coupland, J. (ed.) 2000. *Small Talk.* Essex: Pearson Education.

Coupland, N. and V. Ylänne-McEwen 2000. Talk about the weather: Small talk, leisure talk and the travel industry. In J. Coupland (ed.) *Small Talk.* Essex: Pearson Education, pp. 163–82.

Cuff, E.C. 1994. *Problems of Versions in Everyday Situations: Studies in Ethnomethodology and Conversation Analysis.* Lanham, Maryland: University Press of America.

Curcio, F. 1978. Sensorimotor functioning and communication in mute autistic children. *Journal of Autism and Childhood Schizophrenia,* 8(3): 281–92.

Dautenhahn, K. and I. Werry 2000. Issues of robot-human interaction dynamics in the rehabilitation of children with autism. *Proc. From Animals to Animats, The Sixth International Conference on the Simulation of Adaptive Behaviour* (SAB2000) 11–15 September 2000, Paris, France.

Davidson, J. 1984. Subsequent versions of invitations, offers, requests and proposals dealing with potential rejection. In J.M. Atkinson and J. Heritage (eds) *Structures of Social Action: Studies in Conversation Analysis.* Cambridge: Cambridge University Press, pp. 102–28.

Day, R., A. Chenoweth, A. Chun and S. Luppescu 1984. Corrective feedback in native–nonnative discourse. *Language Learning,* 34(2): 19–46.

De Gelder, B. 1987. On not having a theory of mind. *Cognition,* 27: 285–90.

Deutsch am Telefon. Ein Lernprogramm für Migrantinnen und Migranten. 2001. Teachers Manual with CD-ROM. Carl von Ossietzky Universität Oldenburg, Zentrum für Wissenschaftliche Weiterbildung und Institut für Bildung und Kommunikation in Migrationsprozessen.

Dobbinson, S., M.R. Perkins and J. Boucher 1998. Structural patterns in conversations with a woman who has autism. *Journal of Communication Disorders,* 31: 113–34.

Donato, R. 2000. Sociocultural contributions to understanding the foreign and second language classroom. In J. Lantolf (ed.) *Sociocultural Theory and Second Language Learning.* Oxford: Oxford University Press, pp. 27–50.

Doughty, C., and C. Varela 1998. Communicative focus on form. In C. Doughty and J. Williams (eds) *Focus on Form in Classroom Language Acquisition.* Cambridge: Cambridge University Press.

Drew, P. 1984. Speaker's reportings in invitation sequences. In J.M. Atkinson and J. Heritage (eds) *Structures of Social Action: Studies in Conversation Analysis.* Cambridge: Cambridge University Press, pp. 129–51.

Drew, P. 1991. Asymmetries of knowledge in conversational interactions. In I. Marková and K. Foppa (eds) *Asymmetries in Dialogue.* Hemel Hempstead: Harvester Wheatsheaf, pp. 29–48.

Drew, P. 1997. 'Open' class repair initiators in response to sequential sources of troubles in conversation. *Journal of Pragmatics,* 28: 69–101.

Drew, P. 2004. Conversation Analysis. In K. Fitch and R.Sanders (eds) *Handbook of Language and Social Interaction.* Mawah, NJ: Lawrence Erlbaum.

Drew, P. and J. Heritage 1992a. *Talk at Work. Interaction in Institutional Settings.* Cambridge: Cambridge University Press.

Drew, P. and J. Heritage 1992b. Analyzing talk at work: An introduction. In P. Drew and J. Heritage (eds) *Talk at Work: Interaction in Institutional Settings.* Cambridge: Cambridge University Press, pp. 3–65.

Drew, P. and M. Sorjonen. 1997. Institutional Dialogue. In T. van Dijk (ed.) *Discourse as Social Interaction (Discourse Studies: A Multidisciplinary Introduction, Volume 2)*. London: Sage, pp. 92–118.

Drummond, K. and R. Hopper. 1993a. Acknowledgement tokens in series. *Communication Reports*, 6: 47–53.

Drummond, K. and R. Hopper. 1993b. Back channels revisited: Acknowledgment tokens and speakership incipiency. *Research on Language and Social Interaction*, 26: 157–77.

Drummond, K. and R. Hopper. 1993c. Some uses of *Yeah*. *Research on Language and Social Interaction*, 26: 157–77.

Duffy, J. 1995. *Motor Speech Disorders: Substrates, Differential Diagnosis, and Management*. St Louis: Mosby.

Eckman, F.R. 1994. The competence-performance issue in second-langue acquisition theory: A debate. In E. Tarone, S. Gass and A. Cohen (eds), *Research Methodology in Second Language Acquisition*. Hillsdale, NJ: Lawrence Erlbaum, pp. 3–15.

Egbert, M.M. 1997. Schisming: The collaborative transformation from a single conversation to multiple conversations. *Research on Language and Social Interaction*, 30: 1–51.

Egbert, M.M. 1998. Miscommunication in language proficiency interviews of first-year German students: A comparison with natural conversation. In R. Young and A. He (eds) *Talking and Testing: Discourse Approaches to the Assessment of Oral Proficiency*. Amsterdam: Benjamins, pp. 147–69.

Egbert, M.M. 2002. Der Reparatur-Mechanismus in deutschen und interkulturellen Gesprächen [The repair mechanism in German and intercultural conversation]. Habilitation. University of Oldenburg, Germany.

Egbert, M.M. 2004. Other-Initiated Repair and Membership Categorization – Some Conversational Events that Trigger Linguistic and Regional Membership Categorization. *Journal of Pragmatics*, 36: 1467–98.

Ellis, R. (2003). *Task-based Language Learning and Teaching*. Oxford: Oxford University Press.

Ervin-Tripp, S.M. 1981. How to make and understand a request. In H. Parret, M. Sbisà and J. Verschueren (eds) *Possibilities and Limitations of Pragmatics*. Amsterdam: John Benjamins.

Ervin-Tripp, S.M. 1982. Ask and it shall be given you: children's requests. In H. Byrnes (ed.) Georgetown Roundtable on Languages and Linguistics. Washington, DC: Georgetown University Press, pp. 235–45.

Ervin-Tripp, S.M., A. Strage, M. Lampert and N. Bell 1987. Understanding requests. *Linguistics*, 25: 107–43.

Felder, R. and R. Brent 1996. Navigating the bumpy road to student-centred instruction. *College Teaching*, 44: 43–7.

Firth, A. 1995. Talking for change: Commodity negotiating by telephone. In A. Firth (ed.) *The Discourse of Negotiation: Studies of Language in the Workplace*. Oxford: Pergamon Press, pp. 183–222.

Firth, A. 1996. The discursive accomplishment of normality: On 'lingua franca' English and conversation analysis. *Journal of Pragmatics*, 26(2): 237–59.

Firth, A. and J. Wagner 1997. On discourse, communication, and (some) fundamental concepts in SLA research. *Modern Language Journal*, 81: 285–300.

Firth, A. and J. Wagner 1998. SLA Property: No Trespassing! *The Modern Language Journal*, 82: 91–4.

Ford, C. and S. Thompson 1996. Interactional units in conversation: syntactic, intonational, and pragmatics resources for the management of turns. In E. Ochs, E. Schegloff and S. Thompson (eds) *Interaction and Grammar*. Cambridge: Cambridge University Press, pp. 134–84.

Ford, C., B. Fox and S. Thompson 1996. Practices in the construction of turns, the TCU revisited. *Pragmatics*, 6(3): 427–54.

Foster, P. (1998). A classroom perspective on the negotiation of meaning. *Applied Linguistics*, 19, 1–23.

Francis, B. 1999. Lads, lasses and (New) Labour: 14–16-year-old students' responses to the 'laddish behaviour and boys' underachievement' debate. *British Journal of Sociology of Education*, 20(3): 355–71.

Francis, B. 2000. *Boys, Girls and Achievement: Addressing the Classroom Issues*. London: Routledge.

Freeling, P. 1983. The doctor–patient relationship in diagnosis and treatment. In D. Pendleton and J. Hasler (eds) *Doctor–Patient Communication*. London: Academic Press, pp. 161–75.

Frith, U. 1989. *Autism: Explaining The Enigma*. Oxford: Blackwell.

Fry, J. 1993. *General Practice: Facts*. Oxford: Radcliffe Medical Press.

Gaertner, S.L. and J.F. Dovidio 1986. The aversive form of racism. In J.F. Dovidio and S.L. Gaertner (eds) *Prejudice, Discrimination, and Racism*. Orlando, FL: Academic Press, pp. 61–89.

Gafaranga, J. 1999. Language choice as a significant aspect of talk organization: The orderliness of language alternation. *Text*, 19: 201–25.

Gafaranga, J. 2000. Medium repair vs. other-language repair: Telling the medium of a bilingual conversation. *International Journal of Bilingualism*, 4 (3): 327–50.

Gafaranga, J. 2001. Linguistic identities in talk-in-interaction: Order in bilingual conversation. *Journal of Pragmatics*, 33: 1901 25.

Gafaranga, J. and M.C. Torras 2001. Language versus medium in the study of bilingual conversation. *International Journal of Bilingualism*, 5 (2): 195–219.

Gafaranga, J. and M.C. Torras 2002. Interactional otherness: Towards a redefinition of code-switching. *International Journal of Bilingualism*, 6 (1): 1–22.

Gallagher, T. (1977). Revision behaviours in the speech of normal children developing language. *Journal of Speech and Hearing Research*, 20(2): 303–18.

Gallagher, T. 1981. Contingent query sequences within adult–child discourse. *Journal of Child Language*, 8(1): 51–62.

Gallagher, T. and B. Darnton 1978. Conversational aspects of the speech of language disordered children. Revision behaviours. *Journal of Speech and Hearing Research*, 21(1): 118–35.

Gardner, H. 1986. An investigation of maternal interaction with phonologically disordered children as compared to two groups of normally developing children. Unpublished M.Sc thesis University of London, Institute of Neurology.

Gardner, H. 1989. An investigation of maternal interaction with phonologically disordered children as compared to two groups of normally developing children. *British Journal of Disorders of Communication*, 24(1): 41–61.

Gardner, H. 1994. Doing Talk about Speech: A study of Speech/Language Therapists and Phonologically Disordered Children Working Together. Unpublished D.Phil thesis, University of York.

Gardner, H. 1997. Are your minimal pairs too neat? The dangers of 'phonemicisation' in phonology therapy. *European Journal of the Disorders of Human Communication*, 32(2): 167–75.

Gardner, H. 1998. Social and Cognitive Competencies in Learning: Which is Which? in I. Hutchby and S. Moran Ellis (eds) *Children and Social Competence*. Falmer Press, pp. 115–33.

Gardner, R. 1997. The Conversational Object Mm: A Weak and Variable Acknowledging Token. *Research on Language and Social Interaction*, 30(2): 131–56.

Gardner, R. and Wagner, J. (eds). 2004. *Second Language Conversations*. London: Continuum.

Garfinkel, H. 1967. *Studies in Ethnomethodology*. Englewood Cliffs, NJ: Prentice Hall.

Garvey, C. 1975. Requests and responses in children's speech. *Journal of Child Language*, 2: 41–63.

Gass, S.M. 1997. *Input, Interaction and the Second Language Learner*. Mahwah, NJ: Lawrence Erlbaum.

Gass, S.M. 1998. Apples and oranges: Or, why apples are not oranges and don't need to be. A response to Firth and Wagner. *Modern Language Journal*, 82: 83–90.

Gass S.M. and E.M. Varonis 1984. The effect of familiarity on the comprehensibility of non-native speech. *Language Learning*, 34: 65–89.

Gass, S. and E. Varonis 1994. Input, interaction, and second language production. *Studies in Second Language Acquisition*, 16: 283–302.

Gass, S.M., A. Mackey and T. Pica 1998. The role of input and interaction in second language acquisition: Introduction to the special issue. *Modern Language Journal*, 82: 299–307.

Givon, T. 1983. Topic continuity in discourse: A quantitative cross-language study. *Typological Studies in Language, Vol. 3*. New York: John Benjamins.

Goffman, E. 1967. *Interaction Ritual: Essays on Face-to-face Behavior*. New York: Random House.

Goffman, E. 1971. *Relations in Public*. New York: Harper.

Goffman, E. 1981. *Forms of Talk*. Philadelphia: University of Pennsylvania Press.

Goodwin, C. 1981. *Conversational Organization. Interaction between Speakers and Hearers*. New York: Academic Press.

Goodwin, C. 1987. Forgetfulness as an interactive resource. *Social Psychology Quarterly*, 50: 115–31.

Goodwin, C. 1995. Co-constructing meaning in conversations with an aphasic man. *Research in Language and Social Interaction*, 28(3): 233–60.

Goodwin, C. 2003a. Conversational Frameworks for the Accomplishment of Meaning in Aphasia. In C. Goodwin (ed.) *Conversation and Brain Damage*. Oxford: Oxford University Press.

Goodwin, C. 2003b. Pointing as situated practice. In Sotaro Kita (ed.) *Pointing: Where Language, Culture and Cognition Meet*. Mahwah, NJ: Lawrence Erlbaum, pp. 217–41.

Goodwin, M.H. 1980. Directive/Response speech sequences in girls' and boys' task activities. In S. McConnell *et al*. (eds) *Women and Language in Literature and Society*. New York, NY: Praeger, pp. 157–73.

Goodwin, M., and C. Goodwin 1986. Gesture and coparticipation in the activity of searching for a word. *Semiotica*, 62: 51–75.

Gordon, D. and S. Ervin-Tripp, 1984. The structure of children's requests. In R.L. Schiefelbusch and J. Pickar (eds) *The Acquisition of Communicative Competence*. Baltimore: University Park Press, pp. 295–321.

Greatbatch, D. 1988. A turn taking system for British news interviews. *Language in Society*, 17 (3): 401–30.

Greatbatch, D. 1992. The management of disagreement between news interviewees. In P. Drew and J. Heritage (eds) *Talk at Work: Interaction in Institutional Settings*. Cambridge: Cambridge University Press, pp. 268–301.

Greatbatch, D. and R. Dingwall 1998. Talk and identity in divorce mediation. In C. Antaki and S. Widdicombe (eds) *Identities in Talk*. London: Sage, pp. 121–32.

Grice, H.P. 1975. Logic and conversation. In P. Cole and J. Morgan (eds) *Syntax and Semantics, vol. 3: Speech Acts*. New York: Academic Press, pp. 41–58.

Gumperz, J. 1982. *Discourse Strategies*. Cambridge: Cambridge University Press.

Hall, J.K. and L.S. Verplaetse (eds). 2000. *Second and Foreign Language Learning Through Classroom Interaction*. Mahwah, NJ: Lawrence Erlbaum Associates.

Halliday, M.A.K. and R. Hasan 1980. Text and context: Aspects of language in a social-semiotic perspective. *Sofia Linguistica*, 6: 4–91.

Halliday, M.A.K. and R. Hasan 1989. *Language, Context, and Text: Aspects of Language in a Social-Semiotic Perspective*. Oxford: Oxford University Press.

Harren, I. 2001. "ne?" in Alltagsgesprächen – Interaktive Funktion und Positionierungen in Turn und Sequencez. MA thesis. University of Oldenburg, Germany.

Hart, C.W.L., J.L. Heskett and W.E. Sasser 1990. The profitable art of service recovery. *Harvard Business Review*: 148–54.

Hayashi, M. 2000. Practices in joint utterance construction in Japanese conversation. Unpublished PhD dissertation, University of Colorado.

Heath, C. 1981. The opening sequence in doctor–patient interaction. In P. Atkinson and C. Heath (eds) *Medical Work: Realities and Routines*. Aldershot: Gower, pp. 71–90.

Heath, C. 1984. Talk and recipiency; sequential organization in speech and body movement. In J.M. Atkinson and J. Heritage (eds) *Structures of Social Action: Studies in Conversation Analysis*. Cambridge: Cambridge University Press, pp. 247–65.

Heath, C. 1986. *Body Movement and Speech in Medical Interaction*. Cambridge: Cambridge University Press.

Heeschen, C. and E. Schegloff 1999. Agrammatism, adaptation theory, conversation analysis: on the role of so-called telegraphic style in talk-in-interaction. *Aphasiology*, 13: 365–405.

Herbert, J. 2000. *Journalism in the Digital Age: Theory and Practice for Broadcast, Print and On-line Media*. Oxford: Focal Press.

Heritage, J. 1984a. A change-of-state token and aspects of its sequential placement. In J.M. Atkinson and J. Heritage (eds) *Structures of Social action. Studies in Conversation Analysis*. Cambridge: Cambridge University Press, pp. 299–345.

Heritage, J. 1984b. *Garfinkel and Ethnomethodology*. Cambridge: Polity Press.

Heritage, J. 1985. Analyzing news interviews: aspects of the production of talk for an 'overhearing' audience. In T. van Dijk (ed.) *Handbook of Discourse Analysis, vol. 3: Discourse and Dialogue*. London: Academic Press, pp. 95–119.

Heritage, J. 1995. Conversation Analysis: Methodological Aspects. In U.M. Quasthoff (ed.) *Aspects of Oral Communication*. Berlin/New York: Walter de Gruyter, pp. 391–418.

Heritage, J. 1997. Conversation Analysis and Institutional Talk: Analysing Data. In D. Silverman (ed.), *Qualitative Research: Theory, Method and Practice*. London: Sage, pp. 161–82.

Heritage, J. 1999. Conversation analysis at century's end: Practices of talk-in-interaction, their distributions, and their outcomes. *Research on Language and Social Interaction*, 32 (1 and 2): 69–76.

Heritage, J. 2004. CA as Applied Linguistics: Crossing the boundaries of discipline and practice. Discussion of colloquium presented at the 2004 annual conference of the American Association of Applied Linguistics (Portland, 1–4 May).

Heritage, J. and D. Greatbatch 1991. On the institutional character of institutional talk: the case of news interviews. In D. Boden and D.H. Zimmerman (eds) *Talk and Social Structure*. Cambridge: Polity Press, pp. 93–137.

Heritage, J.C. and D.W. Maynard (in press). *Practicing Medicine: Talk and Action in Primary Care Encounters*. Cambridge: Cambridge University Press.

Heritage, J. and A. Roth 1995. Grammar and institution: questions and questioning in the broadcast news interview. *Research on Language and Social Interaction*, 28(1): 1–60.

Heritage, J. and T. Stivers. 1999. Online commentary in acute medical visits: a method of shaping patient expectations. *Social Science and Medicine*, 49(11): 1501–17.

Hermelin, B. 1972. Locating events in space and time: experiments with autistic, blind and deaf children. *Journal of Autism and Childhood Schizophrenia*, 2(3): 288–98.

Hester, S. and P. Eglin (eds) 1997. *Culture in Action: Studies in Membership Categorization Analysis*. Lanham, MD: International Institute for Ethnomethodology and Conversation Analysis and University Press of America.

Higginbotham, D. and D. Wilkins 1999. Slipping through the timestream: Social issues of time and timing in augmented interactions. In M. Maxwell (ed.) *Constructing (In) Competence: Disabling Evaluations in Clinical and Social Interaction*. Mahwah NJ: Lawrence Erlbaum Associates Inc., pp. 49–82.

Holtgraves, T. 1992. The linguistic realization of face management: implications for language production and comprehension, person perception, and cross-cultural communication. *Social Psychology Quarterly*, 55: 141–59.

Hosoda, Y. 2000. Other-repair in Japanese conversations between nonnative and native speakers. *Issues in Applied Linguistics*, 11(1): 39–63.

Hutchby, I. and R. Wooffitt 1998. *Conversation Analysis: Principles, Practices and Applications*. Cambridge: Polity Press.

Iles, Z. 1996. Collaborative repair in EFL classroom talk. *York Papers in Linguistics*, 17: 23–51.

Jacoby, S. (1998a). How can ESP practitioners tap into situated discourse research: And why should we? (Part 1). *English for Specific Purposes News*, 7(1), 1–10.

Jacoby, S. (1998b). How can ESP practitioners tap into situated discourse research: And why should we? (Part 2). *English for Specific Purposes News*, 7(2), 4–10.

Jacoby, S. and T. McNamara 1999. Locating competence. *English for Specific Purposes*, 18: 213–41.

Jefferson, G. 1979. A technique for inviting laughter and its subsequent acceptance declination. In G. Psathas (ed.) *Everyday Language. Studies in Ethnomethodology*. New York: Irvington Publishers, pp. 79–96.

Jefferson, G. 1980. The abominable ne? An exploration of post-response pursuit of response. In P. Schröder and H. Steger (eds) *Dialogforschung*, Düsseldorf: Pädagogischer Verlag Schwann, pp. 53–88.

Jefferson, G. 1983. Two explorations of the organization of overlapping talk in conversation. *Tilburg Papers in Language and Literature*, 28.

Jefferson, G. 1984a. Transcript Notation. In J.M. Atkinson and J. Heritage (eds) *Structures of Social Action: Studies in Conversation Analysis*. Cambridge: Cambridge University Press, pp. ix–xvi.

Jefferson, G. 1984b. On stepwise transition from talk about trouble to inappropriately next-positioned matters. In J.M. Atkinson and J. Heritage (eds) *Structures of Social Action: Studies in Conversation Analysis*. Cambridge: Cambridge University Press, pp. 191–221.

Jefferson, G. 1987. On exposed and embedded correction. In G. Button and J. Lee (eds) *Talk and Social Organisation*. Clevedon: Multilingual Matters, pp. 86–100.

Jefferson, G. 1988. Remarks on 'non-correction' in conversation. Unpublished notes for a lecture at Helsingin Yliopisto, Suomen Kielen Laitos, Helsinki.

Jefferson, G. 1990. List-construction as a task and a resource. In G. Psathas (ed.) *Interactional Competence*. Washington, DC: University Press of America, pp. 63–92.

Jefferson, G. 1996. A case of transcriptional stereotyping. *Journal of Pragmatics*, 26: 159–70.

Jordan, R. 1999. *Autistic Spectrum Disorders: An Introductory Handbook for Practitioners*. London: David Fulton.

Jung, E.H. 1999. The organisation of second language classroom repair. *Issues in Applied Linguistics*, 10(2): 153–71.

Kanner, L. 1943. Autistic disturbances of affective contact. *Nervous Child*, 2: 217–250.

Kanner, L. 1946. Irrelevant and metaphorical language in early infantile autism. *American Journal of Psychiatry*, 103: 242–6.

Kasper, G. 1997. 'A' stands for acquisition: A response to Firth and Wagner. *The Modern Language Journal*, 81: 307–12.

Kasper, G. 2002. Conversation Analysis as an approach to Second Language Acquisition: Old wine in new bottles? Invited talk, SLATE speaker series, University of Illinois at Urbana-Champaign, 13 March, 2002.

Kasper, G. and S. Ross. 2001. 'Is drinking a hobby, I wonder': Other-initiated repair in oral proficiency interviews. Paper delivered at the annual convention of the American Association for Applied Linguistics.

Keenan, E.O. and B.B. Schieffelin 1975. Topic as a discourse notion: A study of topic in the conversations of children and adults. In C.N. Li (ed.) *Subject and Topic*. New York: Academic Press, pp. 335–84.

Kendon, A. 1990. Some functions of gaze in two-person conversation. In *Conducting Interaction: Patterns of Behavior in Focused Encounters*. Cambridge: Cambridge University Press, pp. 51–89. (Originally published 1967).

Kidwell, M. 2000. Common ground in cross-cultural communication: sequential and institutional contexts in front desk service encounters. *Issues in Applied Linguistics*, 11(1): 17–37.

Kim, Young M. 2000. Whites' explanations of blacks' socioeconomic underachievement: Individualism, structuralism, and status inconsistency. *Current Research in Social Psychology*, 5 (8): 126–50.

Koshik, I. 1999. Practices of pedagogy in ESL writing conferences: A conversation analytic study of turns and sequences that assist student revision. Unpublished doctoral dissertation, University of California, Los Angeles.

Kurhila, S. 2001. Correction in talk between native and non-native speaker. *Journal of Pragmatics*, 33: 1083–110.

Kurhila, S. 2003. Co-constructing understanding in second language conversation. Unpublished PhD thesis, University of Helsinki.

Laakso, M. 1997. *Self-initiated Repair by Fluent Aphasic Speakers in Conversation.* Studia Fennica Linguistica, 8. Helsinki: SKS.

Laver, J. 1975. Communicative functions of phatic communication. In A. Kendon, R. Harris and M. Ritchie Kay (eds) *Organisation of Behaviour in Face-to-Face Interaction.* The Hague: Mouton, pp. 215–38.

Lazaraton, A. 1997. Preference organization in oral proficiency interviews: The case of language ability assessments. *Research on Language and Social Interaction*, 30(1): 53–72.

Lazaraton, A. 2000. Current trends in research methodology and statistics in applied linguistics. *TESOL Quarterly*, 34: 175–81.

Leekam, S.R., E. Hunnisett and C. Moore 1998. Targets and cues: Gaze-following in children with autism. *Journal of Child Pychology and Psychiatry*, 39(7): 951–62.

Lerner, G. 1996. On the 'semi-permeable' character of grammatical units in conversation: Conditional entry into the turn space of another speaker. In E. Ochs, E. Schegloff and S. Thompson (eds) *Interaction and Grammar.* Cambridge: Cambridge University Press, pp. 238–76.

Lerner, G. 1996. Finding 'face' in the preference structures of talk-in-interaction. *Social Psychology Quarterly*, 59(4): 303–21.

Lerner, G.H. and T. Takagi 1999. On the place of linguistic resources in the organization of talk-in-interaction: A co-investigation of English and Japanese grammatical practices. *Journal of Pragmatics*, 31: 49–75.

Leslie, A.M. 1987. Pretence and representation: The origins of 'Theory of Mind' *Psychological Review*, 94(4): 412–26.

Levinson, S.C. 1983. *Pragmatics.* Cambridge: Cambridge University Press.

Liddicoat, A. 1997. Interaction, social structure, and second language use: A response to Firth and Wagner. *Modern Language Journal*, 81: 313–17.

Lindblom, B. 1990. On the communication process: Speaker–listener interaction and the development of speech. *Augmentative and Alternative Communication*, 6: 220–30.

Lindenfeld, J. 1990. *Speech and Sociability at French Urban Market Places.* Amsterdam: John Benjamins.

Lindström, A.K.B. 1997. Designing social actions: Grammar, prosody, and interaction in Swedish conversation. Unpublished doctoral dissertation, University of California, Los Angeles.

Local, J. and J. Kelly 1986. Projection and "silences": Notes on phonetic and conversational structure. *Human Studies*, 9:185–204.

Local, J. and A. J. Wootton 1995. Interactional and phonetic aspects of immediate echolalia in autism: A case study. *Clinical Linguistics and Phonetics*, 9: 155–84.

Long, M.H. 1996. The role of the linguistic environment in second language acquisition. In W.C. Ritchie and T.K. Bhatia (eds) *Handbook of Second Language Acquisition.* New York: Academic Press, pp. 414–68.

Long, M.H. 1997. Construct validity in SLA research: A response to Firth and Wagner. *Modern Language Journal*, 81: 318–23.

Long, M.H. 1998. SLA: Breaking the siege. *University of Hawai'i Working Papers in ESL*, 17(1): 79–129.

Long, M., S. Inagaki and L. Ortega 1998. The role of implicit negative feedback in SLA: models and recasts in Japanese and Spanish. *The Modern Language Journal*, 82: 357–71.

Lyster, R. 1998. Negotiation of form, recasts, and explicit correction in relation to error types and learner repair in immersion classrooms. *Language Learning*, 48: 183–218.

Lyster, R. and L. Ranta 1997. Corrective feedback and learner uptake: Negotiation of form in communicative classrooms. *Studies in Second Language Acquisition*, 19: 37–66.

McCarthy, M. 1994. *Discourse Analysis for Language Teachers*. Cambridge: Cambridge University Press.

McCarthy, M. 1998. *Spoken Language and Applied Linguistics*. Cambridge: Cambridge University Press.

McCarthy, M. 2000. Mutually captive audiencies: small talk and the genre of close-contact service encounters. In J. Coupland (ed.) *Small Talk*. Essex: Pearson Education, pp. 84–109.

McConahay, J.B. 1986. Modern Racism, Ambivalence and the Modern Racism Scale. In J.F. Dovidio and S.L. Gaertner (eds), *Prejudice, Discrimination and Racism: Theory and Research*. Orlando, FL: Academic Press, pp. 91–126.

McHoul, A. 1978. The organization of turns at formal talk in the classroom. *Language in Society*, 7: 183–213.

McHoul, A. 1990. The organization of repair in classroom talk. *Language in Society*, 19 (3): 349–78.

McHoul, A. and M. Rapley (eds) 2001. *How to Analyse Talk in Institutional Settings*, London: Continuum.

McKay, S. and N. Hornberger (eds) 1996. *Sociolinguistics and Language Teaching*, Cambridge: Cambridge University Press.

Mackey, A. and J. Philp 1998. Conversational interaction and second-language development: Recasts, responses and red herrings? *Modern Language Journal*, 82: 338–56.

Mangione-Smith, R., T. Stivers, M. Elliot, L. McDonald and J. Heritage. 2003. Online commentary during the physical examination: a communication tool for avoiding inappropriate antibiotic prescribing. *Social Science and Medicine*, 56: 313–20.

Markee, N. 1994. Toward an ethnomethodological respecification of second language acquisition studies. In E. Tarone, S. Gass and A. Cohen (eds), *Research Methodology in Second Language Acquisition*. Hillsdale, NJ: Lawrence Erlbaum, pp. 89–116.

Markee, N. 1995. Teachers' answers to students' questions: Problematizing the issue of making meaning. *Issues in Applied Linguistics*, 6: 63–92.

Markee, N. 1997. SLA research: A resource for changing teachers' professional cultures? *Modern Language Journal*, 81: 80–93.

Markee, N. 2000. *Conversation Analysis*. Mahwah NJ: Lawrence Erlbaum.

Martino, W. 2000. Mucking around in class, giving crap, and acting cool: adolescent boys enacting masculinities at school. *Canadian Journal of Education*, 25(2): 102–12.

Maynard, D.W. 1980. Placement of topic changes in conversation. *Semiotica*, 30 (3/4): 263–90.

Maynard, D.W. and C.L. Marlaire. 1992. Good reasons for bad testing performance: the interactional substrate of educational exams. *Qualitative Sociology*, 15: 177–202.

Mehan, H. 1979. *Learning Lessons: Social Organization in the Classroom*. Cambridge, MA: Harvard University Press.

Merritt, M. 1975. On questions following questions in service encounters. *Language in Society*, 5: 315–57.

Mirenda, P., A.M. Donellan and D.E. Yoder 1983. Gaze behaviour: A new look at an old problem. *Journal of Autism and Developmental Disorders*, 13: 397–409.

Mori, J. 2002. Task design, plan, and development of talk-in-interaction: an analysis of a small group activity in a Japanese language classroom. *Applied Linguistics*, 23: 323–47.

Mundy, P. and M. Sigman 1989. The theoretical implications of joint attention deficits in autism. *Development and Psychopathology*, 1: 173–83.

Mundy, P. and M. Crowson 1997. Joint attention and early social communication: Implication for research on intervention with autism. *Journal of Autism and Developmental Disorders*, 27: 653–76.

Murphy, J. 2003. *Talking Together – Communication Strategies of People with MND and their partners*. Stirling: University of Stirling.

National Autistic Society (NAS). 1999. *The Autistic Spectrum: A Handbook*. London: National Autistic Society.

Nicholas, H., P. Lightbown, and N. Spada 2001. Recasts as feedback to language learners. *Language Learning*, 51: 719–58.

Norrick, N. 1991. Functions of repetition in text. *Text*, 7: 245–64.

Norrie, E. and J. Middleton, 2002. The challenge of induction! Introducing engineering students to higher education: a task-oriented approach. *Innovations in Education and Teaching International*, 39(1): 46–53.

O'Connor, N. and B. Hermelin 1967. The selective visual attention of psychotic children. *Journal of Child Psychology and Psychiatry*, 8: 167–79.

Ochs, E., E. Schegloff and S. Thompson. 1996. *Interaction and Grammar*. Cambridge: Cambridge University Press.

Oelschlaeger, M. and J. Damico 1998. Joint productions as a conversational strategy in aphasia. *Clinical Linguistics and Phonetics*, 12(6): 459–80.

Ohta, A.S. 2000. Rethinking interaction in SLA: Developmentally appropriate assistance in the zone of proximal development and the acquisition of grammar. In J.P. Lantolf (ed.) *Sociocultural Theory and Second Language Learning*. Oxford: Oxford University Press, pp. 51–78.

Oliver, R. 1995. Negative feedback in child NS–NNS conversation. *Studies in Second Language Acquisition*, 17: 459–81.

Oliver, R. 1998. Negotiation of meaning in child interactions. *Modern Language Journal*, 82: 372–86.

Oliver, R. 2000. Age differences in negotiation and feedback in classroom and pair work. *Language Learning*, 50: 119–51.

Panagos, J.M., K. Bobkoff and C.M. Scott 1986. Discourse analysis of language intervention. *Child Language Teaching and Therapy*, 2: 211–29.

Peräkylä, A. 1995. *AIDS Counselling: Institutional Interaction and Clinical Practice*. Cambridge: Cambridge University Press.

Peräkylä, A. and S. Vehvilainen 2003. Conversation Analysis and the Stocks of Interactional Professional Knowledge, *Discourse and Society*, 14(6): 727–50.

Phoenix, A. and S. Frosh 2001. Positioned by 'Hegemonic' Masculinities: A Study of London Boys' Narratives of Identity. *Australian Psychologist*, 36(1): 27–35.

Pica, T. 1988. Interlanguage adjustments as an outcome of NS–NNS negotiated interaction. *Language Learning*, 38/1, 45–73.

Pichler, P. 2002. Between gangsta rap and pet shop boys: the (re)negotiation of middle class femininities in adolescent girl talk. Paper presented at IGALA 2 Lancaster University.

Pike, K. 1967. *Language in Relation to a Unified Theory of the Structure of Human Behaviour*. The Hague: Mouton.

Pomerantz, A. 1984a. Pursuing a response. In J.M. Atkinson and J. Heritage (eds) *Structures of Social Action: Studies in Conversation Analysis*. Cambridge: Cambridge University Press, pp. 152–63.

Pomerantz, A. 1984b. Agreeing and disagreeing with assessments: Some features of preferred/dispreferred turn shapes. In J. Atkinson and J. Heritage (eds) *Structures of Social Action*. Cambridge: Cambridge University Press, pp. 57–101.

Powell, S.D. 1999. Autism. In D. Messer and S. Millar (eds) *Exploring Developmental Psychology: From Infancy to Adolescence*. London: Arnold.

Psathas, G. 1995. *Conversation Analysis: The Study of Talk-in-Interaction*. Thousand Oaks: Sage.

Rae, J. 2001. Organizing participation in interaction: doing participation framework. *Research on Language and Social Interaction*, 34: 253–78.

Ragan, S.L. 2000. Sociable talk in women's healthcare contexts: Two forms of non-medical talk. In J. Coupland (ed.) *Small Talk*. London: Longman, pp. 269–87.

Raymond, G. 2000. The Structure of responding: Type-conforming and Noncon-forming Responses to Yes/No Type Interrogatives. Unpublished PhD dissertation. Department of Sociology, University of California, Los Angeles.

Redman, P. and M. Mac an Ghaill 1997. Educating Peter: the making of a history man. In D.L.Steinberg *et al.* (eds) *Border Patrols: Policing the Boundaries of Hetero-sexuality*. London: Continuum.

Robertson, S.J. 1982. *Dysarthria Profile*. London: Robertson.

Robillard, A. 1994. Communication problems in the intensive care unit. *Qualitative Sociology*, 17(4): 383–95.

Robillard, A. 1999. *Meaning of a Disability – The Lived Experience of Paralysis*. Philadelphia: Temple University Press.

Robinson, J.D. (forthcoming). Soliciting patients' presenting concerns. In J. Heritage and D. Maynard (eds) *Practicing Medicine: Talk and Action in Primary Care Encounters*. Cambridge University Press.

Royal College of Speech and Language Therapists 1998. *Clinical Guidelines by Consensus for Speech and Language Therapists*. London: M and M Press.

Ryave, A.L. and J.N. Schenkein 1974. Notes on the art of walking. In R. Turner (ed.) *Ethnomethodology: Selected Readings*. Harmondsworth: Penguin Education, pp. 265–74.

Sacks, H. 1964–65. The MIR membership categorization device. In G. Jefferson (ed.) 1992, *Harvey Sacks: Lectures on Conversation*, Volume 1. Oxford: Blackwell, pp. 40–8.

Sacks, H. 1972a. An initial investigation of the usability of conversational data for doing sociology. In D.N. Sudnow (ed.) *Studies in Social Interaction*. New York: Free Press.

Sacks, H. 1972b. On the analyzability of stories by children. In J.J. Gumperz and D. Hymes (eds) *Directions in Sociolinguistics*. New York: Holt, Rinehart and Winston, pp. 216–32.

Sacks, H. 1972c. Spring Lecture 5: A single instance of Q–A pair; topical versus pair organisation disaster talk. In G. Jefferson (ed.), 1992, *Harvey Sacks: Lectures on Conversation*, vol. II. Oxford: Blackwell, pp. 161–9.

Sacks, H. 1974. On the analysability of stories by children. In R. Turner (ed.) *Ethnomethodology: Selected Readings*. Harmondsworth: Penguin, pp. 216–32.

Sacks, H. 1987. On the preference for agreement and contiguity in sequences in conversation. In G. Button and J. Lee (eds) *Talk and Social Organisation*. Clevedon: Multilingual Matters, pp. 54–69.

Sacks, H. 1992. *Lectures on Conversation* (Vols. I and II, edited by Gail Jefferson). Oxford: Blackwell.

Sacks, H., E. Schegloff and G. Jefferson 1974. A simplest systematics for the organization of turntaking in conversation. *Language*, 50(4): 696–735.

Sacks, H., E. Schegloff and G. Jefferson 1978. A simplest systematics for the organization of turn taking for conversation. In J. Schenkein (ed.). *Studies in the Organization of Conversational Interaction*. New York: Academic Press, pp. 7–55.

Sarangi, S. and C. Roberts (eds) 1999. *Talk, Work and Institutional Order*. Berlin: de Gruyter.

Schegloff, E.A. 1968. Sequencing in conversational openings. *American Anthropologist*, 70: 1075–95.

Schegloff, E.A. 1979a. Identification and recognition in telephone conversation openings. In Psathas (ed.) *Everyday Language: Studies in Ethnomethodology*. New York: Erlbaum, pp. 23–78.

Schegloff, E.A. 1979b. The relevance of repair in a syntax-for-conversation. In T. Givon (ed.), *Syntax and Semantics 12: Discourse and Syntax*. New York: Academic, pp. 261–86.

Schegloff, E.A. 1982. Discourse as an interactional achievement: Some uses of "uh huh" and other things that come between sentences. In D. Tannen (ed.) *Georgetown University Roundtable on Languages and Linguistics*. Washington, DC: Georgetown University Press, pp. 71–93.

Schegloff, E.A. 1984a. On questions and ambiguity in conversation. In J.M. Atkinson and J. Heritage (eds) *Structures of Social Action: Studies in Conversation Analysis*. Cambridge: Cambridge University Press, pp. 28–52.

Schegloff, E.A. 1984b. On some gestures' relation to talk. In J.M. Atkinson and J.Heritage (eds) *Structures of Social Action: Studies in Conversation Analysis*. Cambridge University Press, pp. 266–96.

Schegloff, E.A. 1986. The routine as achievement. *Human Studies*, 9: 111–51.

Schegloff, E.A. 1987. Some sources of misunderstanding in talk-in-interaction. *Linguistics*, 25: 201–18.

Schegloff, E.A. 1988a. Presequences and indirection. Applying speech act theory to ordinary conversation. *Journal of Pragmatics*, 12: 55–62.

Schegloff, E.A. 1988b. On the virtual servo-mechanism for guessing bad news: A single-case juncture. *Social Problems*, 35: 442–57.

Schegloff, E.A. 1989. Reflections on language, development and the interactional character of talk-in-interaction. In M. Bornstein and J.S. Bruner (eds) *Interaction and Human Development*. Hillsdale, NJ: Erlbaum, pp. 139–53.

Schegloff, E.A. 1990. On the organization of sequences as a source of 'coherence' in talk-in-interaction. In B. Dorval (ed.) *Conversational Organization and its Development*. Norwood, NJ: Ablex.

Schegloff, E.A. 1991. Reflections on talk and social structure. In D. Boden and D. Zimmerman (eds) *Talk and Social Structure. Studies in Ethnomethodology and Conversation Analysis*. Cambridge: Polity Press, pp. 44–70.

Schegloff, E.A. 1992a. Repair after next turn: The last structurally provided defense of intersubjectivity in conversation. *American Journal of Sociology*, 97(5): 1295–345.

Schegloff, E.A. 1992b. On talk and its institutional occasions. In P. Drew and J. Heritage (eds) *Talk at Work*. Cambridge: Cambridge University Press, pp. 101–34.

Schegloff, E.A. 1992c. To Searle on conversation: A note in return. In J. Searle *et al. (On) Searle on conversation*. Amsterdam: John Benjamins, pp. 113–28.

Schegloff, E.A. 1992d. In another context. In A. Duranti and C. Goodwin (eds) *Rethinking Context: Language as an Interactive Phenomenon*. Cambridge: Cambridge University Press, pp. 191–228.

Schegloff, E.A. 1993. Reflection on quantification in the study of conversation. *Research on Language and Social Interaction*, 26: 99–128.

Schegloff, E.A. 1995. *Sequence Organization*. Unpublished manuscript. University of California, Los Angeles.

Schegloff, E.A. 1996a. Turn organization: One intersection of grammar and interaction. In E. Ochs, E. Schegloff and S. Thompson. *Interaction and Grammar*. Cambridge: Cambridge University Press, pp. 52–133.

Schegloff, E.A. 1996b. Confirming Allusions: Toward an Empirical Account of Action. *American Journal of Sociology*, 102(1): 161–216.

Schegloff, E.A. 1997. Whose text? Whose context? *Discourse and Society*, 8(2): 165–87.

Schegloff, E.A. 1998. Reply to Wetherell. *Discourse and Society*, 9(3): 413–16.

Schegloff, E.A. 1999. 'Schegloff's texts' as Billig's data: a critical reply. *Discourse & Society*, 10(4): 558–72.

Schegloff, E.A. 2000a. When 'others' initiate repair. *Applied Linguistics* 21(2): 205–43.

Schegloff, E.A. 2000b. Overlapping talk and the organization of turn-taking for conversation. *Language in Society*, 29(1): 1–63.

Schegloff, E.A. 2001. Discourse as an Interactional Achievement III: The Omnirelevance of Action. In D. Schiffrin, D. Tannen and H. Hamilton (eds) *The Handbook of Discourse Analysis*. Oxford : Blackwell, pp. 229–49.

Schegloff, E.A. (forthcoming). *A Primer on Conversation Analysis: Sequence Organization*. Cambridge, Cambridge University Press.

Schegloff, E.A. (2003). Conversation analysis and communication disorders. In Goodwin, C. (ed.) *Conversation and Brain Damage*. Oxford: Oxford University Press, pp. 21–55.

Schegloff, E., G. Jefferson, and H. Sacks. 1977. The preference for self-correction in the organization of repair in conversation. *Language*, 53: 361–82.

Schegloff, E., I. Koshik, S. Jacoby, and D. Olsher. 2002. Conversation analysis and applied linguistics. *Annual Review of Applied Linguistics*, 22: 3–31.

Schegloff, E.A. and H. Sacks. 1973. Opening up closings. *Semiotica*, 8: 289–327.

Schenkein, J. 1978a. Identity negotiations in conversation. In J. Schenkein (ed.) *Studies in the Organization of Conversational Interaction.* New York: Academic Press, pp. 57–78.

Schenkein, J. 1978b. *Studies in the Organization of Conversational Interaction.* New York: Academic Press.

Schiffrin, D. 1977. Opening encounters. *American Sociological Review*, 42 (5): 679–91.

Schiffrin, D. 1994. *Approaches to Discourse.* Oxford: Blackwell.

Seedhouse, P. 1996. Learning Talk: A Study of the Interactional Organisation of the L2 Classroom from a CA Institutional Discourse Perspective. Unpublished D Phil thesis, University of York.

Seedhouse, P. 1997. The case of the missing "No": The relationship between pedagogy and interaction. *Language Learning*, 47: 547–83.

Seedhouse, P. 1998. CA and the analysis of foreign language interaction: A reply to Wagner. *Journal of Pragmatics*, 30: 85–102.

Seedhouse, P. 1999. The relationship between context and the organization of repair in the L2 classroom. *International Review of Applied Linguistics*, 38: 59–80.

Seedhouse, P. 2004. *The Interactional Architecture of the Language Classroom: A Conversation Analysis Perspective.* Malden, MA: Blackwell.

Selting, M. 1996. On the interplay of syntax and prosody in the constitution of turn-constructional units an turns in conversation. *Pragmatics*, 6(3): 357–88.

Seppänen, E.-L. 1998. *Läsnäolon Pronominit* [The pronouns of presence]. Helsinki: SKS.

Siller, M. and M. Sigman 2002. The behaviours of parents of children with autism predict the subsequent development of their children's communication. *Journal of Autism and Developmental Disorders*, 32(2): 77–89.

Silverman, D. 1997. *Discourses of Counselling: HIV counselling as social interaction.* London: Sage.

Silverman, D. (1999). Warriors or collaborators: Reworking methodological controversies in the study of institutional interaction. In: C. Roberts and S. Sarangi (eds) *Talk, Work and Institutional Order.* Berlin: Mouton de Gruyter, pp. 401–25.

Sinclair, J. and M. Coulthard 1975. *Towards an Analysis of Spoken Discourse: The English used by Teachers and Pupils.* Oxford: Oxford University Press.

Sonnenmeier, R. 1993. Co-construction of messages during facilitated communication. *Facilitated Communication Digest*, 1(2): 7–9.

Sorjonen, M.-L. 2001. *Responding in Conversation.* Amsterdam: Benjamins.

Steinmetz, D. and H. Tabenkin 2001. The 'difficult patient' as perceived by family physicians. *Family Practice*, 18: 495–500.

Stokoe, E.H. 1995. Gender differences in undergraduates' talk: contrasting analyses and what they offer. *Feminism and Psychology*, 5(1): 99–104.

Stokoe, E.H. 1997. An evaluation of two studies of gender and language in educational settings. *Gender and Education*, 9(2): 233–44.

Stokoe, E.H. 1998. Talking about gender: the conversational construction of gender categories in academic discourse. *Discourse and Society*, 9(2): 217–40.

Stokoe, E.H. 2000. Constructing topicality in university students' small-group discussion: a conversation analytic approach. *Language and Education*, 14(3): 184–203.

Streeck, J. 1996. A little Ilokano grammar as it appears in interaction. *Journal of Pragmatics*, 26(2): 189–213.

Takahashi, T. and L. Beebe 1993. Cross-linguistic influence in the speech act of correction. In G. Kasper and S. Blum-Kulka (eds) *Interlanguage Pragmatics*. New York: Oxford University Press.

Tannen, D. 1989. *Talking Voices: Repetition, Dialogue, and Imagery in Conversational Discourse*. Cambridge: Cambridge University Press.

Tarone, E. and G. Liu 1995. Situational context, variation, and second language acquisition theory. In G. Cook and B. Seidlhofer (eds) *Principle and Practice in Applied Linguistics: Studies in Honour of H.G. Widdowson*. Oxford: Oxford University Press, pp. 107–24.

Tarplee, C. 1993. Working on Talk: The Collaborative Shaping of Linguistic Skills within Child–Adult Interaction. Unpublished PhD thesis, University of York.

Tarplee, C. 1996. Working on young children's utterances: prosodic aspects of repetition during picture labelling. In M. Selting (ed.) *Prosody in Conversation*. Cambridge: Cambridge University Press, pp. 406–35.

Tarplee, C. and E. Barrow 1999. Delayed echoing as an interactional resource: A case study of a 3-year old child on the autistic spectrum. *Clinical Linguistics & Phonetics*, 13(6): 449–82.

ten Have, P. 1999. *Doing Conversation Analysis: A Practical Guide*. London: Sage.

Torras, M.C. 1998. Code Negotiation and Code Alternation in Service Encounters in Catalonia. Unpublished MA thesis, University of Lancaster.

Torras, M.C. 2002. Language Choice, Social Identity and the Order of Service Talk-in-Interaction: A Study of Trilingual Service Encounters in Barcelona. Unpublished PhD thesis, Lancaster University.

Torras, M.C. and J. Gafaranga 2002. Social identities and language alternation in non-formal institutional bilingual talk: Trilingual service encounters in Barcelona. *Language in Society*, 31 (4): 527–48.

Travers, M. and J.F. Manzo 1997. *Law in Action: Ethnomethodological and Conversation Analytic Approaches to Law*. Aldershot: Dartmouth.

Tuckett, D., M. Boulton, C. Olson and A. Williams 1985. *Meetings Between Experts: An Approach to Sharing Ideas in Medical Consultations*. London: Tavistock Publications.

Van der Geest, J.N., C. Kemner, M.N. Verbaten and H. Van Engeland 2002. Gaze behaviour of children with pervasive developmental disorder toward human faces: A time fixation study. *Journal of Child Psychiatry & Psychology*, 43(5): 669–78.

van Dijk, T. 1984. *Prejudice in Discourse*. Amsterdam: Benjamins.

van Dijk, T. 1987. *Communicating Racism*. Newbury Park, CA: Sage.

van Lier, L. 1988. *The Classroom and the Language Learner*. London: Longman.

van Lier, L. 1994. Forks and hope: Pursuing understanding in different ways. *Applied Linguistics*, 15(3): 328–46.

van Lier, L. 1996. *Interaction in the Language Curriculum: Awareness, Autonomy and Authenticity*. Harlow: Longman.

Varonis, E.M. and S. Gass 1985. Non-native/non-native conversation: A model for negotiation of meaning. *Applied Linguistics*, 6: 71–90.

Ventola, E. 1987. *The Structure of Social Interaction. A Systemic Approach to the Semiotics of Service Encounters*. London: Frances Pinter.

Volkmar, F.R. and L.C. Mayes 1990. Gaze behaviour in autism. *Development and Psychopathology*, 2: 61–9.

Wagner, J. 1996. Foreign language acquisition through interaction – a critical review of research on conversational adjustments. *Journal of Pragmatics*, 26: 215–35.

Wagner, J. 1998. On doing being a guinea pig – A response to Seedhouse. *Journal of Pragmatics*, 30: 103–13.

Watson, D.R. 1992. Ethnomethodology, conversation analysis and education: an overview. *International Review of Education*, 38(3): 257–74.

Werry, I., K. Dautenhahn, B. Ogden and W. Harwin 2001. Can social interaction skills be taught by a social agent? The role of a robotic mediator in autism therapy' *Proceeding CT 2001, The Fourth International Conference on Cognitive Technology: Instruments of Mind (CT2001) 6–9 August 2001 University of Warwick UK, Springer-Verlag Lecture Notes in Computer Science.*

Wetherell, M. 1998. Positioning and interpretative repertoires: conversation analysis and post-structuralism in dialogue. *Discourse and Society* 9(3): 387–412.

Whalen, M.R. and D.H. Zimmerman 1987. Sequential and institutional contexts in calls for help. *Social Psychology Quarterly*, 50(2): 172–85.

Whalen, J. and R.E. Vinkhuyzen 2000. Expert systems in (inter)action: Diagnosing document machines problems over the telephone. In P. Luff, J. Hindmarsh and C. Heath (eds) *Workplace Studies: Recovering Work Practice and Informing Design.* Cambridge: Cambridge University Press, pp. 92–140.

Whalen, J., D.H. Zimmerman and M.R. Whalen 1988. When words fail: A single case analysis. *Social Problems*, 35(4): 335–62.

Whalen, J., M.R. Whalen and K. Henderson 2002. Improvisational technology in teleservice work. *British Journal of Sociology*, 53(2): 239–58.

Whalen, M., J. Whalen, R. Moore, G. Raymond, M. Szymanski and E. Vinkhuyzen (in press). Studying Workscapes. In P. LeVine and R. Scollon (eds), *Georgetown University Round Table on Languages and Linguistics 2002: Discourse and Technology: Multimodal Discourse Analysis.* Washington, DC: Georgetown University Press.

Widdowson, H.G. 2000. On the limitations of linguistics applied. *Applied Linguistics*, 21(1): 3–25.

Wilkinson, C., K. Yorkston, E. Strand and M. Rogers 1995. Features of spontaneous language in speakers with amyotrophic lateral sclerosis and dysarthria. *American Journal of Speech-Language Pathology*, 4: 139–42.

Wilkinson, R., S. Beeke and J. Maxim 2003. Adapting to conversation: On the use of linguistic resources by speakers with fluent aphasia in the construction of turns at talk. In C. Goodwin (ed.) *Conversation and Brain Damage.* New York: Oxford University Press, pp. 59–89.

Willey, B. 2002. Examining a 'communicative strategy' from a conversation analytic perspective: Eliciting help from native speakers inside and outside of word search sequences. Unpublished Master's thesis, University of Illinois at Urbana-Champaign.

Willis, J. 1992. Inner and outer: spoken discourse in the language classroom. In M. Coulthard (ed.), *Advances in Spoken Discourse Analysis.* London: Routledge, pp. 161–82.

Willis, P. 1977. *Learning to Labour: How Working Class Kids Get Working Class Jobs.* Aldershot: Saxon House.

Wilson, T.P. 1991. Social structure and the sequential organisation of interaction. In D. Boden and D.H. Zimmerman (eds) *Talk and Social Structure.*

Studies in Ethnomethodology and Conversation Analysis. Oxford: Polity Press, pp. 22–43.

Wing, L. 1993. The Definition and Prevalence Of Autism: A Review. *European Child and Adolescent Psychiatry*, 2: 61–74.

Wodak, R. (ed.) 1989. *Language Power and Ideology: Studies in Political Discourse.* London: Benjamins.

Wodak, R. and T. van Dijk (eds) 2000. *Racism at the Top. Parliamentary Discourses on Ethnic Issues in Six European States.* Klagenfurt: Drava Verlag.

Wolff, S. and S. Chess 1964. A behavioural study of schizophrenic children. *Acta Psychiatrica Scandanavia*, 40: 438–66.

Wong, J. 1984. Using conversational analysis to evaluate telephone conversations in English as a second language textbooks. Unpublished master's thesis, University of California, Los Angeles.

Wong, J. 1994. A conversation analytic approach to the study of repair in native–nonnative speaker English conversation: The element 'yeah' in same turn repair and delayed next turn repair initiation. Unpublished doctoral dissertation, University of California, Los Angeles, CA.

Wong, J. 2000a. Delayed next turn repair initiation in native-nonnative speaker English conversation. *Applied Linguistics*, 21(2): 244–67.

Wong, J. 2000b. The token 'yeah' in nonnative speaker English conversation. *Research on Language and Social Interaction*, 33(1): 39–67.

Wong, J. 2000c. Repetition in conversation: A look at 'first and second sayings'. *Research on Language and Social Interaction*, 33(4): 407–24.

Wong, J. 2002. 'Applying' conversation analysis in applied linguistics: Evaluating dialogue in English as a second language textbooks. *International Review of Applied Linguistics (IRAL)*, 40(1): 37–60.

Wong, J. 2004. Some preliminary thoughts on delay as an interactional resource. In R. Gardner and J. Wagner (eds) *Second Language Conversations*. London: Continuum.

Wong, J. and D. Olsher 2000. Reflections on conversation analysis and nonnative speaker talk: An interview with Emanuel A. Schegloff. *Issues in Applied Linguistics*, 11(1):111–28.

Wootton, A.J. 1981. The management of grantings and rejects by parents in request sequences. *Semiotica*, 37: 59–89.

Wootton, A.J. 1984. Some aspects of children's use of 'please' in request sequences. In P. Auer and A. Di Luzio (eds) *Interpretive Sociolinguistics: Migrants – Children – Migrant Children*. Tübingen: Narr.

Wootton, A.J. 1989. Remarks on the methodology of Conversation Analysis. In D. Roger and P. Bull (eds) *Conversation: an Interdisciplinary Perspective*. Clevedon: Multilingual Matters.

Wootton, A.J. 1999. An investigation of delayed echoing in a child with autism. *First Language*, 19: 359–81.

World Health Organisation 1993. *The ICD-10 Classification of Mental and Behavioural Disorders: Diagnostic Criteria for Research*. WHO: Geneva.

Yirmiya, N., T. Pilowsky, D. Solomonica-Levy and C. Shulman 1999. Gaze behaviour and theory of mind in individuals with autism, Down syndrome and mental retardation of unknown etiology. *Journal of Autism and Developmental Disorders*, 29(4): 333–41.

Yorkston, K. and D. Beukelman 1981. *Assessment of Intelligibility of Dysarthric Speech*. Austin TX: Pro-Ed.

Yorkston, K., D. Beukelman and L. Ball 2002. Management of Dysarthria in Amyotrophic Lateral Sclerosis. *Geriatrics and Aging*, 5(1): 38–41.

Young, R.F. and A. He (eds) 1998. *Talking and Testing: Discourse Approaches to the Assessment of Oral Proficiency*. Amsterdam: John Benjamins.

Yule, G. 1997. *Referential Communication Tasks*. Mahwah, NJ: Lawrence Erlbaum Associates.

Zimmerman, D.H. 1992. Achieving context. Openings in emergency calls. In G. Watson and R.M. Seiler (eds) *Text in Context: Contributions to Ethnomethodology*. London: Sage, pp. 35–51.

Zimmerman, D.H. 1998. Identity, context and interaction. In C. Antaki and S. Widdicombe (eds) *Identities in Talk*. London: Sage, pp. 87–106.

Zuengler, J. and J. Mori (eds) 2002. Microanalysis of Classroom Discourse, *Applied Linguistics* special issue, 23(3).

Index